All about Poodles

Books by Margaret Sheldon and Barbara Lockwood

POODLES
CLIPPING YOUR POODLE
BREEDING FROM YOUR POODLE
POODLE OWNER'S ENCYCLOPAEDIA
FIRST AID FOR YOUR DOG
VIMS DOG CARE BOOK
DOGS AND HOW TO SHOW THEM
DOGS AND HOW TO GROOM THEM
THE POODLE GUIDE (U.S.A.)
(in collaboration with Margaret Geddes)
FEEDING YOUR POODLE
THE TOY BREEDS
ALL ABOUT CROSSBREEDS AND MONGRELS

All about Poodles

MARGARET SHELDON,
BARBARA LOCKWOOD
and MARGARET GEDDES

PELHAM BOOKS

This Book is Dedicated to
RAZZLE DAZZLE,
RANDY,
and PRUE
The present much loved
companions of the authors.

First published in Great Britain by
Pelham Books Ltd
44 Bedford Square
London WC1B 3DU
1983

Sheldon, Margaret
    All about poodles.
    1. Poodles
    I. Title   II. Lockwood, Barbara
    III. Geddes, Margaret
    636.7′2   SF429.P85
    ISBN 0-7207-1440-0

Phototypeset in Linotron 202 by
Graphicraft Typesetters Hong Kong

Printed in Great Britain by
Butler & Tanner Ltd, Frome and London

Contents

Illustrations

Photographs

Line Drawings by Margaret Geddes

Figures

© PHOTO CREDITS

Allbrooks Ltd 25, 51; Frank Carwood 46; Stanley Dangerfield 1, 2; Miss Eachus 54; George A. Eliot 55; T. Fall 11; Dave Freeman 7; Margaret Geddes 3, 4, 6, 20, 33, 48, 49, 50, 52; Margaret Worth 13; Keith 16; Barbara Lockwood 17, 22, 26–28, 31, 32, 34–42, 44, 53, 57; J.K. McFarlane 10, 12, 15; L.A.R. Mitchell 43; R. Mitchell 23, 24; Diane Pearce 9; J. Youel 5.

Acknowledgements

The authors would like to express their very grateful thanks to the following: The Kennel Club for their help and co-operation and for allowing publication of the breed Standards; Dr S. Peacock of Pennsylvania for help with the American breed Standard; Mr Keith Butt, M.A. Vet M.B. (Cantab), M.R.C.V.S. for his invaluable veterinary advice; Mr Stanley Dangerfield, championship show judge; Messrs Denes for their advice on natural feeding; Messrs Allbrooks for all their help over grooming requisites; Mrs Margaret Watson for her advice on show trimming; Miss Honor Sherry for her advice on first aid; Mr Ronald Mitchell for his assistance with a great many photographs; Mrs Abbey for typing the manuscript so faultlessly; Mrs Winifred Brown for her advice and Dr and Mrs Wohl of Louisiana for their help and advice. Last, but by no means least, all those who have allowed us to publish photographs of their lovely poodles.

Reproduction of the front page of a Parliamentary broadsheet dated 1642 referring to the famous white poodle owned by Prince Rupert.

1 Early History of the Poodle

MANY theories have been propounded regarding the real history of the poodle. Some dove-tail in, while others completely contradict each other. Certainly as far as England is concerned, the poodle was known as a hunting dog in the early 1500s. However, this breed of dog was known much earlier than this in many European countries. The late Mr Howard Price, who was rather an authority on the antiquity of the poodle tells us in his book *The Miniature Poodle* that he had been able to 'trace evidence of Roman and Greek coins which clearly show a dog with a large lion-like mane and hind quarters clipped short'. He also tells us that he believes small poodles were 'represented on some monuments about the time of the Emperor Augustus, approximately A.D. 30'.

Of course, it is comparatively easy from these somewhat indistinct examples to imagine that the dog shown is definitely a poodle, and in some cases one could talk oneself into thinking they could be almost any full coated breed. However, one of the earliest pictures of a dog which looks very like a poodle appears on the front page of a parliamentary broadsheet of 1642 to be found in the British Museum. The wording is fascinating for it says 'PRINCE RUPERT'S WHITE DOG CALLED BOY: Carefully taken by T.B. For that purpose imployed by some of quality in the City of London. Printed in the YEERE MDCXLII'. Boy has a lion-like appearance with a large mane of curly hair, a shaved lower half to his body, enormous feet, and a long tail with large tufts of hair on the end. Although he is always said to be a poodle, it is possibly more correct to say that he resembles to a greater degree the European or Portuguese Water Dog (Cao D'aqua). The story of Boy holds one's imagination for he was no ordinary dog. He was said to have been brought to this country by Prince Rupert after his imprisonment in Europe, when he came to England to help King Charles I fight the Roundheads, but Boy was also supposed to have been endowed with supernatural powers, and was even credited with speaking several foreign languages. It was believed that he would live for ever, but unfortunately this was also a myth for he died bravely defending his master at the Battle of Marston Moor in 1644. There is another engraving, less well known, which appears on the title page of *A Dog's Elegy, or Rupert's Tears* published in London in 1644 and which can be seen in the British Museum Collection of Pamphlets. Boy is shown here lying on his back finally at rest on the field of battle, with Prince Rupert heartbroken at his side.

It was in the middle 1500s that the 'Pudel' became known in Russia and Germany. There was great variation in size from the huge hunting dog weighing some 80 lb down to the tiny pet somewhat resembling the toy poodle of today. His popularity took him to Holland and Belgium where he was known as the *Poedel*, and then on into France where he was called *Barbet*. Until the 1930s he was known in England as the *French* poodle, but nowadays the word 'French' has been dropped, probably rightly for it does not appear from history that France could really claim that the poodle originated in that country. Indeed, the very name surely derives from the German verb meaning to 'splash in water'.

Poodles, apart from Boy and his princely owner, seem to have had their niche in high places for the Prince Regent, afterwards George IV, was said to own a poodle which was his constant companion, and also the Empress Josephine had her own small poodle. There are so many prints which include a poodle as for instance one entitled *Bond Street Loungers* which shows four gentlemen of quality one of whom is leading a poodle, and there is also a painting of Sancho, which the late Miss Clara Bowring told us was a white dog with brown ears which belonged to the Marchioness of Worcester, having been rescued by her husband from the grave of a French officer whose body Sancho was devotedly guarding. And of course in our own day, a poodle bore the status of friend to a Prime Minister of Britain – Sir Winston Churchill and his brown miniature Rufus.

It is interesting to note that in Goethe's *Faust*, translated by A. Swannick, Mephistopheles is described as a black poodle and indeed there is an etching showing the poodle standing on his hind legs menacing poor old Faust. In a book of paintings of Fragonard compiled by Georges Wilderstein in 1960 there are two which include poodles, and also a fine lithograph by Toulouse-Lautrec in a book of his lithographs and dry points compiled by Jean Adhmar, with the poodle as the central figure.

Better known probably is *The Dancing Dog* by Jan Steen, (about 1660) which shows a small white poodle in lion clip entertaining a group of onlookers by dancing on his hind legs while a boy plays the flute and then there is another *Dancing Dog* by Gerard Terborch, which shows a white poodle on his hind legs either dancing or begging for a bird perched on a lady's wrist. There are two prints by Le Bon Genre one of which shows 'Munito, the Calculating Poodle' picking out numbered cards for his trainer in front of an admiring audience; and the second print entitled *The Toy Poodle at Dinner* shows a tiny white poodle sitting up at the table, wearing a smart bow in his topknot while his mistress feeds him the wishbone from the chicken, but at the side somewhat

'Les Tondeuses de Chiens', a coloured lithograph engraving by J.J. Chalon, dated 1820 from the collection owned by Mr Stanley Dangerfield. This shows the equivalent of the modern Poodle Parlour, here operated by the women 'barbers' of France in the market place.

forlornly sitting on a chair is the lady's maid pathetically nibbling what appears to be a crust of bread. There was a beautiful bronze model of French origin (dated about 1775) which shows a poodle seated on a cushion. This model was originally owned by Mrs Bonney of the States, and appears to be a poodle in lion clip, but could equally refer to the Cao d'Agua or Portugese Water Dog. The photograph reproduced here was kindly lent by Mr Stanley Dangerfield from his collection, as was also the photograph of the lithograph *Les Tondeuses de Chiens*. This latter coloured lithograph engraving by J.J. Chalon dated 1820 must surely presage the modern poodle parlour for it shows two French women busily putting some poodles into the lion clip in the Market Square with several more poodles queueing up awaiting their turn. It is interesting to note that one of the poodles is white with black ears and black patches on the body, which perhaps means that 'mis-marks' were not frowned upon in France 150 years ago as they are in England today. Another amusing etching is that by Theodore Lane, also 1820, called *Innocent Amusements*. Here the proverbial old spinster in mob cap and spectacles on the end of her nose is grooming her pet poodle who sits on a table with the hair of his coat rolled in curl papers. Although he is obviously in the lion clip, he also has a long undocked tail with a plume on the end.

This amusing example of the work of George Cruikshank (1792–1878) who was an English book illustrator and caricaturist and famous for his work in 'Oliver Twist'.

Between 1830 and 1848 a tax was levied on all pet dogs kept as luxuries in France, and in a lithograph from *Miroir Caricatural* a poodle owner is shown hotly disputing her case while the tax collector points accusingly at the somewhat haughty white poodle who is sitting on a chair disdainfully reviewing the situation. The tax collector's 'mate' is uncovering a basket in which a bitch with a litter lies. With typical broad French humour, a little terrier is joyfully lifting his leg against the tax collector's trousers. A most detailed and fascinating reproduction entitled *Behind the Scenes* by Ludwig Knaus (1880) appears in *The Book of the Poodle*. Here obviously is the makeshift dressing-room behind the circus, and several poodles are sitting about resting between the acts in front of a heating stove. The detail in the picture is immense, for one sees the clown feeding a baby from a bottle, the ringmaster chatting with the equestrienne, various circus clothes hanging on a line and also scattered on the floor, while in the background one can see children sitting in the audience and a tight-rope walker giving her performance.

Poodles have, of course, been used as circus turns for generations, and the original French clowns always worked a poodle or two as part of their act. There is a theory that the style of pompoms on the wrists and ankles of the poodles was evolved to match the large poms on the clown's dress. Whether this is true or not is hard to say, for equally it is said that the hair was left long over the wrist, ankle and stifle joints to keep the dogs warm and protect them from rheumatism while working as gun dogs and water fowlers in the reeds. The authors are not particularly in favour of performing poodles but fairly recently a very amusing poodle act appeared on television. The redeeming feature of this act was that the canine performers never stopped wagging their tails and really *did* appear to be loving every minute of their performance.

Perhaps one of the most interesting examples, which was reproduced in the magazine *In Britain* quite recently, was a colour photograph of an etching by Landseer of 1840 entitled *Laying Down the Law*. This shows a large white standard poodle in the role of judge surrounded by at least twelve dogs of various breeds sitting round listening to his words of wisdom. The original can be seen in the art collection at Chatsworth House.

When one is considering the poodle in the sphere of art one must not forget recent photography which has undoubtedly produced some breath-taking pictures of the modern poodle. One such photograph is that of Ch. Tarrywood Starlight Glow owned by the late Mrs Longworth Birch and photographed by her husband Geoffrey. It is a glorious head study which has caught the true poodle expression. There is also an

An unusual piece of Staffordshire china of a model clock and three poodles. About mid-19th century.

amusing trick photograph called *The Flying Poodle* which shows a small black poodle apparently flying through the air above the chimney pots. All these photographs appear in *The Book of the Poodle* published by the Harvill Press. Another photograph which has always appealed to the authors has the caption 'They *look* nice sort of people' and one sees only the back views of three white poodles, all in Dutch clip. The largest is standing up against a closed door presumably looking through the key-hole, while the other two are squatting down waiting for information. This photograph was taken by George Elliot, and appears in Stanley Dangerfield's book *Your Poodle and Mine*. The frontispiece of the same book also has a delightful photograph of a white standard stretched flat out in front of a mirror and bears the caption 'Relax, Madame'. Another fine photograph was of those two lovely white miniatures Rothara the Rake and his son U.S.A. Champion Rothara the Cavalier standing side by side and taken by the grand old man of photography, Thomas Fall. Another miniature from the authors' kennel was Triple International Champion Rothara the Gamine photographed by Miss Eachus. Gamine is curled up in an armchair, presumably snoozing but with one eye on events. It is a brilliant example of natural photography for wherever the portrait is hung Gamine is watching one! In Mrs Sherman Hoyt's book *Your Poodle*, a photograph of Blakeen Glacier sitting in the snow is particularly attractive.

A glorious photograph taken by Lisa Grey quite recently must join the gallery for it is really lovely. It is a picture of Knotroms Jaffatan of Merrymorn with Champion Merrymorn Golden Rod below him. Both these lovely apricot toy poodles are owned by Mrs Lucy Ellis and Miss Honor Sherry.

Opposite: A really magnificent example of modern photography. Two beautiful apricot toy poodles owned by Mrs. L.E. Ellis – Knotroms Jaffatan of Merrymorn (top) and his son Ch. Merrymorn Hot Rod.

2 The Standards of the Breed

THE points of the perfect poodle are laid down in what is known as the official Standard of the breed. This Standard is the result of much thought and deliberation of usually the breed club or representatives from a number of clubs, who draw up a code or list of attributes which the perfect poodle should possess and which includes various bad points which should either disqualify the dog from competition in the show ring or alternatively penalise him to a greater or lesser extent in competition. This carefully drawn up code is then laid before a select committee of the Kennel Club who, after a further period of deliberation either accept the Standard or make various alterations to it. In due course, the Official Standard of each breed is published by the Kennel Club and is accepted as the yardstick by which every judge, competitor or breeder of the particular breed must work. Every serious judge, breeder or exhibitor should not only read this Standard carefully many times but should learn it by heart. It is only by learning the Standard in this manner, or continually comparing this ideal with the poodle he is judging, or exhibiting or trying to breed, that he will find the picture of the perfect poodle growing in his mind's eye. It is no uncommon fact that quite knowledgeable breeders can become 'kennel blind' and will not see where their dogs fail simply because they do not continually compare them with the Official Standard.

Another way in which an exhibitor can miss the faults in his own stock is by never watching his show dogs go through their paces handled by someone else. Such matters as soundness of gait and general outline cannot be adequately assessed by the exhibitor if he always has a hold on the other end of the lead. So all really serious poodle enthusiasts will live with the Official Standard almost *ad nauseam* and will also welcome the help of another person to show off their stock so that they can avoid the great danger of self-complacency. Certainly the Standard must be studied most carefully before buying a puppy, for although some attributes are not discernible until the youngster gains maturity, a great many are very obvious right from the start, and the bad points will show up if only enough 'homework' has been carried out in advance.

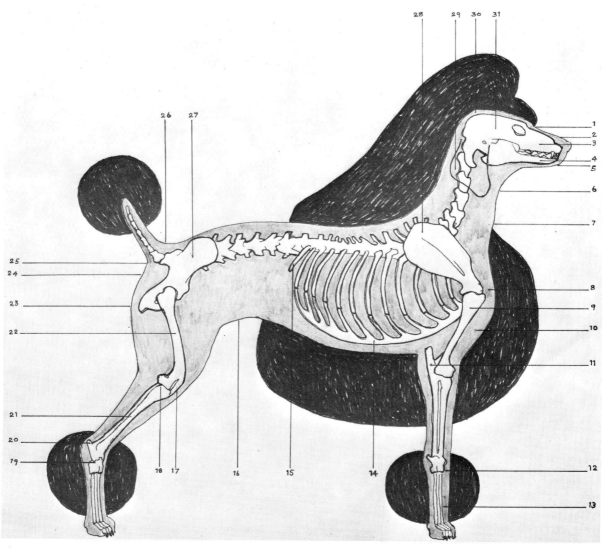

KEY TO FIG 1. SKELETON

Fig. 1 Skeleton

1. Stop.
2. Muzzle.
3. Upper Jaw.
4. Lower Jaw.
5. Chin.
6. Neck.
7. Adam's Apple.
8. Chest.
9. Humerus.
10. Brisket.
11. Elbow.
12. Wrist.
13. Pastern.
14. Ribcage.
15. Last rib.
16. Flap.
17. Flat bone of stifle.
18. Stifle Joint.
19. Hock.
20. Hock point.
21. Tibia.
22. Femur.
23. Rump.
24. Anal glands.
25. Anus.
26. Tail root.
27. Hipbone or pelvis.
28. Shoulder blade or scapula.
29. Ear Leather.
30. Peak or occiput.
31. Skull.

The Official Standard

The Official Standard of the poodle (all three sizes) can be obtained from the Kennel Club, 1 Clarges Street, London, W1, but the secretary of the Kennel Club has given permission for the Standard to be printed here, for which privilege the authors give their grateful thanks.

Characteristics and General Appearance That of a very active, intelligent, well balanced and elegant looking dog with good temperament, carrying himself very proudly.

Gait Sound, free movement and light gait are essential.

Head and Skull Long and fine with slight peak at the back. The skull not broad and with a moderate stop. Foreface strong and well chiselled, not falling away under the eyes; bones and muscles flat. Lips tight fitting. Chin well defined, but not protruding. The whole head must be in proportion to the size of the dog.

Eyes Almond shaped, dark, not set too close together, full of fire and intelligence.

Ears The leather long and wide, low set on, hanging close to the face.

Mouth Teeth – white, strong, even, with scissor bite. A full set of forty-two teeth is desirable.

Neck Well proportioned, of good length and strong to admit of the head being carried high and with dignity. Skin fitting tightly at the throat.

Forequarters Shoulders – strong and muscular, sloping well to the back, legs set straight from the shoulders, well muscled.

Body Chest – deep and moderately wide. Ribs – well sprung and rounded. Back – short, strong, slightly hollowed, loins broad and muscular.

Hindquarters Thighs well developed and muscular, well bent stifles, well let down hocks, hind legs turning neither in nor out.

Feet Pasterns strong, tight feet proportionately small, oval in shape, turning neither in nor out, toes arched, pads thick and hard, well cushioned.

Tail Set on rather high, well carried at a slight angle away from the body, never curled or carried over the back, thick at the root.

Coat Very profuse and dense of good harsh texture without knots or tangles. All short hair close, thick and curly. It is strongly recommended that the traditional lion clip be adhered to.

Colour All solid colours. White and cream poodles to have black nose, lips and eye rims, black toenails desirable. Brown poodles to have dark amber eyes, dark liver nose, lips, eye rims and toenails. Apricot poodles to have dark eyes with black points or deep amber eyes with liver points. Black, silver and blue poodles to have black nose, lips, eye rims and toenails. Cream, apricot, brown, silver and blue poodles may show varying shades of the same colour up to eighteen months. Clear colours preferred.

Size 38cm (15″) or over.

Faults Heavy build, clumsiness, long back, snipy in foreface, light or round or prominent eyes, lippiness, bad carriage, heavy gait, coarse head, over or undershot or pincer mouth, flesh coloured nose, coarse legs and feet, long flat toes, open soft coats with no curl, particolours – white markings on black or coloured poodles, lemon or other markings on white poodles, vicious temperament.

Note: Male animals should have two apparently normal testicles fully descended in the scrotum.

POODLE (MINIATURE)
The poodle (miniature) should be in every respect a replica, in miniature, of the poodle (standard). Height at shoulder should be under 38cm (15″) but not under 28cm (11″).

POODLE (TOY)
The Standard of the poodle (toy) is the same as that of the poodle (standard) and poodle (miniature) except that the height at shoulder should be under 28cm (11″).

It must be pointed out that the English Kennel Club is currently reviewing the Standards of all breeds, but it is not certain when the revised Standards will be published and thus be put into action. This coming major review is probably the first to be undertaken since 1950, so obviously there will be changes. This probably will also apply to the American, German and French Standards as there is a certain amount of co-operation on an international basis between the Kennel Clubs of other countries, who produce their own official Standards of the various breeds. The Standards drawn up by other countries are by no means identical in every way, though they do have a great deal in common with each other. For those who intend to judge abroad or export show stock to other countries it is essential that the relevant official Standard should be obtained and studied so that any differences may be noted. After all, a small difference in perhaps only an inch in the permitted size or a regulation as to a permitted colour could mean that a valuable show dog according to English standards was completely valueless in some other country.

The American Kennel Club has afforded the authors the same privilege of publishing the *Official American Standard for Poodles*, for which they are grateful.

The American Standard of the Breed Poodle

General Appearance, Carriage and Condition That of a very active, intelligent and elegant-appearing dog, squarely built, well-proportioned, moving soundly and carrying himself proudly. Properly clipped in the traditional fashion and carefully groomed, the poodle has about him an air of distinction and dignity peculiar to himself.

Head and Expression *a. Skull*: moderately rounded, with a slight but definite stop. Cheekbones and muscles flat. Length from occiput to stop about the same as length of muzzle. *b. Muzzle*: Long, straight and fine with slight chiseling under the eyes. Strong without lippiness. The chin definite enough to preclude snipeyness. Teeth white, strong, and with a scissor bite. *c. Eyes*: very dark, oval in shape and set far enough apart and positioned to create an alert intelligent expression. *d. Ears*: hanging close to the head, set at or slightly below eye level. The ear leather is long, wide, and thickly feathered; however, the ear fringe should not be of excessive length.

Neck and Shoulders Neck well proportioned, strong and long enough to permit the head to be carried high and with dignity. Skin snug at throat. The neck rises from strong, smoothly muscled shoulders. The shoulder blade is well laid back and approximately the same length as the upper foreleg.

Body To insure the desirable squarely-built appearance, the length of body measured from the breastbone to the point of the rump approximates the height from the highest point of the shoulders to the ground. *a. Chest*: deep and moderately wide with well sprung ribs. *b. Back*: the topline is level, neither sloping nor roached from the highest point of the shoulder blade to the base of the tail, with the exception of a slight hollow just behind the shoulder. The loin is short, broad, and muscular.

Tail Straight, set on high and carried up, docked of sufficient length to insure a balanced outline.

Legs *a. Forelegs*: Straight and parallel when viewed from the front. When viewed from the side the elbow is directly below the highest point of the shoulder. The pasterns are strong. Bone and muscle of both forelegs and hindlegs are in proportion to size of dog. *b. Hindlegs*: Straight and parallel when viewed from the rear. Muscular with width in the region of the stifles which are well bent; femur and tibia are about equal in length; hock to heel short and perpendicular to the ground.

When standing, the rear toes are only slightly behind the point of rump. The angulation of the hindquarters balances that of the forequarters.

Feet The feet are rather small, oval in shape with toes well arched and cushioned on thick firm pads. Nails short but not excessively shortened. The feet turn neither in nor out. Dewclaws may be removed.

Coat *a. Quality* (1) curly: of naturally harsh texture, dense throughout. (2) corded: hanging in tight even cords of varying length; longer on mane or body coat, head, and ears; shorter on puffs, bracelets, and pompoms. *b. Clip*: A poodle under twelve months may be shown in the 'Puppy' clip. In all regular classes, poodles twelve months or over must be shown in the 'English Saddle' or 'Continental' clip. In the stud dog and brood bitch classes and in a non-competitive parade of champions, poodles may be shown in the 'Sporting' clip. A poodle shown in any other type of clip shall be disqualified. *1. 'Puppy'*: A poodle under a year old may be shown in the 'Puppy' clip with the coat long. The face, throat, feet and base of the tail are shaved. The entire shaven foot is visible. There is a pompom on the end of the tail. In order to give a neat appearance and a smooth unbroken line, shaping of the coat is permissible. *2. 'English Saddle'*: In the 'English Saddle' clip the face, throat, feet, forelegs and base of the tail are shaved, leaving puffs on the forelegs and a pompom on the end of the tail. The hindquarters are covered with a short blanket of hair except for a curved shaved area on each flank and two shaved bands on each hindleg. The entire shaven foot and a portion of the shaven leg above the puff are visible. The rest of the body is left in full coat but may be shaped in order to insure overall balance. *3. 'Continental'*: In the 'Continental' clip, the face, throat, feet and base of the tail are shaved. The hindquarters are shaved with pompoms (optional) on the hips. The legs are shaved, leaving bracelets on the hindlegs and puffs on the forelegs. There is a pompom on the end of the tail. The entire shaven foot and a portion of the shaven foreleg above the puff are visible. The rest of the body is left in full coat but may be shaped in order to ensure overall balance. *4. 'Sporting'*: In the 'Sporting' clip, a poodle shall be shown with face, feet, throat and base of tail shaved, leaving a scissored cap on the top of the head and a pompom on the end of the tail. The rest of the body and legs are clipped or scissored to follow the outline of the dog leaving a short blanket of coat no longer than one inch in length. The hair on the legs may be slightly longer than that on the body. In all clips the hair of the top-knot may be left free or held in place by no more than three elastic bands. The hair is only of sufficient length to present a smooth outline.

Color The coat is an even and solid color at the skin. In blues, grays silvers, browns, cafe-au-laits, apricots and creams the coat may show varying shades of the same color. This is frequently present in the somewhat darker feathering of the ears and in the tipping of the ruff. While clear colors are definitely preferred, such natural variation in the shading of the coat is not to be considered a fault. Brown and cafe-au-lait poodles have liver-colored noses, eye-rims and lips, dark toenails and dark amber eyes. Black, blue, gray, silver, cream and white poodles have black noses, eye-rims and lips, black or self colored toenails and very dark eyes. In the apricots while the foregoing coloring is preferred, liver-colored noses, eye-rims and lips, and amber eyes are permitted but are not desirable. Parti-colored dogs shall be disqualified. The coat of a parti-colored dog is not an even solid color at the skin but is of two or more colors.

Gait Straightforward trot with light springy action, strong hindquarters drive. Head and tail carried up. Sound effortless movement essential.

Size The standard poodle is over 38cm (15″) at the highest point of the shoulders. Any poodle which is 38cm (15″) or less in height shall be disqualified from competition as a standard poodle.

The miniature poodle is 38cm (15″) or under at the highest point of the shoulders, with a minimum height in excess of 25cm (10″). Any poodle which is over 38cm (15″) or is 25cm (10″) or less at the highest point of the shoulders shall be disqualified from competition as a miniature poodle.

The toy poodle is 25cm (10″) or under at the highest point of the shoulders. Any poodle which is more than 25cm (10″) at the highest point of the shoulders shall be disqualified from competition as a toy.

Value of points

General appearance, temperament, carriage and condition	30
Head, expression, ears, eyes and teeth	20
Body, neck, legs, feet and tail	20
Gait	20
Coat, color and texture	10

Major faults Any distinct deviation from the desired characteristics described in the breed standard with particular attention to the following:

Temperament: Shyness or sharpness.

Muzzle: Undershot, overshot, wry mouth, lack of chin.

Eyes: Round, protruding, large or very light.

Pigment: Color of nose, lips and eye-rims incomplete, or of wrong color for color of dog.

Neck and shoulders: Ewe neck, steep shoulders.

Tail: Set low, curled or carried over the back.

Hindquarters: Cowhocks.

Feet: Paper or splayfoot.

Disqualifications *Clip*: A dog in any type of clip other than those listed under 'Coat' shall be disqualified. Parti-colors: the coat of a parti-colored dog is not an even solid color at the skin but of two or more colors. Parti-colored dogs shall be disqualified. *Size*: A dog over or under the height limits specified shall be disqualified.

The authors are very much indebted to Dr and Mrs Wohl of New Orleans for obtaining the American Standard of the Breed, and their particular thanks are offered to Dr Peacock and the American Kennel Club.

Perhaps the greatest difference occurs in the sizes of poodles in various countries and here a comparison may be interesting:

	England	*U.S.A.*	*Germany & France*
Standard Poodles	38cm (15″) or over	Over 38cm (15″)	45cm (17¾″) to 55cm (21¾″) (In Germany acceptable up to 60cm (25″)
Miniature Poodles	38cm (15″) but not under 28cm (11″)	38cm (15″) or under with a minimum height in excess of 25cm (10″)	35cm (14″) to 45cm (17¾″)
Toy Poodles	Under 28cm (11″)	Under 25cm (10″)	Under 35cm (13¾″)

In Germany, the three sizes are known as Grosspudel, Kleinpudel and Zwergpudel; while in France they are Grand, Moyen, and Nain. There are also some very tiny poodles in Holland known as Dwergpoedel. Poodles are known by different names in different countries, for instance in Italy they are *Cane Barbone* (meaning dogs with the grey beards) and the toys are *Barbinos*; in Spain they are *Perro de Lanas* (woolly dogs); in France they were known as *Grands Barbets* and the tiny ones as *Petit Barbets* (bearded), but now they are generally known as *Caniche* or *Chien Caniche*. In Germany he is just *Pudel*, but there were at one time no less than six different varieties – *Schaf Pudel* (curly poodle), *Schur Pudel* (corded poodle), *Gros Pudel* (great), *Mittlere Pudel* (middle), *Kleine Pudel* (little) and the *Zwergpudel* (tiny).

So it really does pay all poodle breeders to be sure of the sizes and the appropriate names by which poodles of other countries are known.

One has cause to be extremely grateful to the various Kennel Clubs for keeping such a watchful eye on breed points for unless it was incumbent on breeders to produce stock as near as possible to a drawn-up standard it is quite certain that a great many different types of very queer poodles would progressively appear.

However, it is not always easy to know exactly what the Official Standard of the breed really means when you are looking at your own poodle, and we will do our best to explain the relevant points with the aid of diagrams.

BALANCE

First of all, the balance of your poodle. It is obvious from this drawing that a poodle who pokes his head forward is not properly balanced as this immediately leads to possibly a low set tail or one that is carried horizontally rather than at about 90°, and in turn this fault is really all due to the hindquarters, where a vertical line from root of tail to backfeet occurs. From the diagram it will be seen that if the poodle carries his head proudly erect with an imaginary line running from top-knot over ears to front feet, and with rear hocks well placed out behind, this will cause his tail to be in the correct position, and thus in this matter of conformation he is a well balanced, elegant looking poodle, carrying himself proudly.

Fig. 2
(a) Correct structure with good angulation, head carriage and tail carriage.
(b) Incorrect structure showing poking head, straight shoulder and dipping tail.

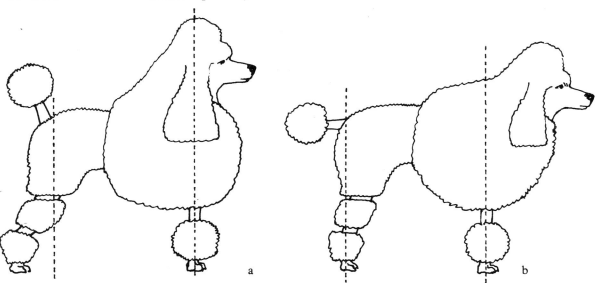

a   b

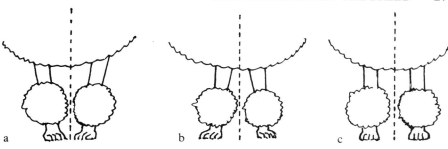

Fig. 3
(a) Too wide in chest causing toes to turn inwards.
(b) Too narrow in chest causing splayed out feet.
(c) Correct straight front with legs parallel.

GAIT

A poodle with a very wide chest is probably also 'out at elbow' and will also turn his toes in. Equally, a narrow chested poodle is going to turn his feet outwards, so neither will help him to walk in the correct manner. Thus, a poodle with neither a too-wide nor too-narrow chest must be looked for, and the ideal chest will lead to straight parallel front legs. Young puppies up to about a year may 'paddle' their front legs, which means they are inclined to weave as they walk. Usually this simply means that the shoulders have not finally tightened up and as the poodle grows to adulthood, this weaving will remedy of its own accord, providing of course that the above points are correct.

SHOULDERS

Another important point for correct gait is shoulder formation. There can be no free movement which is essential in a poodle if the shoulder bones do not have proper angulation. Look well at Fig. 4.
The shoulder blade must be well laid back, and if the scapula is felt with the fingers from top to bottom, the slanting is quite obvious in the well constructed poodle.

Fig. 4
(a) Shoulder not sufficiently angulated.
(b) Correctly angulated with shoulder well laid back.

HIND ACTION

Again angulation is the operative word and if Fig. 5 is studied this angulation is well demonstrated. With the poodle standing sideways, the hip joint can be felt and there should then be a good slant down the femur towards the stifle joint, and another slant the opposite way to the hock at the back, and down to the sole of the foot. If these three angles are well pronounced the poodle should be capable of correct gait, but if there is practically no angulation, then he would be termed 'straight in stifle', causing a very stilted action with no easy freedom in it.

Turning the poodle so that his rear faces you, his hind legs should be reasonably straight from hip to hock, slightly widening out towards the feet. If his legs are bending slightly outwards half way down the legs he will be, as a result, what is known as 'cow-hocked', i.e. his hocks will be touching each other as he walks, or at any rate be too close for good action. (See Fig. 6.)

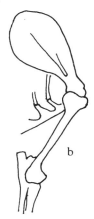

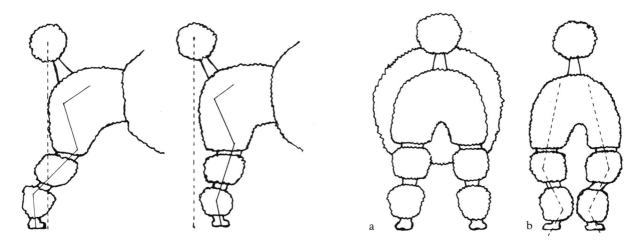

Fig. 5 (*above left*) Correct hindquarters and angulation giving good driving action.

Fig. 6 (*above right*) Straight in stifle causing little angulation.

Fig. 7 (*far right*) (a) Rear view of well constructed poodle. (b) Incorrect hindquarters – cow hocks.

HEAD AND SKULL

The head should be long and fine from occiput to end of nose. The chin should be well defined. A chin which falls away, or recedes, gives the poodle a 'snipey' look which is weak and unpleasing. Equally a too-heavy chin takes away from what should be a fine and elegant head. The whole effect of the face and jaw should be clean and well fitting with no flabbiness in either lips, cheeks or under the chin.

EYES

Eyes should be dark and almond shaped. They should never be large, round and prominent, as this immediately leads to a thick skull. Equally, eyes must not be too small or close-set, as this immediately tends to a

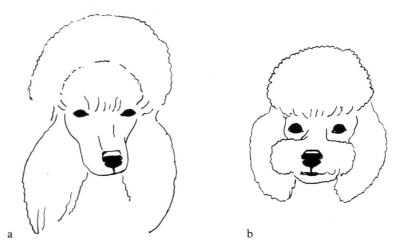

Fig. 8 (a) Eyes. Correct shape, flat and almond shaped. (b) Incorrect shape, round and prominent.

'plain' expression. The expression of the poodle should be alert, full of fire and also denote a sense of humour. The eye rims should be clean and neat. Occasionally in white and apricot poodles, there is an unsightly red or brown staining under the eyes. This can be due to one or two conditions – for instance, the lashes may be sweeping over the eyeball, thus causing weeping. This could be a hereditary condition. Or it might be caused by a blocked tear duct or ducts. However, the authors have come to the conclusion that this unsightly staining in many cases is due to lack of healthy condition, and it would appear that the poodle who is fed on *good quality* food containing all necessary vitamins, and who is also well exercised and cleanly housed, will quite likely never suffer from this unpleasant condition. It does seem that 'running' eyes are synonymous with the poodle being off colour and ill conditioned.

EARS

Correct set of ear can make or mar the poodle's beauty. Ears should be low set, that is just below a line drawn from the outside corner of the eye. They should fall closely to the side of the head. The leathers should be wide and long, but not too thick, and with plenty of long fringes. Both high set ears (rather like a terrier) or ears which stand away from the head give the poodle a very untypical expression. In some extreme cases the ears may even turn backwards which really *is* a bad fault. Puppies, sometimes up to nine months, may have a tendency to fly their ears, but this is a fault which usually rights itself by adulthood.

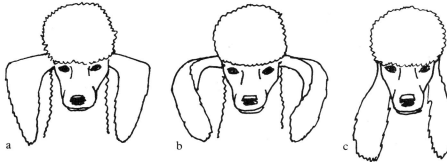

a   b   c

Fig. 9 Ear Set
(a) Incorrect – high set.
(b) Incorrect – standing out.
(c) Correct – falling close to head.

TEETH

The teeth should be strong, even, and white. The top teeth should tightly overlap the bottom teeth, which is called a scissor bite, though the teeth often meet edge to edge. Both are considered correct. If the top teeth considerably overlap the bottom teeth, this is known as 'overshot', and gives the poodle a weak, characterless expression and generally goes with a receding chin. If the bottom teeth extend over the top, then this is 'undershot', and gives the poodle a slightly pugilistic expression which again is not characteristic of the breed. (See Fig. 10.)

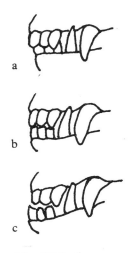

Fig. 10 Teeth
(a) Scissor bite.
(b) Edge to edge.
(c) Undershot.

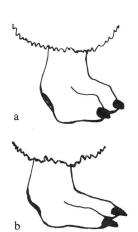

Fig. 11 Feet
(a) Correct – well muscled arched foot.
(b) Incorrect – flat foot with very little muscle.

The jaw should contain forty-two teeth and these are divided into 6 'incisors' (small front teeth) in both upper and lower jaws, and these are sub-divided into 'nippers' which are the two middle teeth, 'intermediates' which are those next to the nippers, and 'corners' which come next. Then there is one long 'canine' on either side of the six teeth. Behind these come the 'molars' and 'pre-molars', of which there should be six on each side of the upper jaw, and seven on each side of the lower jaw. Correct placement should be checked before buying an adult poodle. In a puppy, the milk teeth will be present from about six weeks, or earlier, until the second teeth push them out at four to five months of age. If the puppy has the correct amount of first teeth, he will usually have a perfect adult jaw. However, puppies sometimes are missing a tooth or teeth in their first teeth, but this does not necessarily mean their second teeth will be wrong. Quite often, a normal set of teeth will come through with the second teeth. A complication often occurs when the second teeth are coming through, but the first teeth are so tightly set that they will not drop out, and then both first and second tooth is present. If this should happen, the vet should remove the offending first tooth otherwise the jaw may grow unevenly and spoil the adult mouth.

NECK
The skin of the neck fits tightly at the neck, thus any flabbiness under the chin and by the throat is undesirable. A short neck gives the poodle a stocky and inelegant outline, as equally an over-long neck destroys his balance and gives the impression of a 'gangling' dog.

FEET
Although a poodle should have strong, well muscled, arched feet with thickly cushioned pads, this will depend so much on his condition health wise and also on the amount and type of exercise he receives. If he is well and properly fed, then his condition should be good and he will be up on his toes.

A great aid to this is regular walking every day on hard ground or on the road, with a proportion of his exercise devoted to running flat out on grass to tighten the muscles of his feet. Chasing after a ball is excellent as the fast twisting and turning is so good for his muscles. Fig. 11 gives a very good idea of the correct foot as against the long flabby foot. If the toe-nails are kept short, either as a result of road walking or by nail clipping, this will help considerably. The poodle with long nails is obviously going to be flat footed – a matter of cause and effect.

TAIL SET
The tail should be set on fairly high and carried in a joyous manner. These diagrams ably illustrate the correct and incorrect angle of carriage.

A poodle who carries his tail over his back – and there are some who even have the tail lying horizontally on the back! – and the dog who seems unable to raise his tail, are both faulty. The too-gay tail is usually accompanied by what is known as a 'sway back', while the low set depressed looking tail goes with the roach-backed poodle. If the top line of the back is level, a good tail set usually follows, together with a well carried head.

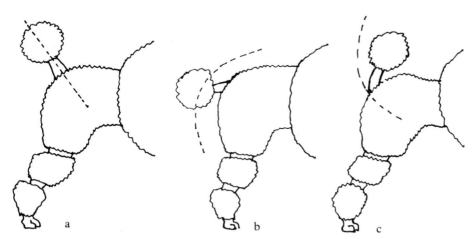

Fig. 12
(a) Correct angle of tail carriage.
(b) Incorrect tail carriage, low set with roach back.
(c) A gay tail, with sway back.

COAT

A most important part of the poodle. The hair should be really dense and springy, and there should be lots of it. Perhaps the word 'springy' is the most important, and to test this if the coat is patted or slightly pressed on with the hand, the hair should resist slightly and spring back to bushiness again. A poodle's coat that really has the right texture will seldom mat or teazle – not that a poodle should ever be so neglected as to have a matted coat, but sadly it does happen quite often. And yet a comb through once a week and matting would never occur. The authors have many times had pet poodles brought to them to clip, and the only method possible was to cut the coat with scissors about 19mm (¾″) from the skin, taking off a thick solid mat, which lies on the grooming table rather like pieces of rug. It must be admitted that the soft, cotton wool coat will tangle and mat more easily, while this trouble will not occur so much with the thin or straight coat. The correct coat certainly must have body in it, density and crispness – a coat condition slightly akin to newly permed human hair which needs only to be combed through or patted into the right shape. Regular brushing, combing and bathing at regular intervals in a good shampoo with added conditioner will help to develop the characteristic coat. A very good additive to feeding which does wonders in producing density and strength to the coat is a daily sprinkling of Bemax over the food. Half a teaspoon for a toy, one teaspoon for a miniature, and two teaspoons for the standard. Incidentally this is also an excellent coat-tonic for the poodle who is past his prime and getting on in years, as at this stage the coat undoubtedly tends to get thinner year by year.

COLOURS

The Standard of the breed lays down that poodles should be of solid colours. Therefore any markings of any colour than the main one is termed 'parti-coloured' and not allowable in the show and really not desirable in the pet poodle. For instance, a white blaze or patch on the chest or perhaps a white foot or feet, is to be avoided on a black or silver or brown poodle. Occasionally the white poodle may have slightly grey tinged ear fringes, or a pale apricot poodle may have tan ear fringes – all to be avoided when selecting a poodle. Of course, many black poodles do produce somewhat grey or grizzled muzzles, top-knots and tail poms as they grow older, but this is only *anno domini* and cannot be avoided. When choosing a special colour in a poodle, it must be remembered that the silver poodle is born practically black and only turns silver maybe in late puppyhood. If an apricot is fancied, then a *very* deep tan is desirable when young. The young puppy which looks 'apricot' at birth or in puppyhood is likely to fade to a dirty cream with a brown nose and pale tan ear fringes when adult. Some years ago, a colour referred to as 'harlequin' was gaining a little popularity, and this was really a poodle with fair sized black and white patches. However, this trend seems to have passed, and solid colours are the norm.

The pigmentation (i.e. the colour of nose, eye-rims and in some cases nails) is important, and the various descriptions are clearly set out in the Standard of the Breed. It is desirable for white poodles to have black toe nails, but in practice this is quite rare, and in no way disqualifies in the show ring. A butterfly nose (one where the black pigment is interspersed with pink spots) is very undesirable.

The correct balance of the poodle. (i.e. relation of height of leg to length of back) is so important. In fact, he should resemble a square box for he should measure exactly the same from root of tail to floor Y to X as from foot of tail to shoulder Y to Z (Fig. 13a). If he measures more from Y to Z than from Y to X (Fig. 13b) then he is either long in back or short on leg. Equally, if he measures more from Y to X than from Y to Z (Fig. 13c) then he is too high on the leg. Either of these last two examples show that he is a wrongly balanced poodle.

All the faults have been considered already in this chapter, but to sum up the poodle must always be elegant in the extreme and a real joy to look at. Any tendency to heaviness, or coarseness in build is to be

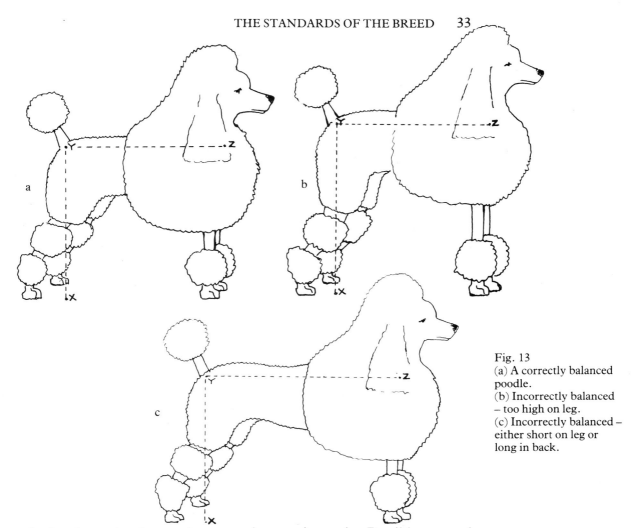

Fig. 13
(a) A correctly balanced poodle.
(b) Incorrectly balanced – too high on leg.
(c) Incorrectly balanced – either short on leg or long in back.

deplored, as is also a clumsy and stumping gait. Possibly a good description of the poodle is that he will resemble a ballet dancer – elegant, graceful with a real spring in all his movements. However, a male poodle must never appear effeminate or 'bitchy'. Equally a bitch must not appear 'doggy' which would mean slightly coarse or heavy. She must have more finesse and femininity than the dog.

All the foregoing is particularly relevant if you are buying a show dog or trying to breed one. For the prospective owner of a companion poodle it is not quite so important – one will love him just as dearly whatever his faults. However, it is pleasant to own a dog which is continually admired when taking him for his daily walks, for if the poodle is elegant, well constructed, and well clipped you will not be shamed by remarks such as 'Goodness me, is that supposed to be a poodle!'

3 The Standard Poodle

IT is really incorrect to refer to the large-sized poodle as a 'standard poodle'. His real designation always was in the olden days, and possibly should be in these modern times 'the poodle'. But as miniatures and toys have for many years joined the ranks, it has become usual to differentiate between the sizes by tacking the word 'standard' on to the big fellows, and so to avoid confusion we will refer to them by this name.

The late Mrs Alida Monro in her book *The Popular Poodle* told us that the first standard poodles were actually mentioned in the Kennel Club Stud Book in 1874 when five dogs were registered – Don, Elmer, Flo, Frank and Lion, and that these were followed in 1877 by Charlie, Fecken, Michael Angelo and Touche. In those days the poodles were practically all 'corded'. They were, apparently, quite fantastic to look at for they grew long cords of hair which trailed on the ground. These long cords fell from the middle of the back and down the sides to the floor, from the docked tail, and also, from each ear leather. These cords were seldom if ever combed out, and when the dogs were not actually in the show ring, the cords were wrapped in rag curlers having been heavily coated with oil or grease beforehand. The length of the cords well exceeded the height of the dog, and therefore swept the ground. This must have impeded his walking ability very considerably, and been very uncomfortable.

Towards the end of the century a great controversy was developing, for another style of poodle had come into being – the non-corded or curly poodle. Two prominent poodle breeders of these days held widely divergent views, for Miss Brunker of the Whippendell prefix was convinced that corded and non-corded poodles were *not* the same, while Mrs Leonard Crouch of the Orchard prefix contended that they were basically identical except for a different 'hair-do'. However, in 1904 the breed was divided into two varieties – the corded variety and the non-corded variety.

Corded poodles are never seen these days, and all now have the characteristics of the curly poodle, although it must be admitted that occasionally one comes across the coat which is inclined to twist itself into tight cords, especially if the coat is long and the dog has been out in the rain.

Head study of Penpens Firefly of Dorlin ('Prue'), a young black standard poodle at only six months of age.

Early Registrations

By the early 1900s, poodles were becoming really quite popular. A great many imports from America, Germany and France, were finding their way to England, and during the first thirty years of this century poodles were quite widely shown and also used extensively as gun-dogs. Unfortunately World War II played havoc with the breed, and many prominent breeders and exhibitors faded out. From a registered total of around 500 a year in the 1940s to 1950s, they showed a downward trend between 1950 and 1960, dropping to the 300s up till 1964. In 1965 they increased to 417, but dropped again in 1966 to 376, but in 1967 and 1968 they increased again to 474 and 495 respectively. But from 1969 to 1975 there was a tremendous rise in registration totals, even attaining 970 in 1973. But from 1st April 1976, registration figures show only those standards placed on the active register and for two years the figures were lower, for 1976 they were 436, for 1977 they were 246 and in 1978 they were going up again to 583. In 1979 the rise was considerable to 995, and again in 1980 they were 983. No figures have yet been published for 1981. But in view of almost double the amount of registrations from 1968 to the present time perhaps we can look forward to seeing a great many more of these elegant and graceful dogs in the show ring and also beautifying our private homes.

Early Pioneers

Amongst the early pioneers of the standard poodle must be remembered Miss Brunker (Whippendell), Mrs D'Arcy Thompson (Rathnally), Miss Jane Lane (Nunsoe) who incidentally owned the magnificent dog Int. Champion Nunsoe Duc de la Terrasse, who was imported into this country from Switzeland, and made a tremendous stir in England by winning everywhere he was shown, and then was exported to America to join Mrs Sherman Hoyt's celebrated Blakeen Kennel, where he quickly became an American Champion and Triple International Champion; Mrs Boyd (Piperscroft) who owned the celebrated dog King Leo; Mrs Murray-Wilson (Stillington); and Mrs Ionides (Vulcan Champagne). Many of these famous kennel names appear way back in current poodle pedigrees, although only the Vulcan Champagne Kennel appears to be still actively functioning, for on the death of the Hon. Mrs Ionides, the prefix was transferred to her partner Miss Shirley Walne, who was then joined by Miss Coppage.

During the past years, many lovely poodles have achieved high honours – for instance, Mrs Proctor's Ch. Tzigane Aggri of Nashend gained the award of Supreme Best in Show at Crufts in 1955 out of a total

Champion Groomar Mixed Blessings, winner of 5 Ch. Certs when only 20 months old. Owned and bred by Mrs M. Cleaver.

Mrs A. Proctor with her Champion Tzigane Aggri of Nashend, the first Poodle to be judged Surpreme Best in Show at Crufts in 1955.

of 6,127 dogs, while Mrs Fraser's lovely black standard poodle Bibelot's Tall Dark and Handsome was judged Reserve Best in Show all breeds at Crufts in 1967. However, many more lovely standards have been exhibited since this latter date, and the following challenge certificate winners at some of the principal shows over the last few years will be of interest to enthusiastic owners of this variety. It should be noted that an asterisk (*) denotes best of breed.

Crufts Championship Show (Standard Poodles)

Year	Sex	Challenge Certificate Winner	Owner	Judge
1976	Dog	Ch. Tiopepi Baymer Golden Sunrise	Mrs C. Coxall	Mrs M. Sharpe
	*Bitch	Ch. Captains Lady from Malibu	Mrs B & Miss K. Sillito	
1977	Dog	Ch. Josato Capability Brown of Tragapanz	Mrs C. Flatt	Miss J. Johnson
	*Bitch	Ch. Kelrarmo Lily the Pink	Mrs A.V. Timson	
1978	*Dog	Ch. Leighbridge Catmint	Mrs C.A. Saunders	Miss R. Gregory
	Bitch	Ch. Vanitonia Prunella Prune	Messrs R. Stone & G. Thompson	
1979	*Dog	Ch. Torpaz Gambit	Mrs P. Ashwell	Mrs C.G. Sutton
	Bitch	Ch. Vicmars In Demand	Mrs I. Pine	
1980	*Dog	Ch. Midshipman at Kertellas Supernova	Mr & Mrs K.A. Nathan	Mrs C. Kellard
	Bitch	Ch. Sablecombe Colomba	Mrs H. Stanley	
1981	*Dog	Sablecomb White Polar at Leander	Mesdames Stanley & Streatfield & Mr Williams	Mr H. Glover
	Bitch	Ch. Kertellas South Pacific	Mr R. Bayliss	
1982	*Dog	Ch. Montravia Gay Gunner	Mrs P. Gibbs	Mrs M. Willis-Pritchard
	Bitch	Ch. Kelrarmo Pink Annie	Mrs A.V. Timson	

Champion Kelrarmo Pink Annie, owned by Mrs Timson. A magnificent black standard in perfect Continental Clip.

The International Poodle Club Championship Show
(Standard Poodles)

Year	Sex	Challenge Certificate Winner	Owner	Judge
1977	*Dog	Torpaz Zorro	Mrs P. Ashwell	Mr P. Howard-Price
	Bitch	Kelrarmo Lily the Pink	Mrs A.V. Timson	
1978	*Dog	Ch. Lentella Stagestruck of Glyndale	P. Parkinson P.M. Cox & Mrs D. Poole	Mr W. Siggers
	Bitch	Vulcan Champagne Star Turn	Mesdames Wright & Kellard	

Year	Sex	Challenge Certificate Winner	Owner	Judge
1979	*Dog	Ch. Midshipman at Kertellas Supernova	Mr & Mrs K. Nathan	Mr J.A. MacDougal
	Bitch	Chestall Sarah Jane	Miss B. Peake	
1980	*Dog	Dassin Diablo at Tiopepi	D.R. Coxall	Mr L. Harwood
	Bitch	Kelrarmo Call Me Kate	Mrs A.V. Timson	

No certificates were on award in 1981, but the Best Dog was judged to be Ch. Montravia Gay Gunner owned by Mrs P. Gibbs, while the Best Bitch and also Best of Breed was Ch. Kertella's South Pacific owned by Mrs R. Bayliss.

As there were no certificates at the International Poodle Club Show for 1981, readers might like to know that the following were the certificate winners at the Standard Poodle Club Show for that year:

Year	Sex	Challenge Certificate Winner	Owner	Judge
1981	Dog	Poolbank Cream Whip at Peppadene	Mrs W. Hamilton	Mrs B. Sillito
	*Bitch	Ch. Groomar Mixed Blessings	Mrs M. Cleaver	Miss S. Spear

The Poodle Club Championship Show (Standard Poodles)

Year	Sex	Challenge Certificate Winner	Owner	Judge
1976	*Dog	Ch. Acadia Stage Door Johnny of Leander	Mrs W. Streatfield & Miss J. Sering	Mr F. Sabella
	Bitch	Ch. Vicmar's Royale Debutante	Mrs V. Marshall	
1978	*Dog	Ch. Roushka's Pacific	R. Bayliss & D. Thomas	Mrs M. Howarth
	Bitch	Ch. Vanitonia Prunella Prune	R. Stone & G. Thompson	

1979	Dog	Janavons Midnight Blue	Mrs E. Geeson	} Mrs G. Flatt
	*Bitch	Ch. Sablecome Colomba	Mrs H. Stanley	
1980	*Dog	Ch. Midshipman at Kertellas Supernova	Mr & Mrs K.A. Nathan	} Miss V. Hincks
	Bitch	Lentella With Love	P. Parkinson & P.N. Cox	
1981	*Dog	Ch. Montravia Gay Gunner	Mrs P. Gibbs	} Mrs O. Bullock
	Bitch	Ch. Kertellas South Pacific	Mr R. Bayliss	

There were no challenge certificates on offer for 1977.

Challenge Certificates

It should be explained that the number of challenge certificates allotted by the Kennel Club to any breed of dog is dependant on the number of registrations received. Thus in the case of standard poodles there may not be sufficient registrations to warrant challenge certificates for every championship show. It therefore behoves every breeder of standard poodles to register as many dogs as possible so that challenge certificates may be available at many more championship shows. Certainly all standard poodle lovers should get together to help this lovely variety to remain at any rate moderately popular, and to this end those interested might well join the Standard Poodle Club. The secretary is Mrs A. Rawlinson, Viewswood Kennels, Buxted Park, Near Uckfield, E. Sussex. Also, of course, the Poodle Club and the International Poodle Club and any other regional poodle clubs. Addresses of secretaries appear in Chapter 21.

The standard poodle is such a lovely animal that he must never be allowed to fade into insignificance. The elegance of his gait, his sweet temperament, his wonderful sense of humour are all attributes so well worth while for the perfect companion.

It is hoped that readers will not imagine that the authors have any bias towards any of the three sizes of poodle. They have all three owned, bred and loved one or all of the sizes, and while standards, miniatures and toys differ in temperament quite considerably, they are a wonderful breed of dog and all three authors count themselves honoured to have the privilege of owning poodles.

4   The Miniature Poodle

THE miniature poodle is the middle sized variety, and should measure under 38cm (15″) and not under 28cm (11″) at the shoulder. However, the preferred size is between 38cm (15″) and 33cm (13″). By very careful and selective breeding the miniature was reduced in size from the standard poodle, and nothing of the grace and elegance should have been lost in the dwarfing process, but of course the first miniature *did* lose a tremendous amount of quality in the beginning, and long bodies on short legs, uneven mouths, and large eyes were not uncommon faults. After some years the quality improved and this was entirely due to the selective care and perseverance of the early miniature breeders.

Measuring

In 1911 the Kennel Club decided that these smaller poodles should be registered as a separate variety to be known as 'Poodles, Miniature' and must measure under 38cm (15″) at the shoulder. It was also agreed that this new variety should be measured standing on a table in the show ring, and such measuring should be carried out either by a veterinary surgeon or a ring steward. Nowadays, in the case of miniature and toy poodles the show committee or executive at all shows must provide a fixed bridge type metal measure, and before any exhibit receives a class award it must be measured with the appropriate measure by the judge making the award.

The First Miniatures

Miss Millie Brunker was undoubtedly one of the pioneers of this new variety and her Whippendell Cachet, Whippendell Turqu and Whippendell Cabillat were among the first eleven to be registered. Miss Newall, Mrs Cobbold and Mrs Leonard Crouch were others who did noble work in establishing the first miniature poodles.

Before 1911 and official recognition, several miniature-sized white poodles had gained a certain amount of success in the show ring but they had to compete against the large standards. Mrs Pacey (who showed them under her maiden name of Hawley) had considerable success with

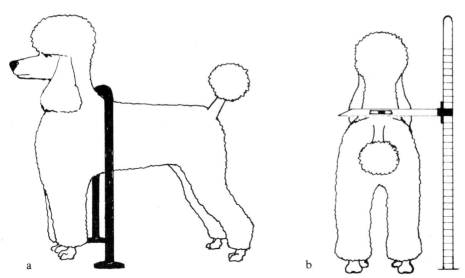

Fig. 14
(a) Fixed bridge type of measure for three sizes of poodles.
(b) Sliding rule type for exact measurement of poodle.

Chaseley Leo, bred by Miss Rose Armitage. Miss Florence Brunker (sister of Millie) was also to the fore with her small whites, as was Miss Moorhouse with her Chieveley strain. Miss Jane Lane, so well known for her Nunsoe Standard poodles, was attracted by the smaller ones, and her Nunsoe Dandy Jim is behind most miniature white pedigrees today. A little later on Mrs Campbell Inglis appeared with her Mannerhead Miniatures and was joined by Mr and Mrs Theo Megroz and the Colernedowns, Mrs Tyndall and the Vendas, Mrs Boyd and the Piperscrofts, Mrs Monro and the Firebraves.

Up till 1946, poodles were registered according to their *size* as either standards or miniatures irrespective of their actual breeding. But in 1946 the Kennel Club decreed that true miniatures must be the *progeny* of miniatures, and if now so-called miniatures were sired by or out of a standard parent, then they must be registered as *inter-bred poodles*. So from that date miniatures were truly a separate variety in every sense of the word.

Dogs in general went through a bad time during the Second World War, and many kennels went to the wall purely because the feeding of dogs in any numbers was well nigh impossible. Thus many of the old breeders were heard of no more, and consequently a new set came into existence. Of those who did manage to withstand the privations of war-time Britain and who came up smiling again in the post-war show rings were Mrs Campbell Inglis, Mrs Alida Monro, Mrs G.L. Boyd, Mrs Fife-Failes, Mrs Tyndall, and Mr and Mrs Megroz, Mrs L.E. Ellis and a few others. Amongst the 'newcomers' were Mrs Austin Smith (Braeval), Miss Joan Eddie (Nashend), Mrs Coventon (Adastra), Mrs Elsie Thomas

(Fircot), Mrs Diana Waugh (Berinshill), Commander Hinton (Panoply), Mrs Gwen Birch (Tarrywood), and the authors Mrs Sheldon and Miss Lockwood with their Rotharas, most of whom favoured the white miniatures. Amongst those who bred the blacks, were Mr Philippe Howard-Price (Montfleuri), Mrs Atkinson (Pixholme), Mrs Conn (Montmartre), Mrs Mick Watson (Bidabo) and many others.

Well known for the lovely silver miniatures were Mr and Mrs Booth (Gypsyheath), Mr and Mrs Gundry (Walditch), Miss Chris Seidler (Burdeisel), and Mr Donald Wickens (Silcresta); while Mrs Proctor (Tzigane) and Mrs Davies (Heatherton) produced some lovely browns. Mrs Ellis (Merrymorn) exhibited the first cream post-war Champion Cremola of Swanhill, while her sister Miss 'Mouse' Sherry campaigned the outstanding white dog Ch. Blakeen Oscar of the Waldorf, who was owned by Mrs Hall of the Wychwood Kennels and imported from Mrs Sherman Hoyt of the famous Blakeen strain of Connecticut. Ch. Oscar made a tremendous impact on miniatures in Britain, and a long way back is behind most of the outstanding whites in the country today. He was extensively used at stud and sired the breath-taking Ch. Adastra Magic Flame, Ch. Adastra Magic Fame and Ch. Adastra Magic Foam for Mrs Coventon in one litter. Oscar was also the sire of Rothara the Courtesan, who in turn was the dam of Triple International Champion Rothara the Gamine, both owned and bred by the authors.

There are of course many other breeders and exhibitors who played their part in perfecting the lovely miniature poodle, and indulgence is sought from those not specifically mentioned.

Registrations

By the late 1950s and early 1960s, miniature poodles had become so popular that the number registered at the Kennel Club in 1960 was more than three times the number of any other single breed. For eleven years from 1954 to 1964 (inclusive) they had stayed at the top of the popularity poll, more having been registered each year by a very wide margin than any other breed.

In fact, in 1960 the registrations numbered a record 23,216. After that they dropped gradually until in 1968 the number was 6,536 and miniatures were then in sixth place of all breeds. From 1970, registrations dropped very considerably until in 1975 they were only 2,941. From 1st April 1976, only dogs placed on the active register were taken into account, and the registrations were 1976 – 1,676, 1977– 1,003, 1978 – 2,330, 1979 – 2,790, and 1980 – 2,353.

However, the period from 1954 to 1964 was not a particularly happy state for miniatures for whenever a breed becomes so outstandingly popular, the quality runs the risk of not being maintained. The demand far exceeded the supply and as a result breeding programmes by many were not properly planned. Unpleasant faults began to appear and many breeders whose main object was to make as much money as possible while the harvest was ripe, simply did nothing to obviate or breed out such faults. Miniatures became the 'rave' breed in America as well as in Britain, and mushroom puppy factories started up everywhere so that ready dollars could be snatched. A great many kennel owners of other breeds kept a poodle bitch or two because puppies could be sold as quickly as they could be bred, and this helped to keep the other breeds which were not so easy to sell. Consequently crates of immature poodle puppies were flown across the Atlantic every week by dealers and breeders some of whom appeared to care little for the comfort, health or ultimate well-being of the puppies. The minimum age for puppies to fly was supposed to be twelve weeks, but many which were very considerably younger than that were exposed to the noise and horror of air flight and all the other attendant privations. Stud dogs were, in many cases, over-used as they were in great demand. Unsoundness crept in as a result of all this, and such horrors as progressive retinal atrophy (blindness), slipping stifles, hipdysplasia and nervousness, were terms which were becoming linked with the breed. This appeared to be the fall and decline of the lovely miniature poodle. But it was not quite that for many of the conscientious and serious breeders became even more selective in their breeding plans, and worked unendingly to prevent the rot from spreading.

Now in the 1980s the bad times are over and the miniature has become again the alert, elegant, delightful animal which he was before the tragedy of too much popularity overtook him. A wrong impression must not be conceived from the foregoing, for only a proportion of kennels served the breed badly, only a proportion of the dogs were unsound and this proportion was not too large to be stamped out once the demand for puppies at any price had dwindled. There is no doubt that now one has only to attend a championship show such as Crufts, or a specialist club championship show such as those held yearly by the Poodle Club and the International Poodle Club to see walking around the ring miniatures which are now perhaps far more sound and far more beautiful than perhaps they have ever been, due entirely to those careful, knowledgeable breeders who were not going to allow their beloved breed to deteriorate into oblivion. One of these breeders is Mrs Margaret Worth of the Piccoli Poodles, who is also the untiring and very efficient secretary of the Midland Poodle Club. Mrs Worth was the breeder of Rothara the Ragamuffin, owned by Mrs Sheldon and Miss Lockwood. 'Rags' was a delightful character and achieved a great many wins before, as the first Rothara, he went to the States where he quickly became an international champion. He was exported to Dr and Mrs Wohl of New

Champion Piccoli Polichinelle, an outstandingly lovely white miniature dog owned and bred by Mrs Margaret Worth.

Orleans, U.S.A. who have been intimate and lasting friends of the authors for over 25 years. The friendship is renewed every year when Dr and Mrs Wohl visit England, and the authors have visited them in New Orleans where they were greeted by at least ten Rothara poodles who had flown across the Atlantic, and lived in the lap of luxury, all ten seemingly sleeping on Dr and Mrs Wohl's bed!! One of the latest stars in Mrs Worth's family of miniature poodles is the glorious white Ch. Piccoli Polichinelle who is rapidly making a great name for himself in the poodle world. This lovely miniature already has gained four challenge certificates and three bests of breed. To Mrs Worth's delight his six-month-old son won the miniature poodle puppy class under Mrs Sheila Cox at a recent International Poodle Club Championship Show.

Many years ago, Margaret Geddes called at the Rothara Kennels and chose a very nice miniature bitch puppy which we agreed to name Rothara Pilgrim's Penny and which was by a son of Phillipe Howard-Price's famous Ch. Braebeck Toni of Montfleuri and out of Jessica of Rothara. This bitch was the foundation of the Penpens Poodles, and in their time they made their mark, for Penny's son Penpens Potentate ('Spud') was exported to Norway and became a Norwegian Champion and one of Penny's daughters, Penpens Portia, won a great deal in this country. Several other Penpens puppies were exported to the States. Now Margaret Geddes owns a magnificent black standard bitch Penpens Firefly of Dorling ('Prue') who was extensively shown when younger and undoubtedly would have gained championship status but for the fact that Margaret, who is a professional painter was extremely busy arranging exhibitions of her work all over the country and thus could not spare the time that campaigning a poodle to his or her championship involves. This would have been a full time job and Margaret had to make the choice.

There are so many beautiful miniatures who have been collecting the highest honours over the last few years that it is difficult to pick and choose. Certainly Mrs Coxall's Tiopepi Tycoon, a magnificent dog and in 1976 he was judged best of breed at both Crufts and the Poodle Club Championship Show, and in 1977 the dog challenge certificate at the International Poodle Club Show was gained by Tiopepi Typhoon, and in 1980 Mrs Coxall has come up with yet another – Ch. Tiopepi Tempest. Mrs Gibb's Montravia Poodles are nearly always competing for the top honours. It would be pleasant to mention all the lovely poodles prancing about the rings these days but they would fill a book by themselves.

The authors find it most interesting that so many of the current top judges were newcomers to poodles when the authors themselves were also starting with their first show dogs who, it went without saying, were all going to become Crufts supreme winners! These breeders and owners who are now first class judges got to the top through learning the hard way, working seven days a week the whole year through, going to shows full of trepidation and nerves and coming home full of joy at winning a first prize and then at the next show being cast into the doldrums at being sent out of the ring without a card! Many of these judges who are now at the top must have experienced these emotions – Mrs Sheila Cox, Mrs Jill Ellis, Miss Gregory, Miss Christine Hawkes, Miss Hincks, Mrs Howard-Price, Miss Machon, Mrs Price Jones, Miss Kathleen Rees, Miss Seidler, Miss 'Mouse' Sherry, Miss S. Walne, Mrs 'Mick' Watson, Mrs Margaret Worth and so many others.

We have explored the history of the miniature poodle from his beginnings to the present day and considered some of the breeders and owners who did a lot of pioneer work. But so far we have not mentioned many of the dogs themselves. There have been many who have been outstanding either as sires or dams, as top show winners, or as ambassadors in foreign countries. Many of the following lovely dogs did so much to keep the miniature poodle on the right rails by the splendid type of sound offspring which they sired or produced over the difficult years when the whole variety was in danger of being swamped by a glut of weak, unsound specimens, and therefore they must not go unsung. While one cannot possibly remember or note every dog and bitch who has contributed his or her bit towards the emergence of the near perfect poodle, here are some which readily spring to mind.

Bonny Forget-Me-Not, bred by Mrs Tyndall and owned by Mrs Campbell Inglis produced in one litter those two lovely black dogs The Laird and Limelight of Mannerhead, and in another litter, Flashlight of Mannerhead. Others in the Mannerhead kennel were Dare Devil Dink and Eric Bright Eyes. Firebrave Cupidon was the founder of Mrs Monro's kennel, with the fabulous Firebrave Gaulois following on. Another headliner was Mrs Boyd's Top Hat of Piperscroft, and then followed Mrs Austin Smith with Bob, Brioche, Bolero and Biscuit all of Braeval. Mrs Atkinson was much to the fore with Pixholme Firebrave Gustav and Milada. Mrs Coventon was nearly always at the top with Adastra Magic Beau, Magic Action and many others. Perhaps one of the most glorious blacks of all time was the late Mr Philippe Howard-Price's Braebeck Toni of Montfleuri, followed by Jonella of Montfleuri and Trilla of Montfleuri. Mr and Mrs Price throughout the years seemed to have that enviable knack of picking a winner for at almost every championship show another likely Montfleuri came prancing along to take the first prize. Another beautiful white was Mrs Birch's Tarrywood Starlight Glow, while Mrs Diana Waugh's Berinshill Dancing Boy won countless awards in this country, and continued his winning ways in Canada and the States. Mrs Ressenaar's Binkie of Piperscroft must not be forgotten, and Mrs Worth's Piccoli Peacock's Pride and Miss Pantlin's Rothara the Smuggler. For over fourteen years the authors' Rothara Kennel of white miniatures had considerable success, until their retirement from the show ring in 1960. That fine stud force Rothara the Rake scored countless bests-in-show, was the founder of the strain and lived to the ripe old age of seventeen years. Perhaps the outstanding female member of the kennel was Rothara the Gamine who won her championship in Britain and then went to the States where she gained Triple International Championship Status. Others of this strain who were all best-in-show and first prize winners, were Rothara the Roysterer, The Rascal, The Courtesan, The Ragamuffin, The Centurion, The Ragman, and many others.

A study of the certificate winners over the past years at some of the main shows will prove interesting for it shows the modern exhibitors and their dogs. Even more interesting is a study of the pedigrees behind these winners which confirms the splendid foundation which was laid by the old-time dedicated breeders, but unfortunately there is not room in a book of this size to quote such pedigrees. The asterisk (*) denotes best of breed.

Rothara the Rake, owned and bred by Margaret Sheldon and Barbara Lockwood. The winner of countless Bests-in-Show in the early 1950's, and foundation sire of the Rothara Poodles.

Crufts Championship Show (Poodles Miniatures)

Year	Sex	Challenge Certificate Winner	Owner	Judge
1976	*Dog	Ch. Tiopepi Tycoon	Mrs C. Coxall	Mrs E. Conn
	Bitch	Ch. Aesthete Hell's Bells	J. Currie	
1977	*Dog	Ch. Beritas Banacheke	Mrs R. Gee	Mr S. Jobson
	Bitch	Ch. Florontie Black Orchid	J. Outterside	
1978	Dog	Ch. Minarets the Maverick	Mrs M. Harwood	Miss C. Seidler
	*Bitch	Ch. Florontie Black Orchid	J. Outterside	
1979	*Dog	Ch. Jolanta By Jove	Mrs J. Porter	Mr N. Butcher
	Bitch	Ch. Montravia Lavinas Snow Blanche	Mrs P. Gibbs	
1980	*Dog	Ch. Suraliam Rupert	Mr & Mrs S & R Holmes	Mrs B.M. Gundry
	Bitch	Ch. Lochranza Ailsa	Mrs H. Lunnon-Turner	
1981	*Dog	Snowstar Charles	Mrs P. Gregory	Mr J. Outterside
	Bitch	Ch. Jolda Jacquenetta	Mr & Mrs J.A. Macdougall	
1982	*Dog	Ch. Romar Ringmaster	Mrs M. Boulton	Mr J. Braddon
	Bitch	Arrowflight Bista	Mrs H. Lunnon-Turner	

Champion Romar Ringmaster, judged the best Miniature dog at Crufts in 1982 by Mr Joe Braddon. This lovely dog is owned and bred by Mrs M. Boulton.

International Poodle Club Championship Show (Poodles Miniature)

Year	Sex	Challenge Certificate Winner	Owner	Judge
1976	*Dog	Jason of Montfleuri	Miss N. Stott	Miss J. Coram
	Bitch	Ch. Tiopepi Amber Tanya	Mrs C. Coxall	
1977	Dog	Ch. Tiopepi Typhoon	Mrs C. Coxall	Miss M. Dayer-Smith
	*Bitch	Ch. Vasahope Lucille	Mrs R.E. Price-Jones	
1978	*Dog	Eyecote Brandy – snap	Mrs A. Holland-Bignell	Miss B. Ringrose
	Bitch	Ch. Merit Michelle	Mrs J. Merritt	

Year	Sex	Challenge Certificate Winner	Owner	Judge
1979	Dog	Montravia Midnight Marksman	Mrs P. Gibbs	Mrs N. Howard-Price
	*Bitch	Ch. Montravia Lavinas Snow Blanche	Mrs P. Gibbs	
1980	Dog	Ch. Tiopepi Tempest	Mrs C. Coxall	Mrs H. Ridgen (New Zealand)
	*Bitch	Ch. Glayvar Graffitti	Mrs J. Clark	
1981	*Dog	Claridon of Montfleuri	Mrs E.R. Lee	Mrs S.R. Chamberlaine
	Bitch	Suraliam Wonder Woman	Mrs & Mrs R. Holmes	

Poodle Club Championship Show (Poodles Miniature)

Year	Sex	Challenge Certificate Winner	Owner	Judge
1976	*Dog	Ch. Tiopepi Tycoon	Mrs C. Coxall	Mrs A. Stevenson
	Bitch	Maralph Debutante	Mesdames Sillito & Milner	
1977	Dog	Ch. Minarets The Maverick	Mrs M. Harwood	Mrs M. Worth
	*Bitch	Shula of Romar	Mrs M. Boulton	
1978	*Dog	Ch. Jolanta By Jove	Mrs J. Porter	Mr H. Brunotte (Canada)
	Bitch	Lochranza Ailsa	Mrs H. Lunnon	

1979	*Dog	Ch. Lochranza Fozzy Bear of Filigran	Miss H. Smith	} Miss M. Gibbs
	Bitch	Tiopepi Star Attraction of Coelegant	Mrs J.O. Falconer-Atlee	
1980	*Dog	Ch. Suraliam Rupert	Mr & Mrs S. & R. Holmes	} Mrs H. Jennings
	Bitch	Ch. Lochranza Ailsa	Mrs Lunnon-Turner	
1981	*Dog	Frenches Toscanini	Mrs R.E. Price- Jones	} Mrs M. Watson
	Bitch	Ch. Astra of Colandra	Mr & Mrs C. Odell	

In the lists of winners at championship shows, many of the dogs and bitches mentioned have since become champions.

To conclude, it is the present day breeders and exhibitors who, having such enthusiasm and love for the breed, will ensure that the miniature poodle remains the dignified, elegant, modish dog who displays such a marvellous sense of humour and unlimited thinking power (his knowledge of words points to a large vocabulary) that he is without any possible doubt whatever, the most devoted, most entertaining and most intelligent companion that it is possible to own.

5 The Toy Poodle

PROBABLY no other variety of dog has risen to such immense popularity in so short a time. The popularity of the toy poodle has really been phenomenal, but as always seems to happen in such cases, the quality and soundness of this little dog did suffer very considerably during the early dwarfing process. Two methods were used to get the diminutive size. Some breeders felt very strongly that the only way to keep the elegance, and the lovely outline of the true poodle was to breed down from the as-near-as-possible faultless miniature, following the same procedure as had been originally employed to evolve the best miniatures directly down from the best type of standard poodle. Other breeders may have felt this would take too long and thus they imported very tiny toy poodles from America in order to speed up matters. Some of these American toys were sound, but many of them were not very elegant, being rather short on the leg with somewhat large, goggle eyes. Others, while certainly being extremely small, may not have been bred entirely true to poodles over the generations, such breeds as tiny Maltese perhaps having been introduced. These reduced the size quite quickly but brought with them such undesirable points as cotton wool coats, squirrel tails, short legs and long backs. It was really quite easy to see in the early toy poodles whether they had been bred down from miniatures or whether the quicker method had been employed.

Lady Stanier was certainly a pioneer in the breeding of toy poodles and her Seahorses Snow Queen was one of the smallest and most correctly balanced toys, for she was only 23cm (9″) high and measured only 23cm (9″) in length of back. Snow Queen was the dam of the renowned Seahorses Snow Marquess who was behind all Lady Stanier's toy poodles. His sire was Mrs Boyd's Drift of Piperscroft, a miniature who was able to sire small progeny when mated to a tiny bitch. Much later on, the authors' well known miniature poodle Rothara the Roysterer who was Best White Miniature at Crufts in 1958 was also able to sire tiny toys if mated to really small bitches, for he produced out of a small bitch belonging to Mrs Hall the tiny 21½cm (8½″) Rothara Wychwood the Spark and his 23cm (9″) sister. Spark lived to a ripe old age and was behind all the Rothara white toy poodles, and in his turn always reproduced himself in size.

Two of the first tiny toy poodles bred by Margaret Sheldon and Barbara Lockwood in their Rothara kennels in 1950.

The Recognition of Toy Poodles

However it was not until 1957 that toy poodles were recognised as a separate variety by the English Kennel Club. Up till then they were just small miniatures and had to compete against this size in the show ring. But in 1957 they were proclaimed a separate variety with a height maximum of 28cm (11″) at the shoulder. In the United States and Canada, the height of the toy poodle had been for some time 25cm (10″) at the shoulder. This was quite a headache to the toy breeders who wished to export their stock for it was difficult to reduce that extra inch and a great many toys 'grew' more than they should have done after arrival much to the disappointment of the buyers. Also as many English toys were evolved from miniatures they were inclined to throw back in size again in the next generation. So although numberless under 25cm (10″) English toys went to Canada and the States, their progeny often turned out to be well into miniature size. It is generally considered that 'line-breeding', that is breeding together dogs which are related (but not too closely) or of the same line, will produce a smaller size in progeny. (Readers are asked to turn to Chapter 16 which deals with this subject in greater detail). This type of line-breeding must not be confused with 'in-breeding' which is not really to be advocated, for in each case both good and bad faults were doubled in the progeny in greater proportions. It was done in certain cases, but both sire and dam had to be completely sound for it to be successful. This type of 'quick-result' breeding was absolutely disastrous in the hands of inexperienced breeders, and produced such dire results as extreme nervousness, bad temper, sterility and was responsible for stamping in a number of terrible defects which are only now being eradicated by perseverance on the part of careful and selective breeders, but its attraction for many of the more impatient breeders was the time factor.

Toy poodles were first accepted for registration as a separate variety of poodle by the Kennel Club in 1957, and 2,169 toys were registered in that year, and the number more than doubled to 4,590 in 1958. The number of miniature registrations for the same period was 18,340 and 21,239 respectively so the little toys had a long way to go.

A number of breeders, many of whom up to then had concentrated on miniatures, now began to breed toys. A lot of study and forethought was carried out and among those who were responsible for evolving through careful and selective breeding (and after a certain amount of trial and error), some of the best early toys must be noted: Mr and Mrs Andrews (Wendoley); Mrs Austin-Smith (Braeval); Mrs Barratt (Great Westwood); Mrs Brauer (Tenaver); Mrs Clarke (Filigree); Mrs Conn (Montmartre); Mrs Coventon (Adastra); Mrs Cox (Sudbrook); Mrs Davies (Cameo); Mrs Ellis (Merrymorn); Mrs Hall (Wychwood); Mrs Hilliard (Peaslake); Mrs Huxham (Emmrill); Mrs Price-Jones (Frenches); Miss Rees (Conersk); Lady Stanier (Seahorses); Mrs Strawson (Tophill); Mrs Thomas (Fircot); Mrs Proctor (Tzigane); Mr Walkden (Capilon); Mrs Wren (Braxted); and the authors' (Rothara).

Some of the first toys to do well in the show ring were Mrs Spencer's Poupon of Braxted, Mr and Mrs Andrews' Wendoley Annette, Mrs Bond's Tammy of Manapouri, Mrs Cox's Sudbrook Sunday Suit, Mrs Turner's Andavian Silver Dollar and the authors' Rothara Wychwood the Spark.

In 1958, which was the first time the toys were scheduled at Crufts there was an entry of 262 from 184 dogs, and ten years later in 1968 there were 332 entries from 206 dogs. In 1962 when it could be said that they were at their zenith there was an entry at Crufts of 410 from 242 dogs. The co-author of this book, Mrs Sheldon, was called on to judge an entry of no less than thirty-nine in the puppy dog class and fifty-five in the puppy bitch class – an almost insurmountable task with only three cash prizes available to award to the winners in each class.

Registrations

The registrations of toy poodles over the years makes interesting reading for in 1959 they totalled 7,132 and were in fifth place of all breeds. They went on from strength to strength with 11,305 (1961), 11,810 (1962) and 11,013 (1963). In 1966, toys came to within 200 of the miniature registrations, and in 1967 beat them by just on 1,000 when miniatures dropped to fourth place (all breeds) and in 1968 the toy still stayed ahead by over 1,500 registrations, but were in fourth place pushing the miniature down to sixth place. But the totals began to drop, possibly because exports fell due to some of the very unsound toys which were being sent abroad, and this was the best thing that could happen as the selective, honest breeders went doggedly on and to their great credit produced more and more really lovely toy poodles. Perhaps a result of

This tiny apricot toy poodle Champion Oakington Puckshill Amber Sunblush, owned by Mrs Perry and bred by Mrs Myles Dobson was the first toy poodle to gain Best in Show all breeds at Crufts in 1966.

this careful and untiring selection of only the best has culminated in 1982 with Mrs Leslie Howard's glorious little chocolate bitch Champion Grayco Hazelnut gaining the award of Supreme Best in Show at Crufts. In all, only three poodles have ever gained this great award – Mrs Proctor's standard poodle Champion Tzigane Aggri of Nashend bred by Miss Joan Eddie. This was in 1955. Then in 1966, Mrs Perry's Champion Oakington Puckshill Amber Sunblush, a tiny apricot poodle bred by Mrs Myles Dobson, and now this lovely chocolate Ch. Grayco Hazelnut in 1982.

To return to registration totals, in 1975 the numbers had fallen to 5,174. From April 1976, only those dogs on the active register of the Kennel Club were included in the totals, and thus for 1976 – 2,957, 1977 – 2,025, 1978 – 3,920, 1979 – 5,170, and 1980 – 4,344, but still well ahead of their bigger brothers and sisters – the standard and miniature poodles.

Having mentioned many of the early toys and their breeders, it may prove of interest to look at some of the challenge certificate winners of both sexes, together with their owners, and the judges at some of the principal shows which scheduled toy poodles over the last few years. The asterisk (*) denotes best of breed.

The Poodle Club Championship Show (Poodles Toy)

Year	Sex	Challenge Certificate Winner	Owner	Judge
1976	*Dog	Sumbuddy of Silcresta	D. Wickens	Mrs A. Rogers-Clark
	Bitch	Ch. Benidorm Daisy's Image of Great Westwood	Mrs G. Barratt	
1977	Dog	Bareza Bonaparte	Mrs S. Breeze	Mrs B.P. Perry
	*Bitch	Ch. Bartat Burnt Almond of Grayco	Mrs L. Howard	
1978	Dog	Ch. Dourado Dashing of Roseala	Mr & Mrs T.W. Mott	Miss R. Gregory
	*Bitch	Ch. Ridingleaze Dainty Toes of Valetta	Miss V.M. Dunn	
1979	No challenge certificates on offer			
1980	No challenge certificates on offer			
1981	No challenge certificates on offer			

Cruft's Championship Show (Poodles Toy)

Year	Sex	Challenge Certificate Winner	Owner	Judge
1976	Dog	Ch. Sunnitoun Black Everard of Branslake	Mrs S.J. Beech	Mr K. Bullock
	*Bitch	Ch. Benidorm Daisy's Image of Great Westwood	Mrs G. Barratt	
1977	Dog	Ch. Sumbuddy of Silcresta	D. Wickens	Miss H. Sherry
	*Bitch	Ch. Clopton Tiger Bay	Mrs S.P. Jones	
1978	*Dog	Ch. Sumbuddy of Silcresta	D. Wickens	Mrs R. Gee
	Bitch	Ch. Aspen Arethusa	Mrs S. Mackenzie-Spencer	
1979	Dog	Ch. Lotsmoor Honky Tonk	P. Young	Miss C. Hawkes
	*Bitch	Ch. Ridingleaze Dainty Toes of Valetta	Miss V.M. Dunn	
1980	Dog	Persan Barnaby Fudge	Mrs S.R. Chamberlaine	Miss K. Machon
	*Bitch	Ch. Grayco Hazelnut	Mrs L. Howard	
1981	Dog	Ch. Valencia Mr Wonderful	Miss A. Hayland	Mrs O. Bullock
	*Bitch	Ch. Grayco Hazelnut	Mrs L. Howard	
1982	Dog	Ch. Suraliam Boogy Woogy From Velveteen	Mrs P. Morris	Mrs M. Watson
	*Bitch	Ch. Grayco Hazelnut	Mrs L. Howard	

and Hazelnut also gained the top award of Best in Show all breeds.

The International Poodle Club Championship Show (Poodles Toy)

Year	Sex	Challenge Certificate Winner	Owner	Judge
1976	*Dog	Ch. Sudbrook Sunday Glad Rags	Mrs H. Cox	Miss Warren Wise
	Bitch	Ch. Great Westwood Halloween of Benidorm	Mrs G. Barratt	
1977	*Dog	Ch. Sumbuddy of Silcresta	D. Wickens	Mr J. Cartledge
	Bitch	Embercourt Time goes by	Mrs J. & Miss Sheard	

1978–80 No challenge certificates in Kennel Club calendar for toy poodles

Year	Sex	Challenge Certificate Winner	Owner	Judge
1981	*Dog	Suraliam Boogy Woogy from Velveteen	Mrs P.A. Morris	Mrs B. Sillito
	Bitch	Vanitonia School for Scandal	Messrs Stone & Thompson	

As no challenge certificates were on offer for toy poodles in 1978, 1979 and 1980 at the International Poodle Club Championship Show, nor in 1979, 1980 and 1981 at the Poodle Club Championship Show, it may be interesting to record the results of the British Toy Poodle Club Championship Show, and some of the regional club championship shows in 1980 and 1981.

The British Toy Poodle Club Championship Show

Year	Sex	Challenge Certificates Winner	Owner	Judge
1980	Dog	Snowstar Ray	Mr & Mrs Gregory	Mrs Phillips
	*Bitch	Ch. Grayco Hazelnut	Mrs L. Howard.	Mrs S. Coupe
1981	*Dog	Ch. Malibu Son of a Bear at Tuttlebees	Mr Norman Butcher	Mr H. Jordan
	Bitch	Ch. Malibu the Sinful Skinful	Miss K. Sillito	Mr W. Taylor

Champion Malibu Son of a Bear at Tuttlebees, a fine little black toy owned by Mr and Mrs Norman Butcher.

The Mercia Toy Poodle Association Championship Show

Year	Sex	Challenge Certificates Winner	Owner	Judge
1980	Dog	Merrymorn Golden Sorrell	Mrs L.E. Ellis	Mr B. Gregory
	*Bitch	Ch. Grayco Hazelnut	Mrs L. Howard	Mr J. Hiddlestone
1981	*Dog	Malibu Son of a Bear at Tuttlebees	Mr and Mrs N.E. Butcher	Mr Bayliss
	Bitch	Stonesby Aria of Aesthete	Mesdames Howard & Heron	Mr P. Parkinson

The Northern Toy Poodle Club Championship Show

Year	Sex	Challenge Certificates Winner	Owner	Judge
1980	Dog	Vallencia Mr Wonderful	Miss A. Hyland	Mr P. Frederico
	*Bitch	Ch. Grayco Hazelnut	Mrs L. Howard	
1981	Dog	Kivox Rustler of Ranjis	Messrs Walkden and Helm	Mrs P. Rose
	*Bitch	Risette Country Attraction	Mr R. Bayliss	

From these results it will be seen that Mr Donald Wickens, Mrs Barratt, Mrs Harold Cox and Miss Dunn were nearly always at the top, and it is interesting to note that Mrs Howard's Ch. Grayco Hazelnut was judged best of breed at Crufts in 1980, a forerunner to the exciting day at Crufts in February 1982, when she won the supreme award.

Many, many other outstanding toy poodles have distinguished themselves – for instance Mrs Ellis and Miss Sherry's Ch. Merrymorn Golden Sorell, who seems so often to have had a ding-dong battle with 'Hazelnut' for best of breed at so many of the championship shows up and down the country – in fact, both owners must often have wished the other had stayed at home! Mrs Ellis and Miss Sherry have certainly made a name for themselves in the toy poodle world, particularly with their apricots. The lovely little dog Ch. Merrymorn Hot Rod, a very worthy companion of Ch. Golden Sorrell also comes from these kennels, and a lovely up and coming son of Hot Rod named Merrymorn Phoenix who has already gained a reserve challenge certificate and reserve best of breed.

It is very obvious the toy poodle is really a V.I.P. in the English show ring and can obviously stand up to all contenders.

A word about the British Toy Poodle Club which is entirely devoted to this variety. The club was founded by Lady Stanier in 1956 and now has a flourishing membership. Mrs Sheila Cox of the Sudbrook toys is the untiring secretary of the club and she is always willing to help toy poodle enthusiasts. There is also the London and Home Counties Toy Poodle Club, the Mercia Toy Poodle Association, and the Northern Toy Poodle Club, and of course many of the regional poodle clubs have thriving toy poodle sections. All those who are really interested in the toy poodle and are contemplating showing this delightful breed should get in touch with

Champion Grayco Hazelnut, possibly the most outstanding chocolate toy poodle of all times, owned by Mrs Leslie Howard. This tiny little bitch was judged Best of Breed by Margaret Watson at Crufts 1982, went on to win Best of Utility Group under Rita Price-Jones, and then finally Mr Reg Gadsden awarded her Supreme Best in Show.

the secretary of the selected club for the interest and experience – to say nothing of the fun – to be gained from membership is enormous. A list of clubs and secretaries is given in Chapter 21.

Certainly the toy poodle is a little aristocrat of a dog, with loads of courage and a delightful sense of humour. He has tremendous devotion to his owner yet never fawns. There are, of course, the odd nervous toys, but generally speaking the temperament is becoming more and more comparable with that of his bigger cousins, the standards and the miniatures. If only all toy breeders will be selective in their breeding programmes, always putting the best to the best, then the toy poodle will yet again rise above all other breeds as happened at Crufts in 1982.

6 Selecting a Puppy

THE selection of just the right puppy needs a lot of thought. After all, the puppy is going to be your constant companion for at least twelve years, or if you are lucky for an even longer period. Therefore it is not an undertaking that can be embarked on lightly. If you were buying a house you would want to know that it was structurally well built, you would want one which was in good condition and which would not need a lot of repairs, you would choose one which appealed to your eye, and was pleasant to look at, and probably you would want a house which had a pleasant atmosphere. Now the same considerations apply when selecting a puppy but in a rather different way. You will wish to have a puppy which is well built and not one which is out of proportion and moves badly, you will want a healthy puppy stemming from healthy, fit parents and one which will not involve you in a lot of veterinary expense, you will want a good looking dog and one which has a pleasant temperament so that the atmosphere of your house is improved by the presence of the new puppy. All these points can be achieved provided sufficient care and thought are expended in the first instance.

But perhaps the primary consideration is to be sure that you are the right person to own a dog, the kind of person who can make your poodle happy and comfortable. Not everyone can do this. For those who spend most of the day either out on social occasions or who work at a job away from home from nine to five a poodle, or indeed any kind of dog, would not find himself in the ideal home. Poodles like company, both human and canine, and are inclined to mope a little if left by themselves for too long. They are such companionable and devoted dogs, and it is not fair to subject them to loneliness and boredom. So in these circumstances it might be better to wait until you can look forward to being at home most of the day and can give your poodle all the company he needs. If you are newly married a dog is nice to have – but will you have any time for him when the first baby comes along, and also would he be jealous at having to take second place? This latter position really depends on you, because if you are sufficiently fond of your poodle you will train him to love the new baby and guard it with his life. Poodles, if brought up with children, become tremendous friends and playmates, and are certainly wonderful guard dogs but the introduction to either a new baby or to small children must be done tactfully and slowly, and the poodle must not feel resentful or feel that he is being pushed out.

SELECTING A POODLE PUPPY 65

Spoilt Poodles

Poodles are so super-intelligent that they can easily wreck a home, but if they do, it is almost invariably the fault of the owner. This sounds rather exaggerated, but often a puppy is so indulged and spoilt that everything and everybody in the home is sacrificed to him. He knows his power and uses it and as a result no one is really happy – least of all the poodle. He soon learns to bring about a state of affairs where he spoils every meal by worrying for food, where he is so noisy with strangers or callers that no one can make themselves heard, where owners cannot attend any small social affairs such as a cinema or a dinner date, because the dog 'couldn't be left alone'. Holidays abroad or to some place where dogs are not welcome cannot be even contemplated because the dog 'would be unhappy in kennels'. This is all absolute nonsense, and provided the poodle is trained right from the start to stay quietly alone for periods that are not *too long* and not *too frequent*, and provided he is given toys with which to play and amuse himself, then he will be a very pleasant chap to have about the house and one who will be the pivot of the family in a nice way for all the days of his life. It is all a matter of training the puppy carefully and not allowing yourself to lay up a lot of trouble through spoiling and lack of kind, firm discipline. The character of the poodle is almost invariably a reflection of that of his owner – a salutary thought indeed! But more about training in the relative chapter. Here we are dealing with earlier considerations of puppy selection.

Poodle Guards

In these days of thugs and vandals, a dog can be a good deterrent. Even if the dog will not actually bite, he will make a lot of noise if strangers attack or break-in. Therefore a poodle with plenty of spirit is needed, and not a cringing, nervous type. On the other hand, any poodle who is too aggressive is to be avoided, and temperament, while difficult to assess in the eight-week-old, can often be guessed at by meeting the sire and dam, for temperament is an inherited factor in most cases. So ideally one needs the poodle who is loving and friendly to his immediate family, polite but not too gushing to outside-the-family friends, suspicious of strangers, and definitely aggressive and noisy to any whom he thinks might cause trouble to his owners. All this is not too difficult to come by as it more or less sums up the typical poodle's character.

What Sex?

Then, of course, there is the question of whether it shall be a dog or a bitch. This really must be a matter of personal choice. Some say bitches are more affectionate, others say dogs are more loyal. Dogs may be more aggressive, while bitches may be more clinging and inclined to jealousy. Bitches have the inconvenience of coming in season every six months – this may cause a little trouble with children, and also may occasion a certain amount of mess at the time. Equally dogs may be inclined to roam, particularly when a bitch in an interesting condition is anywhere in the neighbourhood. But the drawbacks in either sex are really negligible in most cases. Dogs can be castrated and bitches spayed if really necessary which will obviate the nuisance. It is often said that castrated dogs and spayed bitches become lethargic and sometimes tend to obesity in old age. The authors have never found this to be so, and when living in a town or in a flat where there are dogs of the opposite sex around, it is quite a blessing. Dogs should be castrated around nine to ten months before they have learned to be interested in bitches, while if possible it is better for bitches to have one litter before spaying, but this is not really important and the veterinary surgeon will advise on the best time. Certainly castrated dogs will not stray and this is a great consideration especially where there is no fenced-in garden, for instance in a block of flats. In the case of the bitch, spaying will of course obviate the nuisance of her coming in season and the accompanying trouble of visiting suitors. It also helps when making holiday arrangements. Having said all that, if none of these conditions are important to the owner then it is obviously better for the poodle to have a normal sex life.

Size

The matter of size is another consideration. The large standard poodle is ideal for the big house with plenty of grounds, or in places where it is possible to give a lot of exercise. He measures anything from 58cm (23") from top of shoulder to ground and weighs possibly over 18kg (40lb). The big fellows are also excellent with children and splendid guards. They can be trained to the gun with the greatest of ease and have good mouths for game. The miniature poodle, who measures under 38cm (15") at the shoulder and weighs 5½–8kg (12–18lb), is an excellent companion for nearly all grades of society. He fits well into the moderate sized house, can be taken almost anywhere, is a good guard, has a moderate appetite (and in these days of high-priced dog meat this is a consideration), and he is not so expensive to clip, shampoo or board as his big brother, the standard. The toy poodle is an equally good companion, very easy to carry under the arm into any shop or on a bus, for he measures under 28cm (11") and weighs a mere 4½kg (10lb) or less, is a small feeder, needs negligible exercise and is therefore very suitable for life in a flat or small town house, and in view of his light weight is an ideal pet for the not-so-young. So really choice in the matter of size rests on individual living conditions and circumstances and it should not be too difficult to make the right choice.

Two wicked little puppies thinking up some devilment!

Colour

Colour again is a completely personal matter. Whites have very placid, quiet temperaments as a rule but need rather frequent shampooing if they are to look smart. Blacks are full of energy and verve, as are browns. Apricots are lovely to look at if they are a deep colour, but disappointment may occur here for the colour often fades as they mature. The perfect apricot-coloured puppy may well turn into a dirty cream at a year old. The best success in this colour would come from choosing a puppy that is a really dark tan when six or eight-weeks-old. Silvers are extremely pretty, but perhaps slightly highly strung. Again, silvers are almost black when puppies and may not completely turn to an even silver all over until three-years-old. So it would appear that if you want to be absolutely sure that as a novice you get the colour you want, the whites or blacks would be the best buy.

Age

Age is our next consideration, and provided always that your *circumstances allow of this* then the young puppy would be the best proposition. In the eight-week-old puppy you can start from the beginning to train him in your own ways, and what he learns between eight and sixteen weeks of his life usually sticks with him for always. Also at this age he is easier to train providing you are firmly kind. If you take on a youngster of six months to a year or older then you may find instilled in him so many traits and habits that you do not like and which are extremely hard to eradicate. Also it must be remembered that there must be some reason why an older dog is offered for sale – perhaps he has never been taught to be clean, perhaps he is unreliable in temper, perhaps if a dog he is embarrassingly 'sexy', perhaps he is a roamer, perhaps he is destructive. There are so many 'perhaps' in cases like this where you have not been able to train him in your own ways from the word 'go'. Admittedly, there may be perfectly legitimate reasons such as the owner going abroad or having to move to a flat where dogs are not allowed, change of job – but all such reasons need close investigation. If buying a really good show puppy it is generally better to buy a youngster who has a good potential, that is appears to have all the good points rather than an older 'potential show dog'. If, when he is older, he were potentially outstanding it is unlikely the present owners would wish to sell. He may be good, but he may not be *quite* right in every detail, and in view of his age he will certainly be far more expensive than a puppy.

Health

Now the health of the puppy offered for sale must be carefully considered. It is often recommended when selecting a puppy, that he should be taken to a vet for a qualified opinion before making a decision. This is all right for the prospective owner, but the vendor may feel very loath to let the puppy out of his possession especially if he is to be taken to a vet's surgery where he could pick up any kind of infection, and bring this back to all the other puppies in the litter, for he is probably too young to be protected by inoculation. Therefore it seems hardly fair to suggest this. A safer way might be to ask the vet to come to the puppy but of course this will cost £6 to £10. There are pointers, though, in the matter of health which should reassure the would-be buyer when examining a puppy. Firstly, the eyes should be bright, dark and sparkling. A dull eye may mean presence of worms, unhygienic living conditions and general lack of condition. The coat should be shining, thick and clean, and the skin should be loose. A dull, sticky, unpleasant smelling coat means bad conditions, while a scurfy coat usually denotes parasites of some sort, and a tight skin points to worms or general unhealthiness. Any soreness around the anus means that the puppy has, or has had a certain amount of diarrhoea, again pointing to worms or sour feeding. Any yellow discharge from nose, eyes, penis or vulva is a bad sign and may mean unhealthiness or disease of some sort. Thus all the external parts should be carefully checked, and if the puppy measures up well to such an examination you can be reasonably sure that he is healthy and well fed and reared.

Two examples of the right kind of temperament when choosing a puppy.

Temperament

Temperament comes next. This can be assessed up to a point in the young pup. The one that waddles or runs to you, wants to nibble your fingers, untie your shoe laces, and wags his small stump of a tail is probably a good natured pup with a good temperament. The puppy who backs into a corner, regards you with apprehension possibly showing the whites in the corners of his eyes, and when touched possibly rolls on his back and urinates slightly is a potentially nervous puppy and should be avoided. The puppy who screams and struggles when picked up may also be highly strung and unstable. So often the apprehensive and nervous puppy appeals to the buyer simply because he is rather pathetic at that age. The nervous shrinking puppy may well touch one's heart, but he is very likely to grow up into a dog who is really spiteful and who can never be trusted even with his owner. But as already said, it is always difficult to be quite sure of temperament at this early age and it may help the prospective buyer to see and get to know the sire and dam of the puppy.

When approaching a young puppy with a view to assessing temperament, go to him slowly and quietly. Hold out the back of your hand for him to sniff. Never pounce on a puppy and pick him up with a swish. Apart from making his head whirl, he is bound to be scared about it and will probably struggle and yelp, and thus give you an entirely wrong idea about his temperament. This of course applies to the approach to any strange dog, whether a puppy or an adult. When picking up a puppy hold him firmly round his middle and support his back legs with the other hand. Always be prepared for the sudden leap out of your arms, as this could lead to broken bones or dislocated joints. Often puppies coming from a distance by rail or plane may be almost unhandleable on arrival. Not too much notice should be taken of this. Give the puppy time to settle, let him be quiet, and speak to him very gently, let him find his own way about for an hour or so. His apparent nervousness may well be due to the terror of the journey, but being young he will quickly get over this and be none the worse, and if his temperament is fundamentally sound he will soon be bouncing around.

Structure

The structural points of the poodle do not always manifest themselves very clearly in the young puppy. However, a good head can usually be discovered for with it will go a flat cheek, a smallish eye not too wide-set, and low ears which fall closely to the side of the head. A slightly Roman nose also points to a long head when mature. Provided the puppy has this kind of a head it is reasonable to expect that it will mature into a good one.

Forelegs should be straight and parallel. A good way to check this is to have the puppy standing on a table facing you, then put a hand on each side of the shoulder and lift the puppy an inch or so from the ground, and then let him drop gently on to the table again. This will usually tell whether his legs are straight, or whether he is bow legged or knock kneed. If he is a little out in the shoulder his toes will turn in, but if he is narrow chested and the shoulder does not slope correctly then his legs will be too close together and his toes will turn outwards. To check on freedom of movement of hind legs, raise the puppy slightly by placing a hand round his neck and with finger and thumb lift him by the end of his tail and view him sideways. If the forelegs and hind legs are parallel and drop down straightly his quarters are good, but if as you lift him his hindlegs shoot towards his front legs at an angle, the quarters and hind angulation are suspect, and his rear action is likely to be stilted with little freedom.

His tail should be set on fairly high, and a low set tail goes with a roach back and pinned-in hind action.

The puppy's back should be short, with ribs well sprung. Balance in the poodle is all important and he should measure the same distance from nape of neck to root of tail as from top of shoulder to ground – in other words he should resemble a square box. (See Fig. 13 in Chapter 2)

These points should be apparent in the young puppy, but various other good points will probably not manifest themselves until the puppy is considerably older. For instance, one can check that a puppy's mouth is even and that he has a level bite but this does not mean to say that the mouth will not become undershot (that is, lower teeth protruding over top teeth) when he gets his second teeth. If his mouth is level as a puppy it is unlikely that it will become overshot (i.e. top teeth considerably further over the bottom teeth). He may be out at elbow or out at shoulder up to about twelve months of age which causes him to 'weave' or cross his front legs when walking, but the shoulders and elbows often tighten as the poodle matures and he will then be perfectly sound.

However, if an adult or near-adult poodle is being considered for purchase, it is suggested that the would-be buyer turns back to Chapter 2 and reads this again very carefully, for the authors have endeavoured to describe therein as simply as possible exactly what the Standard of the breed lays down and means. From that a fairly correct judgement of the quality of the proposed new poodle can be made, and glaring faults would be discovered. If a show dog is required, then faults cannot be tolerated, and the very best specimen that can be afforded is important. If the poodle is required for breeding purposes, again the best you can afford will pay handsome dividends, but here it is very helpful if you can see both the sire and dam of the poodle you wish to buy because faults (and equally good points) skip a generation and come out in the grandchildren. If it is a companion poodle you need, again go for the best your pocket will sanction, and weigh up the small faults you may discover and decide whether they will be all that important. Perhaps the faults which should not be under-rated at any cost would be (1) snappy or nervous temperament; (2) badly overshot or undershot mouth; (3) prominent or bulbous eyes which may lead to 'weeping' or some eye disease; and finally (4) any mis-marking such as white feet and patches on chests of black poodles; apricot or brown ear fringes on whites; a very pale apricot colour in apricot or brown poodle puppies as this will turn to a dirty cream when mature.

If the puppy is a male then the presence of testicles should be checked. Mostly this is possible at eight weeks, although a puppy with both testicles descended in the scrotum at eight weeks may sometimes tuck them away when he is a little older during the adolescent period. However, it is generally safe to say that if the testicles have both been located in a puppy at some time, that he will be 'entire' when adult. If he is to be shown or bred from, the presence of both testicles in the scrotum is essential. Also this is so if he is to be exported. But for the companion poodle who is not to be used for stud it is really of no consequence. A *monorchid*, which is a dog with only one testicle descended into the scrotum can sire puppies but he is not considered to be as reliable in this respect as the dog which has both testicles descended and is said to be 'entire'. A *cryptorchid* is a dog which has neither testicle descended in the

A young standard
poodle puppy waiting for
a game.

scrotum and in this case he cannot sire puppies. It is sometimes extremely difficult to check the young puppy, for one thing he is inclined to wriggle and also the testicles may come and go with any change of temperature. In cold weather they often disappear, while after a warm bath they are easier to find. The puppy should either be stood on a table or held in your arms on his back. The first two fingers should be run gently downwards on either side of the penis towards the anus. If the puppy is entire two small lumps, usually about the size of a pea and rather jelly-like in substance will be felt.

It is often said that the expert can tell the outstanding puppy immediately he is born, and then not again until after five or six months and the authors would agree with that. However, that does not mean to say that a puppy cannot be considered potentially good *before* five or six months – he certainly can. But the operative word is 'potentially' because there is no doubt that the apparently marvellous puppy can 'go off' in a disappointing way. It is not always the breeder's or the vendor's fault if a nice puppy grows up a bit of an ugly duckling – nor can he know that the somewhat plain puppy sold as a pet may sometimes take all before him and land up a champion!

But if you are doubtful as to whether you are competent to pick the best from a litter, take an unbiased knowledgeable friend to help. Poodle owners are friendly people and will usually assist in this way.

In conclusion, it cannot be too strongly stressed that good, healthy, foundation stock is really important. When you are contemplating buying a pet puppy talk to as many knowledgeable poodle breeders as possible, find out who has healthy, sturdy poodles locally. Your vet can probably help, for he, better than anyone, will know which breeders have weedy, temperamentally unsound puppies. Try to see relations of the puppy you have in mind and consider whether these match up to the kind of poodle you wish to buy. Don't be soft hearted and fall for the weak, shy, underfed little fellow who will cause you a great deal of trouble and expense. Recommendation is the very best advertisement – if a particular line or kennel is well recommended, it is worth enquiring if they have a suitable puppy. If it is a show puppy you want, buy the best you can possibly afford from a strain which repeatedly breeds winners and which has a reputation for being temperamentally sound. Attend shows, talk to exhibitors, study the dogs both on the benches and in the ring. If you particularly like a specific dog, find out what he has sired, or even better if there are puppies from his sire or grandsire. Shop around exhaustively, for as with everything else, the more trouble you take the more likely you are to find just the right thing. There is no such thing as the perfect poodle as yet – but you may be lucky and get as near as no matter. And what fun you'll have campaigning him to his championship title!

7 Rearing and Training

THE rearing and training of the poodle puppy calls for a lot of thought and planning on the part of the owner. The poodle usually has a strong character and there is no doubt that he is somewhat pig-headed! Therefore, unless you make up your mind that you are going to be equally strong willed, your poodle will take advantage of this and do exactly as *he* wishes throughout his whole life. It has been noticed that the somewhat flabby, characterless owner who professes to love his or her poodle more than life itself, generally owns a thoroughly spoilt little dog.

The Spoilt Poodle

A dog who can never be left alone because he creates a rumpus, a dog who is noisy and annoys all the neighbours, a dog who will not quietly ride in a car because he has never been properly trained to do so, and one who can never be left with anyone else for even short periods because he frets and won't eat – are all results of being thoroughly spoilt and made a complete fool of by his owners! In fact, he manages completely to spoil the owner's life. Some people will say this is a very hard outlook, but that isn't really the case for the spoilt dog is so often unhappy and disturbed, whereas the well trained dog knows how to behave and enjoys tremendously the companionship he has with his owner through understanding and carrying out the wishes of that owner. The spoilt dog is always at war with humans, whereas the well trained dog is always in accord and therefore a happy dog.

Educating the Poodle

It is worth considering how the young poodle puppy can be educated. There is no doubt he is brainy, and if his training is started when he is really young he will very quickly learn his lessons. It is surprising what a large vocabulary the trained poodle possesses. He will learn not only a lot of words, but whole sentences, and it is a great joy to the owner to find that a really sensible conversation can be carried on between him and his poodle. Although the poodle cannot, unfortunately, reply with actual words, his expression and actions will supply his side of the conversation and it is quite obvious that he is understanding every single word that is said to him. This happy state only occurs if the owner is really going to put himself out to teach him all that he should know. Equally because he has trained the mind of his poodle, the owner must give his dog complete protection in every sphere because he has instilled in him a great sensitivity. He must be sure that when he has to leave him for any period, long or short, that his poodle will be well-cared for and comfortable, he must ensure that his physical comforts such as warmth, good food, proper bedding are all attended to. The poodle has been trained to behave impeccably and therefore this must not be traded on. He must never be subjected to unhappiness, discomfort and anxiety just because the owner knows he will be 'good and not make a fuss'. There is no doubt that the education of a poodle lays a very great responsibility on the owner.

Settling in

To begin with, the new puppy, when he leaves his mother and his brothers and sisters, is going to feel very strange and very homesick. It is a similar feeling to one's first day at school – exciting but terrifying! In the case of a puppy he is so small amongst the humans who tower above him, and there are so many feet about the place. He misses the warmth and security of his nest so very much for a little while – and the nights are so long and dark. The owner will readily understand what a tremendous strain the puppy will undergo when he comes into his new home by himself. And because his nerves are 'edgy', possibly this can cause a bit of a tummy upset. So for the first forty-eight hours after the new puppy is brought home he should be kept as quiet as possible and fed on a light diet. There are possibly friends and relations who want to see the new acquisition, but let him get used to you and the strange house first.

It is advisable to find out from the breeder exactly how he has been fed, and keep to this diet for a few days, even though it is not what you had in mind for him. When he is quite settled you can introduce him to your own ideas of a good diet. Here are some hints for a well balanced menu for the six to twelve-week-old puppy. The quantities are for a miniature poodle and should be slightly less for a toy poodle, and doubled for a standard poodle puppy.

Breakfast: 8.30 a.m. A drink of Farex made with warm milk with a little glucose added. Or alternatively some cereal and milk such as Weetabix, Corn Flakes or Shredded Wheat. A small teaspoonful of honey can be added.

Dinner: 12.30 p.m. 50–75g (2–3oz) or one to two heaped tablespoonfuls

Puppies feeding from a dish about 3″ off the ground which trains them to carry their heads well and prevents them from splaying out their front legs – all good training for the show ring. (These are the puppies at six weeks, which were shown during the whelping in Chapter 18).

of raw or cooked minced beef. This should be slightly warm, (never frozen or too hot). As alternatives tripe, liver, heart, or fish chopped very finely, with a small quantity of brown breadcrumbs, or crumbled Farley rusk, moistened with non-fatty gravy.

Tea: 4.0 p.m. A saucer of warm milk or milky tea.

Supper: 5.30 p.m. As for dinner. Occasionally a hard boiled egg or a scrambled egg may be given as a change.

Bedtime: a *large* bone to gnaw, or a rusk or a crust of brown bread very *lightly* spread with butter, margarine or dripping.

It is better not to give him a milky drink (unless he is *very* young) before bedding him down – he will stay cleaner through the night if he doesn't have one. Clean cold water must be available for him always, and the water pot should be kept in the same place so that he knows exactly where to find it. If the puppy has come on a long car journey or by train it is better not to feed him for at least an hour after his arrival. Then he can have a good drink of milk and honey, or glucose.

Be sure that you have made a list of everything you will want for him, so that it is ready when he arrives.

Now his sleeping arrangements must be considered. Everyone imagines that the silence of the night is bound to be disturbed by blood curdling yells for at least a week. This is not in the least necessary. Puppies usually cry for two reasons – they are either cold, or else they are lost in the dark. Get a large box, a tea-chest is ideal and put a good layer of wood-wool, or failing that, straw, though this is not so cosy, and make a round nest for the puppy. If it is cold weather place a hot water bottle in the bed for ten minutes or so before the pup is put to bed but be sure to remove the bottle then. Pop the puppy into the warm nest, and cover the box with a blanket with the exception of a few inches for air. The puppy is then warm, there is no fear of him getting out of his bed and becoming lost in a strange room, and it is nearly certain you won't hear a sound all night after the first two minutes. After some time he can graduate to a bed into which he can hop whenever he wants to do so. A large cardboard box with one side cut down to about 8cm (3″) is the best, for this is renewable. He is bound to try out his teeth on it and so it is better to wait until he is over this puppy occupation before buying a permanent and more elaborate bed or basket.

The Play Box

You should give your puppy a 'play box' for this will provide him with immense pleasure and also keep him busy when you must go out and leave him. This should be in the form of a cardboard box which is low enough for him to pull out his toys. Some suggestions for toys are a ball, a slipper, a knotted nylon stocking, a large marrow bone, a chewstick and anything else he might fancy. Let him unpack his toys for himself – he will soon learn to do this, but unfortunately it does not seem possible to teach even a poodle to put them away neatly after playtime!

House Training

Then we come to the all important work of training him to be clean. This needs a lot of patience and plenty of planning. He will want to do his business as soon as he wakes up, and also when he has had a meal, and this is where one needs to be quick. Immediately he wakes, pick him up and take him to a special place in the garden, and once he has used this particular place he will always perform there in the future. If you live in a flat or any place that has no garden, you may wish to train your puppy to newspaper, and the same principles apply. As soon as he has performed tell him he is a very good boy, and make a fuss of him. It is not the slightest use to scold or smack him or put him out *after* he has made his puddle, as he simply will not know what you mean. It is much better to work on the principle of anticipating his needs in this direction, and praise him for being good. At first he may need taking out many times a day, but after a little while he will have more control and will not need to relieve himself so often. It must be remembered that a young puppy has virtually no control, and it happens without warning and even without his knowing that it has happened, and therefore it is up to you to plan so that it happens in the right place.

Another important point is to train him to stay alone quietly when you want to go out, and this training must be started when he is as young as possible. There is nothing worse than the poodle who will not be left alone and who, because of initial bad training, becomes a burden to his owner. This is where the play-box comes in and it should be produced when he is to be left. It will take his attention off the fact that he is alone and he will very soon accept this as a foregone conclusion. You *must* be strong-minded when you are teaching him to be quiet, and if he cries don't go to him or he will very soon learn that he has only to cry to get exactly what he wants. Equally he will just as quickly learn that it is no use crying if nothing happens. So leave him, and he will soon be amusing himself.

Lead Training and Road Drill

Lead training forms the next part of his training. Some poodles are extremely 'awkward' about this while others learn at once. It is certainly a matter of patience. First put a very light collar on him, possibly a felt-lined cat collar is as good as anything. Let him get used to this for a day or so. At first he will scratch madly and roll over on his back in an effort to get the collar in his teeth. Take the collar off at night in case of accidents. Play with him for a while and then quite quickly slip a lead on to his collar. He may sit and look at this but usually a puppy does not mind a lead until it is picked up and he feels constraint. Then the fun starts! He may do everything to get rid of it from turning somersaults to chewing it up. Persevere by holding the lead slackly and going where *he* wants to go to begin with. After a little while try offering him a tit-bit that he particularly likes and try to cajole him to come towards you while you gently pull the lead. He will very likely be stubborn and dig his front toes in, completely refusing to move. Drop the lead, picking it up again a few minutes later. He will learn in time especially if he is given something nice every time he co-operates until he has thoroughly learnt his lesson. 'Good Boy' drops or chocolate drops are especially good as rewards in any training exercise.

Another essential is his training in road drill. He cannot be started too early in this. Once he is really used to the lead he should be taught simple commands such as 'Sit', 'Stay', 'Come', 'Over'. When he begins to take walks on the road he should learn to 'Sit' or 'Stay' at the kerb edge. To teach him this, have him on his lead and as you approach the edge of the pavement say sharply 'Sit', pull him back on his lead and gently press his hind quarters down so that he is in the sitting position. Keep him in this position while you make sure the road is clear and then say 'Over' and jerk the lead forward. Make a fuss of him when he does it properly. After he has learned this drill thoroughly it should become second-nature to him to obey the commands even when not on a lead. Another convenient lesson is to teach him to stay anywhere you wish and not join you until you say 'Come'. It is surprising how quickly poodles learn these things. At first, tie him on his lead to a table leg or something similar and say 'Stay' in a commanding voice, pressing him down. Move away a few yeards and then go back and pat him. Again telling him to 'Stay', go further away. Finally you will be able to go out of sight and can expect him to stay without moving or fussing. When you think he has learned the lesson, try it without the lead, telling him to 'Come' after intervals of 'Stay'. But as with all training, the period of instruction must be short. He can concentrate for just so long and then his attention wanders, especially when he is young. So make his lessons five minutes' duration at the most, but possibly several times a day. If you want him to learn more complicated orders you may like to attend training classes. Here both you and your dog will learn a lot. There will be a variety of breeds as trainees and if you have trained your own dog in simple obedience beforehand you will start with a great advantage. If this type of thing appeals to you, you may wish to go on to real 'obedience training' and compete against other owners and their dogs. Poodles do extremely well in the obedience ring and seem to take to it with tremendous interest and intelligence. Many have gained championship status in this sphere.

Show Training

Show training is quite a different method, but equally should be started early in the puppy's life. At eight weeks, the puppy can be 'stood out' on the table in the correct show stance, that is with his head up (here assist him with a finger under his chin), his front legs straight, his hind legs slightly drawn out behind him, and his tail up (again assisted by a finger under the tail). Encourage him to stand like this, at first for a few seconds and gradually increasing the exercise to several minutes. It will also help him to stand properly and improve his head carriage if he is fed standing on a table with the dish held a little high so that he stretches his neck to get the food. Also when feeding on the floor, his dish should be put on a stand or ledge on a level with his chin so that again he stands squarely while eating and does not splay out his front legs and poke his head forward.

The owner who plans to train his poodle for the show ring would be well advised to attend several dog shows to learn the 'drill' and can then come back and teach his dog exactly what to do. Many a puppy class has been won through thorough pre-show training. Judges have little patience with the handler who brings a dog, bucking like a bronco, into the ring with no idea of behaviour and then gushingly says 'of course,

Show Training at an early age. Teaching an eight week old puppy the right way to 'stand out' for showing.

he's never had a lead on till today – but then, he's only a puppy!'. He should be trained to be handled on the table (if he is a miniature or a toy, and on the ground if he is a standard) showing himself off to the best advantage, accepting it quietly when the judge looks at his teeth, measures the length of his ears, examines his paws and gives him a general 'going-over'. The puppy should be accustomed to this because of his training from an early age. Once he is protected by inoculation it will help to get all and sundry to handle him in this manner. Friends who come to the house should be asked to examine him like this so that a stranger's hands will in no way nonplus him. He should also be taught to walk sedately in a ring, and if other dogs can be enlisted with their owners to walk in front and behind him this is a great help. He must learn to be oblivious of them and not walk in a crab-like manner to see what they are doing. He must learn to walk out at the pace you set, on your left hand side, away from the would-be judge for several yards, stop at the top, stand out well, and then walk calmly back again. If all this can be taught to the puppy before he is six-months-old, he is well on the way to being a well-trained show dog.

Immunisation

There are also many matters to be attended to regarding the health of the puppy. For instance he will need to be protected against infectious disease by inoculation. If the breeder had not treated him for worms, he will need to be dosed to rid him of the possible presence of these pests. His teeth, ears and eyes will need inspection, and his coat must be checked from time to time for the presence of parasites such as fleas and other pests. But all such matters of general health are dealt with in a chapter further on in this book. On the whole, poodles are a hardy, healthy breed and given ordinary care and attention, good food and clean and comfortable living conditions, they usually live a trouble-free life. Serious skin diseases are rare in the poodle and they are by no means delicate in either digestion or chest, but they will naturally have their share of the baby-troubles suffered by all breeds, and as long as the owner can recognise the symptoms and know how to cope, then the puppy will soon be his normal, gay self again.

8 Feeding your Poodle

NOW we come to the all important matter of feeding the poodle. It is sometimes said that poodles are choosey feeders and to some extent this is true, but equally this does rather depend on the common sense of the owner. Almost any dog, unless he is really grossly greedy, will be choosey if he is fussed over too much, is given too much at a time, or is fed under uncomfortable and adverse conditions. The golden rule is to feed your poodle on the best quality meat and give him just the right amount so that he leaves a clean dish. If he leaves some of it, then he is being given just too much. It is very important that all food he is given carries the maximum amount of nutriment. He will not thrive if he is given a lot of bulk which contains only a little goodness.

Punctual Feeding

Feeding time, to the healthy poodle, is of paramount importance to him. He should be fed at the same time each day, and he will know to the split second what that time is! If he thinks you have overlooked this pressing matter of dinner, he will become restless, staring at you as if to say 'Could you possibly have forgotten the time?' If he is kept too long before his dinner arrives, he will suffer from indigestion, and from that will follow an indifferent appetite and a loss of condition. Plan his diet with care for he is unable to tell you in so many words of his likes and dislikes, although if you are in sympathy with him you will soon know what suits him best. It is no exaggeration to say that he will enjoy his food more if it is well cooked, well prepared and even well served. For instance, his food must not be too hot, neither must it be too cold and straight out of the fridge; his dish must be clean and specifically 'his'; the place in which he is fed must be in a quiet corner where he is not going to be shuffled about by passing feet, and this must be dry and comfortable. He should not be fed in a place where there is a howling draught, or outside where it may be raining or else too hot from the sun. Since poodles are such creatures of habit, he should be fed in the same place every day. If you have more than one dog, they should not be fed too near each other, however friendly they may normally be, for there is bound to be a certain amount of anxiety and a guarding of 'rights' which in turn may cause gobbling to ensure it goes down the right throat and this may lead to indigestion. On the other hand, a really difficult feeder may be spurred on to eat better simply because there is competition close by. A dog should always have the opportunity to relieve himself before and after a meal, and should never be fed in the hottest part of the day when he is likely to be feeling a little lazy or lethargic and unready for his dinner.

Choosey Feeders

Most poodles become good feeders from about two years old, which can be regarded as the age of maturity. Young poodles between eight and eighteen months are often choosey, simply because this is the time of growing up and their metabolism has not really settled itself. Particularly this applies to male poodles, for often their thoughts and desires are on other matters than food at this time. If one can only be strong minded enough, the way to cure the choosey feeder is almost to starve him for forty-eight hours, and usually then the phobia is broken and he comes back to normal keenness for food. Pregnant bitches often go through a bad time over food round about three weeks after mating, and will cause their owners unbearable anxiety, for this total abhorrence of food can last until the fourth to sixth weeks of pregnancy. It is, of course, an almost certain sign of successful conception. At this time, bitches quite often completely change their eating habits, for instance those who normally will not touch raw meat will not now touch it if it is cooked, or vice versa. The authors had a toy poodle who became a complete vegetarian during most of her pregnancy, spurning all meat, fish or even chicken, relying instead on biscuits, vegetables, milk and eggs. At the other end of the scale, elderly poodles, like some elderly humans, think almost entirely of food, and unless carefully controlled put on a great deal of weight. In these circumstances lean raw meat is the best diet with no added biscuit or cereal.

Planning the Diet

Certainly when planning the diet for the poodle three points must be carefully borne in mind. The diet must be 1. of the highest quality, 2. properly balanced, and 3. of studied variety.

Best quality food, whether it is meat or fish, pays in the end for it obviates to a large degree the necessity of expensive tonics and medicines, and will probably more than halve the vet's bills. For a diet to be balanced it must contain correct proportions of protein (meat, eggs, fish, cheese, etc.), carbohydrates (cereals, biscuits, fatty meat, fish oils, and the butter content of milk). The third maxim of variety is equally important for a dog can get heartily sick of the same old thing, day in and day out. Alternate his main meat meal with fish, or heart, liver, kidney, or tripe.

Possibly a dog's most favourite meal is chicken and in these days boiled chicken or chicken parts are as cheap or cheaper than meat and contain good digestive nourishment. The giblets, cut finely, also help to make the meal more tasty. Boiled rice is an excellent addition, especially if the poodle is choosey over dog biscuit. A little chicken stock over the meat or else used to soak the biscuit will work wonders! Vitamins and minerals are essential, and if quality, balance and variety of the diet has been the keynote, adequate amounts of these two elements will follow as a natural result. As a general guide a poodle will do very well on half an ounce of meat or other protein to every ½kg (1lb) of his own weight – this is excluding a small amount of cereal, rice, biscuit or brown bread to make up the roughage. He should have his daily ration of milk, and two cooked eggs per week. Clean, fresh cold water is an essential and it must always be available to him in the place where he knows it will be.

To illustrate the fact that poodles are creatures of routine, the following story may prove interesting. For many years the authors owned a kennel of some forty poodles. Twelve of these were top show dogs and at feeding time they used to be called in for their dinner at a long low table, which stood about ten inches from the ground. The table had twelve grooves to take the feeding dishes, and above each dish was a small plaque bearing the relative poodle's name. The dogs would roar in and jostle each other until each was in his or her right place, side by side. They never made a mistake and visitors to the kennels were always amused as it appeared that the poodles could read their own names! It was in fact, of course, simply a matter of routine and if for any reason we wanted one to change places it created havoc and everyone was then put off his dinner! In their correct and usual order they felt relaxed and happy, and because there was competition on each side dinners were polished off quickly and neatly. Growls or rude words were practically non-existent. This form of feeding was employed primarily as a means of discipline, and also to improve head carriage. If a dog eats from a dish on the floor he will poke his head forward and splay out his legs from the shoulder, while eating at a height such as this ensures that necks were stretched slightly upwards which improved head carriage, and legs were straight and parallel, with shoulders in position and well laid back. This regular exercise was responsible to quite a degree for the fine head carriage and straight fronts of the Rothara Poodles.

In these modern times a tremendous amount of research goes into the production of dog foods. Tests for palatability, for growth of coat, for steady maintenance of condition all with their supporting clinical studies are carried out by many of the leading dog food manufacturers. Also vitamins and minerals and their corresponding values are exhaustively explored in laboratory tests, and then finally included in many food-stuffs. So there is no reason why the modern dog should not have available and included in his feeding programme every possible supplement that will enhance his condition both of body and coat and also nourish his nervous system to aid the breeding of dogs whose temperaments are steady and whose dispositions are pleasant.

In the following pages, there are various diets and feeding suggestions which have been compiled with a view to suiting a number of poodles who undertake special work or who might be expected to gain too much weight or the reverse, and many other specific conditions.

Weight Check

It is important to keep a weekly check on the weight of your poodle. He should be placed on the scales on the same day in each week and at approximately the same time when similar conditions prevail. For instance, it is better to weigh him in the morning before he has had a meal, and preferably after his bowels have been evacuated. The weight should be noted down with other records which are relevant to him, and then appropriate action taken if he has lost weight or gained more than he should. A small chart is very useful so that it may be seen at a glance if there is any significant deviation from the normal week by week.

As a very rough guide, it has been found that the height of a young poodle in inches very nearly corresponds to his weight in pounds, though as the poodle matures his weight is inclined to exceed the comparative number of inches of his height by about twenty-five per cent. However, a young miniature poodle standing 35cm (14″) at the shoulder should weigh approximately 6kg (14lb), but will increase to possibly 7½–8kg (17–18lb) as he grows older. A 23cm (9″) toy poodle should weigh round about 4kg (9lb) or less. Obviously, this does not always work out as the poodle may be a heavy bodied type on very short legs who may weigh a good 5½kg (12lb) and yet be only 20cm (8″) in height. But in the normal, well balanced poodle this is a reliable guide.

Food Quantities

To gauge the quantity of food required, 15g (½oz) of good quality meat to every ½kg (1lb) of body weight should be sufficient, thus the dog weighing 6–7kg (14–16lb) will need 200–225g (7–8oz) of meat daily. But to this must be added biscuit meal and any other roughage.

If a dog who is normally a good feeder either refuses his food on any day or appears to have little enthusiasm for it, his temperature should be checked immediately as this may well be the first symptom of the onset of some disease or infection. If you are perceptive enough to notice this sign right at the beginning, then you may well obviate some epidemic from running right through your kennels, causing endless work, worry and expense – to say nothing of the discomfort and pain suffered by the dogs.

The following diets are based on the needs of the miniature poodle. The quantities should be doubled for standard poodles, and not quite halved for the toy poodle.

Basic Diet for a Poodle

Breakfast: One tablespoonful of Barley Flakes soaked overnight in cold milk and water (two parts milk, one part water). Add warm milk on feeding.
or Any good quality cereal and warm milk.
or Raw egg beaten up in milk – (twice a week at most).
or One tablespoonful of honey in warm milk.

Main Meal: Meat, fish or selected offal on the basis of 15g (½oz) to each ½kg (1lb) body weight of dog. Raw meat is best, but if cooked it should be roast in the oven possibly wrapped in foil to retain the goodness. If stewed, then very little liquid should be used in cooking, and this should be given to the poodle with the meat.

Many people do not favour the practice of mixing biscuit meal with meat, as it is believed that for good health, proteins and carbohydrates should not be eaten together but at separate meals, but equally many dogs appear to thrive on a mixed diet of meat and biscuit. If the former method is favoured then it is advisable to give breakfast alternated as above. If however the latter diet is used, then for the adult one large meal a day is correct. If he will take this, a certain percentage of raw vegetable should be fed to the poodle such as grated carrot, parsley. Many poodles relish fruit and will enjoy grated apple or pear. It must be ensured that the poodle receives his necessary vitamin and mineral supplements, and if it is considered that the diet does not contain either vitamins or minerals in sufficient quantities, then the poodle should have a daily vitamin supplement pill to keep him in robust health.

Only large beef bones (preferably raw but in the interests of hygiene, these may be scalded) should be given as these aid the digestion by stimulating the gastric juices. Chicken, rabbit, chop and fish bones are extremely dangerous, and should *never* be given.

Special Diet for Stud Dogs

Stud dogs who undertake a fair amount of work will need a specially nourishing and sustaining diet, and the following is considered suitable:

The full basic diet with the following additions:

a. A raw egg added to the breakfast every day on which a stud service is undertaken, or if preferred a raw egg over the meat.

b. An extra 50g (2oz) of red meat every day for at least a month before the usual heavy stud periods (spring and autumn), and also on the day before and the actual day of service.

A course of wheat germ capsules should be given twice yearly, approximately in January and August (if the weather is very hot in August, postpone until cooler). Parsley is particularly beneficial to the stud dog and should be sprinkled on his meat meal, as this is strongly believed to increase fertility.

If the dog likes milk, 150–300ml (¼–½pint) a day helps to keep him well covered and virile. Pieces of cheese as an extra are most valuable, or cheese grated over his main meal.

Special Diet for Pregnant Bitches

The First Five Weeks: The full basic diet should be given.

Last Four Weeks: A raw egg should be added to the usual breakfast.

Last Two Weeks: As above, but meat should be increased by 50 to 75g (2 to 3oz) a day according to appetite. The main meal should be divided into two meals (dinner and supper) and the extra amount added to the evening meal. Carbohydrates and starch (cereals and biscuit) should *not* be increased during pregnancy as this tends to make the bitch put on too much weight which may in turn cause a difficult labour.

Special Additions: Grated cheese over the main meal is beneficial. Also liver should be regularly fed to the in-whelp bitch twice a week. She should be encouraged to drink as much water as possible. Cow's milk should be given as desired, but goat's milk is preferable if obtainable. Towards the end of her pregnancy, one to two teaspoonfuls of olive oil over the main meal helps to obviate constipation at this time. The administration of calcium phosphate is an excellent safeguard during the last week or ten days of pregnancy, but this can only be assimilated into her blood stream if given with vitamin D. Calcium and vitamin D are particularly recommended in cases where the female has suffered from eclampsia or shown any hint of calcium deficiency. (See Chapter 10.)

During pregnancy the bitch often suffers from morning sickness and a sudden loss of appetite three to four weeks after mating. This is quite normal and food at this time should not be pressed upon her. The dish should be put down for her so that she can eat or not as she feels inclined.

After a few days, or sometimes as long as a week, she will come right back on her food, and from this moment her appetite should increase progressively. Any sudden loss of appetite at the seventh of eighth week of pregnancy must be regarded with misgiving and the opinion of the veterinary surgeon sought.

Special Diet for Nursing Mothers

First twenty-four hours after whelping: The mother should be given three-hourly drinks of a milk food manufactured for dogs or puppies, or failing this a suitable milk preparation intended for babies. If there is a rise in temperature or the mother is very upset or excitable, the milk diet should be continued until the temperature returns to normal and she is less excitable. Thereafter the diet should be as follows, at three-hourly intervals:

Breakfast: Milk drink of approximately 300ml (½pint).

Mid-morning: A piece of cheese or sponge cake.

Dinner: One or two slightly scrambled eggs, mixed with brown bread cut into small pieces, or rice.

Tea: Milk drink 300ml (½pint).

Supper: Raw meat (approximately 175g (6oz) for miniature poodles and 100g (4oz) for toy poodles).

Bedtime: A milk drink, or else creamed rice or semolina pudding made with half milk and half water.

If the bitch has produced a large litter she may need a milk drink in the night, for the first three or four days. All drinks should be given just slightly warm, and should be diluted with about one-third water to stimulate milk production and also to avoid acidity. Clean, fresh water and raw meat are the best milk producers, and the lactating poodle should have plenty of both.

If the mother suffers from diarrhoea while nursing a litter, this is quickly cleared up by reducing the proportion of fresh milk and increasing the water content, as the percentage of fat in the milk may be too rich for her to digest at this time. Honey is excellent for nursing mothers, and a large teaspoonful should always be added to milk drinks. Honey should be natural and direct from the bees, and not blended or synthetic in any way.

When the puppies are about five-weeks-old, the mother may begin to regurgitate her food for them. This is quite natural and is an excellent weaning food for the puppies as it is thus pre-digested. However the food must be given to the mother finely minced or chopped so that it can be easily consumed by the offspring. But remember always to give the mother a *second* meal for her own nourishment afterwards and keep her away from the puppies for a short while.

Special Diet for Bitches after Weaning

When the mother has finished the work of rearing her puppies, she needs a particularly nourishing diet to build her up after the strain of feeding a litter. She needs a tempting and concentrated diet, and it is the least we can do since she has done her part in looking after her family so carefully. The following diet should be given for at least four weeks after the puppies have left her:

Breakfast: Scrambled egg with brown bread.

Dinner: Sponge cake or a piece of cheese.

Supper: A liberal helping of meat, liver, heart or fish with soaked biscuit or brown bread.

Bedtime: A small milk drink.

Conditioners: A course of vitamin tablets should be given, and honey in her bedtime drink will greatly benefit her and help to build her up again.

Special Diet for Young Puppies (six to twelve weeks)

Breakfast: Milk drink with honey, or cereal and milk.

Dinner: Raw minced beef (50g (2oz) for miniature poodles and 40g (1½oz) for toy poodles).

Tea: Drink of milk and honey.

Supper: Raw minced beef (as for dinner).

Bedtime: Milk pudding such as creamed rice or semolina.

Puppies which are born and weaned in the winter time will benefit from two drops of cod liver oil or one drop of halibut liver oil daily. If the puppies are at all loose in their motions, this usually indicates that worming is now necessary, and it is safe to dose for these parasites from the age of six weeks onwards. If, on the other hand, the puppies are slightly constipated, a few drops of olive oil will remedy this condition. Large beef bones should now be given to assist the puppies to cut their teeth.

Special Diet for Growing Youngsters (three to six months)

Breakfast: 75g (3oz) raw meat (or cooked) for miniatures and 50g (2oz) for toys.

Dinner: Milk drink with honey added.

Supper: Raw or cooked meat as above, with a small quantity of brown bread or soaked wholemeal puppy meal.

As an alternative scrambled egg may be given for breakfast, or an occasional semolina pudding with honey added.

Extra Conditioners: Cod liver oil or halibut liver oil once daily. Raw carrot grated on meat is excellent for youngsters and it is useful to get them used to this when they are at the greedy stage, and they will then always take it. It must be remembered that dogs of this age are using a great deal of energy in growing and need additional conditioners as a routine measure to build eventual robustness, and also as disease resisters and intestinal cleansers.

Special Diet for Young Show Dogs (six to twelve months)

The full basic diet should now be given, but in addition a midday dinner of 75g (3oz) raw meat (50g (2oz) for toy poodles). As much milk as will be reasonably taken. Goat's milk is ideal if procurable, and occasional pieces of cheese are usually liked. Olive oil over the supper meal, commencing with half a teaspoonful and working up to a tablespoonful for miniatures (half quantities for toys) is nourishing and in addition will create tremendous growth of coat. A course of wheat germ or a suitable vitamin tonic is most useful during the poodle's adolescent life. Large beef bones containing plenty of marrow are also most beneficial to the young show dog, and help to keep his teeth clean and in good healthy condition.

Special Diet for Over-Weight Poodle

The poodle who carries too much weight is not a healthy animal, and he is also not very pleasant to have as a companion. Most too-fat dogs have offensive breath and are also prone to chest and heart complaints. To reduce the weight of a dog, the owner must be strong minded and plan carefully. The dog's weight should be checked and recorded weekly, and the reduction should not be more than 225g (½lb) per week until the right weight is reached. The diet should be as follows:
The basic diet but delete all cereals, flakes or biscuit meal. No fatty meat. Meat should be reduced by 25 to 50g (1 to 2oz) daily, and should be fed raw if possible. A piece of cheese may be given at breakfast time if

the dog seems exceptionally hungry. Raw bones may be given providing the marrow has been removed and all fat taken off – they keep up the morale of the normally greedy dog who is overweight and who takes a great interest in food, thus making the reduced diet not quite so rigorous. Plenty of hard walking exercise will help the obese poodle. Definitely no chocolate drops, pieces of sugar or 'bits' at table.

Special Diet for Under-Weight Poodle

Young stud dogs, or dogs in the adolescent stage, and also young bitches before producing their first litters are often difficult and choosey feeders, and consequently very much under weight. The diet for difficult feeders can be built up as follows: The full basic diet, but with the addition of a raw or scrambled egg for breakfast. Sometimes a piece of bacon with the egg will be tempting. 75 to 100g (3 to 4oz) of raw meat at midday, or two or three pieces of cheese. One teaspoonful of olive oil over meat daily.

To tempt the bad feeder: liver or meat fried in butter or dripping. Small knobs of butter from time to time will often be licked off the finger and help to add a little weight. If any chicken stock or chicken gravy is available, this can with advantage be put over the meat to make it additionally tasty. Beef bones (with plenty of marrow) help to put on flesh. A piece of home-made sponge cake at bedtime is a good idea. Definitely no bits or in-between meals should be given as these only blunt the appetite for normal meals.

But really the best advice is that you must not try to force your under-weight dog to eat. If you can adopt a take-it-or-leave-it attitude you will have more chance of fattening him. Prepare his meals carefully and make them as tasty as you can. Put his bowl on the floor and leave him alone in the room. Don't stand over him coaxing him with little pieces and almost praying for him to eat. After leaving him alone with his food for ten minutes, take up his bowl if he has not touched it or has not completely finished. Throw what is left right away, and give him *nothing at all* until the next meal comes round. Then repeat the procedure. A laxative such as olive oil will help to stimulate an appetite, and if you can take him for a really energetic scamper just before you produce his meal, this may help him to eat. But don't let him know you are worried, and don't give him any between-meal tit-bits *at all*. When his appetite begins to improve, don't, in your relief, over-load him. Keep to a very moderate diet so that he always cleans up the dish, but ensure that what you give him is of the very best quality and full of solid nourishment.

Special Foods for Invalid Dogs

For any poodle who is slightly indisposed, or at the first sign of a temperature, complete starvation is essential for at least twenty-four hours. After that drinks of honey and boiled cold water should be given at three hourly intervals until the temperature is again normal. Honey and water is excellent in the case of chills, or sudden slight sickness, the honey being particularly healing to the lining of the stomach and intestine, and any solid food given at such a time will only irritate the poodle's condition. At the first sign of any sickness, the veterinary surgeon should be called, but until diagnosis is made the only food that should be given is honey and water.

For the dog who has been seriously ill, first essence of chicken and then beef is excellent, and for the first solid food chicken. Also rabbit and sheep's head (both well sifted for all small bones) are excellent. After this, minced raw beef is the safest food to give and will quickly build up the debilitated dog. Drinks of pure Casilan, glucose and boiled cold water may be given, and as the dog grows stronger milk may be substituted for the water.

The poodle who has been ill is going to need food which is tastily prepared, and cut up in small pieces. He will not have the energy to tackle large pieces of food of a solid nature. Everything that is given must be very easily digested. We give three recipes which are especially beneficial in invalid feeding.

A DIET FOR THE SERIOUSLY ILL POODLE
A heaped dessertspoonful of calcium caseinate milk protein powder (which is made by Glaxo under the name Casilan) mixed with hot water to the consistency of *very thick* cream. Add a teaspoonful of honey, and a few drops of concentrated vitamins. Then whisk in enough cold milk to bring to the consistency of *very thin* cream. This will make about 200ml (7fl oz or ⅓pint). Feed a small quantity to the poodle at intervals of one or two hours. The Casilan powder contains 90 per cent protein, and is therefore an excellent means of providing the very sick poodle with the maximum of nourishment in the least amount of bulk. Most poodles are extremely fond of the taste of this food, and it has the added advantage of being utterly digestible. 'Complan' is also much recommended.

BLAND MIXTURE
This is particularly useful in cases of vomiting, diarrhoea and general stomach upsets.

1 *white* of an egg.
1 teaspoonful of glucose powder.
1 tablespoonful of *cold* water which has been previously boiled.

Beat the three ingredients together, and give one teaspoonful of the mixture every hour. A few drops of brandy may be added. All other food should be withheld until condition has improved.

Some poodles do appear from time to time to suffer from indigestion or 'upset tummies'. When this occurs, the poodle has a great desire to eat grass. Actually this is not a bad thing as the grass provides the very necessary chlorophyll which is a good internal cleanser, so it is good to let him graze as he wishes. He may be slightly sick after such grazing, and vomit the grass but this equally helps to clear his stomach of the matter that is upsetting him. Often, when suffering from indigestion, his tummy will make 'squelching' or 'siphoning' noises. All meat, fish and biscuit should be withheld, and the poodle fed exclusively on boiled chicken and boiled rice until he is back to normal. Again honey and milk or water is an excellent drink at this time.

WEANING OR CONVALESCENT MIXTURE
This is a milky mixture evolved by the authors and used extensively now by many breeders of poodles.

Mix the following powders, which are all made by Glaxo, together in a bowl:

2 parts Farex
1 part Casilan
½ part Glucodin

Add sufficient hot water to beat into a mixture of the consistency of *thick* cream. Then add sufficient cold milk and stir well to the consistency of *thin* cream. The milk drink may be given in all cases of convalescence, to bitches in-whelp and to mothers immediately after the birth of their puppies, and it is also a splendid weaning and puppy food. Quantities of the powders in proportions as given may be stored in large tins for instant use. In this case, two tablespoonfuls of the blended powder should be beaten with 150ml (¼pint) of hot water, with 150ml (¼pint) cold milk then added.

Home made sponge cake
This type of light and extremely nourishing cake is most useful for tiny toy poodles or when it is necessary to tempt a poodle with food. The ingredients are:

2 eggs
100g (4oz) granulated sugar
100g (4oz) butter
100g (4oz) flour

Cream the butter and sugar, beat in the eggs, then mix in the flour. Bake in a moderate oven for approximately 25 to 35 minutes.

Natural Feeding

As an alternative to the foregoing diets, many poodle owners favour the Natural Feeding System. It is not a cheap diet, but the authors have yet to see a poodle who has been faithfully and regularly fed on these principles who does not posses a shining, glossy coat, bright eye, and continual good health. 'Buster' Lloyd-Jones, who carried on a very successful veterinary practice until he was sadly struck down by polio, was a great advocate of natural feeding and the prevention of disease and sickness through administration of herbal remedies. He founded the well known firm of Denes, who produce a completely comprehensive range of veterinary herbal remedies and health foods, which were perfected by Mr Lloyd-Jones, and for those who are interested leaflets are available, free of charge, from Denes, 14 Goldstone Street, Hove, East Sussex BN3 3RL outlining the herbal treatments for the more common ailments.

The basis of natural feeding is raw meat, herbal supplements and one day's complete fasting each week, and the following diets have been worked out by Mr Lloyd-Jones for the various ages.

PUPPIES FROM TWO TO FIVE MONTHS (five meals a day)
8 a.m. Milk and water and honey.
11 a.m. Cereal such as barley flakes, wheat flakes, corn flakes etc., soaked the night before and then strained, and milk and honey added.
2 p.m. Raw red meat, together with one tablet of 'All-in-One', and one Naturebone tablet. In winter time, one cod liver oil capsule may be given.
5 p.m. Repeat the 2 p.m. meal but leave out the 'All-in-One'.
8 p.m. 'Naturemeal' biscuits, or cereals as given in the 11 a.m. meal.

PUPPIES FROM FIVE TO NINE MONTHS (three meals a day)
Noon meal. 'Naturemeal' biscuits.
5 p.m. Exactly as for the 2 p.m. meal above but increase the amount of meat.
8 p.m. 'Naturemeal' Biscuits.

All puppies *over six months* should be fasted for half a day once a week, and given honey and water only.

ADULT DOGS (one main meal only a day)
This one meal should be given between 5 and 6 p.m. and should consist of raw red meat together with chopped raw green vegetables. Quantities would be about 100g (4oz) meat for toys, 175g (6oz) for miniatures and possibly 350–500g (12–16oz) for standards. Supplements of 'All-in-

One' should be given as this provides in herbal form seaweed, parsley, watercress and wheat germ oil.

Three hours after this main meal, an adult poodle should be given 'Naturemeal' biscuits.

But the important part of the above diet is that the poodle should be fasted for one whole day each week – and not even the odd tit-bit! Honey and water can be given during the day and rhubarb tablets should be given the night *before* the fast day.

There is no doubt at all, that if a poodle is fed on these lines he will be a poodle who enjoys roaring good health, but it does mean extra trouble for the owner and possibly extra expense, and let's face it, it is awfully difficult to withstand the expectant looks and wheedling pressure from your pet! The value of the fast day allows the digestive organs from mouth to rectum to have complete rest for twenty-four hours, during which time the entire system is cleansed of all impurities. The value of the various herbs such as garlic, chlorophyll, nettles, seaweed, elderberry, and rhubarb is tremendous, especially in these days when it is increasingly difficult for dogs to find clean grass to graze on to help their digestions. Fast days are not recommended for elderly dogs.

There is no doubt that if you are to feed your poodle successfully and to his physical and mental advantage, a good deal of time, trouble, forethought, patience and even psychology must be employed. But if intelligent thought is given to the matter, the poodle will be a happy, healthy and mentally stable animal who will obviate for his owner those expensive visits to the local veterinary surgeon, and the purchase of a mass of expensive tonics and appetizers.

9 In Health or in Sickness

THIS chapter has been divided into two parts – how to maintain your poodle in good health, and what to do for your poodle if he is ill.

There are four things the owner can do to help to keep his or her poodle in good health. Firstly, feed him on good nourishing food, and to this end attention is particularly drawn to Chapter 8 which deals with feeding. Secondly, give him adequate daily exercise so that his lungs are full of fresh air, and his skin is toned up with energetic scampering. Thirdly, arrange judicious immunisation against disease by inoculation, with regular booster injections. Lastly, and by no means least, ensure psychological security by considering your poodle's comfort and needs and letting him know you are there when he wants you.

With regard to inoculation, there are of course divided opinions over the use of vaccines or the use of natural rearing methods. In these days of the horrible diseases of hard pad, hepatitis, leptospirosis and parvo disease which can be picked up from other animals like foxes, rats and from such sources as fleas, lice or even from items as pieces of straw, wool etc., taken by birds from an infected place and dropped where the poodle is able to pick up the infection, it does appear that some sort of vaccine is the answer. Surely the benefit dogs have derived from such preventive inoculations as have been so widely used over the last twenty-five years does prove that they are without doubt immensely successful. Of course, immunity after vaccine is not 100 per cent certain but usually even if the dog is unlucky and contracts one of the mentioned diseases, the attack will not be so severe as in the non-inoculated dog. But no doubt those who are still in favour of natural rearing and herbal remedies are able to make out a very good case for this method and since the authors have in the past employed both methods with considerable success, they would not wish to be dogmatic. But it must in all fairness be stated that they used natural rearing methods before the present-day vaccines had reached such a high standard of research and efficiency, and nowadays they would not dare to neglect inoculation for the puppy with careful yearly boosters for the adult dogs.

Many manufacturing chemists have carried out invaluable research work resulting in the production of a great many immunising vaccines, such firms as Burroughs Wellcome & Co, Glaxo, Duphar Veterinary Ltd., and Smith, Kline Ltd. There is now an excellent all-in-one vaccine against distemper, hepatitis and two types of leptospirosis produced by Glaxo, but really one should seek advice from the veterinary surgeon as he or she will have the latest information on the subject and will know what would be the most suitable for your particular poodle. All vets have their favourite products, and most vets will insist on yearly booster inoculations for maximum protection. BUT DON'T PUT IT OFF.

The new killer which struck concurrently in many parts of the world in 1978 is called parvovirus. It is lethal and heartbreaking, for it seems usually to hit the best of your stock, and a puppy or dog can die literally in a matter of *hours*. Basically, at the present, there is no specific treatment or cure for parvo. If the poor poodle is lucky enough to survive the first few hours, your vet may be able to help. The symptoms are sudden and extreme quietness, vomiting, diarrhoea either all blood or with some blood in it, a sudden dramatic loss of weight (and remember this in only a few hours). This causes dehydration and death. The only hope is an S.O.S. to your vet day or night and he will give the poodle its only chance – glucose saline injections, possibly under the skin or intravenous drip. As parvo is resistant to most disinfectants the only way to safeguard your puppy or adult dog is by vaccination. However, 'Domestos' *has* been found to be useful to disinfect kennels, etc. but of course there is still great danger of infection anyway. It is a very gloomy and frightening picture. When parvo was first diagnosed the cat enteritis vaccine was used with very mixed results but now Duphar Veterinary has been responsible for a dramatic break-through and have produced the first dog vaccine against parvo, which is safe for puppies and pregnant bitches – a safe inactivated vaccine requiring one yearly booster. The dog world owes Duphar a deep vote of thanks.

The authors are greatly indebted to Mrs Ellis and Miss Sherry (who have owned and bred so many lovely Merrymorn poodles over the years) for the foregoing advice regarding parvo disease. The Merrymorn poodles receive their first shots from their London vet, Keith M. Butt, at eight to nine weeks – Kavak Parvo on one side and Enduracell on the other side, followed by a repeat in three to four weeks' time, and then yearly boosters. When this has been done all owners of poodles can heave a sigh of relief as one more nightmare is conquered, not one hundred per cent but nearly.

Whilst on the subject of inoculations and immunisations, breeders should note that if there is a chance of a puppy being exported to Sweden the veterinary surgeon should be informed and he will then omit the leptospirosis part of the inoculation for if not, even a trace of this will show up in the blood sample required by Sweden and this will cause great difficulties in obtaining the necessary health certificate. The lepto part can always be given at a later date should the puppy not go to Sweden.

Another job for the careful poodle owner is to know and mark down his dog's temperature and pulse rate when he is *perfectly well*. Dogs' normal temperature and pulse rates differ considerably and as long as you know what it *should* be in normal circumstances, you will then know whether there is a dangerous rise or fall when he is 'off-colour'. Another excellent preparation for any bout of illness is to familiarise your poodle with 'dosing'. Give him the occasional spoonfuls of milk or piece of meat as though it were a dose of medicine. You will find if he is accustomed to this he will not upset himself over dosing when he is really ill.

Providing you know how to administer the various types of medicine, dosing is not too difficult. If there is a second person available, it is always an advantage for they can hold or steady your poodle while you give the actual dose. To give liquids by spoon, you should stand on the right hand side of the dog, who should be sitting on a table or chair. Pull out his lower lip at the left side of his mouth to form a small pocket. Pour the spoonful of liquid into the pocket, and while keeping his mouth shut raise his head. The liquid will then slide down his throat. Another method is to put the right amount of medicine into a small bottle, insert the neck of the bottle into the side of the mouth and tip in, while raising the dog's head. Tablets should be given by opening the dog's mouth, placing or throwing the pill on to the back of the tongue, quickly closing the mouth, tipping the head up and gently stroking the poodle's throat until he swallows. Powders may be given in the same way, or if he is a greedy boy then buried in a piece of meat, but in this case it is as well to give several pieces of meat which are free of medicine first, just to hoodwink him!

Below, left: Dosing a poodle with a spoon. The corner of the lower lip is pulled out to make a pocket, and the liquid poured slowly into the dog's mouth.

Below, right: Dosing. Giving a pill or tablet. Open the poodle's mouth and push the pill back as far as possible. Quickly close the mouth and stroke the throat until he swallows.

To take a dog's temperature, use a blunt nosed clinical thermometer. Shake down below 35.5°C (96°F) grease the silvery end with vaseline and very gently insert into the back passage for about one inch and keep there for 1½ minutes. Keep a firm hold on the poodle so that he does not whirl round and send the thermometer flying, or does not sit down and break it which could be dangerous to him. The normal temperature for a dog is 38.6°C (101.5°F) (some thermometers are now metrically marked, but nearly all show both Fahrenheit and Centigrade degrees). To take his pulse, place the first two fingers in the crevice of the groin, and you will easily find the throb. This should be 60–70 per minute. Slightly more for the tiny toy poodle and slightly less for the standard. Take the pulse when the poodle has been sitting quietly for some time, and not immediately after a meal or a scamper.

Get into the habit of always being watchful of your poodle's health. Notice that he eats up his food as usual, notice that he is not excessively drinking, notice that his eyes are bright and sparkling and not dull and rather deep looking, notice that his nose is cool, notice that his stools are of normal consistency and colour, and finally notice that he sleeps contentedly without restlessness. If all these points are automatically checked as routine, you will know immediately if anything is not quite right and can then turn to the relevant chapter which will tell you the First Aid treatment in any untoward circumstances.

Worms

Another subject which should be dealt with in this chapter is the distressing one of worms. This can hardly be called an illness nor a disease, let us call it an unfortunate 'state of affairs' from which most puppies or adults suffer in their lifetime. There are three types *1. thread worms*, *2. round worms*, and *3. tape worms*. There is a fourth type in the hook worm but this is usually only experienced abroad and in this case the dog needs specific veterinary treatment.

A great many puppies harbour worms, indeed the majority are born with these pests. Therefore it is always advantageous to dose the bitch ten days after she has been mated. One should not dose a bitch in this condition later than that in her pregnancy as the purging might bring on an abortion. Get from the vet the right strength of worm pill in accordance with her weight and size. You may then obviate any worms being passed on to the puppy either in embryo or when newly born. Remember also that worms need a 'host' and are not passed directly from dog to dog. The usual method is for the dog to pass either worms or worm eggs, and for flies to land on these and then pass on the infection by blowing on the dog's food, the dog then eating the infected food and incubating the worms. Equally, fleas or lice will bite the dog's skin, the dog will then feel the irritation and nibble the flea or louse and thus the infection will pass into the dog's stomach in that way. From this it will be seen how extremely important it is to pick up and burn all faeces passed by the dog, and also ensure that all food is kept covered and free from flies. If pests such as fleas and lice are suspected it is imperative that a germicidal bath should be given, and for this Cooper's Kur-Mange is excellent, or else the poodle must be kept well dusted with Cooper's Pulvex.

Many puppies can harbour worms from birth and yet show no signs or symptoms of this except perhaps for the occasional loose stool. Other puppies may react very seriously to worm infection and the symptoms they will show will be vomiting and diarrhoea with either dead curled-up worms, or else live, wriggling worms appearing in the excreta. The puppy will be sickly and lackadaisical, with a tight skin, a 'pot belly', a staring dull coat, dull cloudy eye and quite obnoxious breath. His appetite will alternate between madly voracious or else moodily sporadic. All these signs and symptoms must prompt the owner to give an immediate worm dose, providing the temperature is within a point or two of normal – say between 38 and 39.1°C (100.5 and 102.5°F). If the temperature is either below or more particularly above that margin, this may mean the onset of some more serious malady for which the symptoms might be rather similar to that of worm infection. There is not usually a rise in temperature in worm infestation. A puppy can safely be wormed after the age of six weeks. Constant worming, however, is not advocated. The worms should have been despatched in two doses, ten days apart. Some owners like to worm their dogs once a year as a safe precaution, and this is purely a matter of choice, but certainly more frequently than that is inadvisable.

Thread worms resemble pieces of beige cotton, while round worms look like pieces of spaghetti with pointed ends. Tape worm as its name suggests, looks rather like long pieces of tape about ¼″ wide and is often detected by something that looks like grains of rice either in the faeces or adhering to the parts round the anus. In all cases of suspected worms, it is wise to seek veterinary advice, although there are many worm medicines sold in pet shops. Care must be taken about these as the dosage *might* be too strong for your poodle, especially in the case of small toy poodles.

It sometimes happens that very young puppies of anything from two to five weeks may be riddled with worms. This can be seen by the extended pot-belly and by the fact that they are constantly vomiting piles of small round worms. If the puppies appear to be really ill and very thin, then it is really a case of kill or cure. It they are as ill as this with worms at such an early age they will almost certainly die if untreated. Equally, their little constitutions are not really strong enough to cope with the shock effect of a worm dose and they may equally die as a result. If such a decision must be taken, probably a worm dose is the lesser evil but a veterinary surgeon *must* be asked to advise. In any case, after the dose treat the puppy for shock by keeping him in an even, warmer-than-usual temperature. It is at times like this that an infra-red ray lamp is of immense value. If the worm dose is going to be successful, the puppy will turn the corner within a couple of hours, and will very quickly become a normal, healthy, lively little soul with a loose skin, sleek coat and bright eye, with breath which smells of sweet 'bread and milk' instead of something quite horrible! It is believed that more very young puppies die from worm infestation than from anything, so keep a strict watch on that precious litter.

Tape worm is a far more serious affair and usually attacks the young adolescent dog and the mature dog rather than the puppy. Symptoms are much the same, however, for there is the staring dull coat, cloudy eye, very uncertain appetite, complete apathy and above all a most unpleasant odour which emanates from the coat and skin as well as from the breath. Equally the tape worm must have a host, so flies, fleas and lice and the droppings from other tape-infested dogs are the real dangers. A tape worm will continue growing, although segments regularly break off and are passed by the dog, and the worms can attain a length of several feet. It is absolutely essential if the dog is to be well and truly rid of the pests that the head of the worm is actually killed by a strong tape worm dose. The dog will then pass the head so it is usually quite obvious when the dose has been successful. Again the dog will pick up remarkably quickly. Treatment must be carried out by the veterinary surgeon. Fleas are the most general hosts for the flea eats the tape worm eggs, then incubates the head of a tape worm, the dog eats the flea and the tape worm grows and flourishes in the dog. It is so very important to obtain treatment if tape worm is suspected for this type of infection can lead to many deficiency diseases, also tape worm is transmittable to humans. As dogs with this plague develop depraved appetites, they will often eat either their own or other dogs' excreta, which is a very definite sign of infestation, and also the quickest way for the dog to increase the number of worms. Another source of infection is contained in rabbit droppings.

Nursing

As with the human, the poodle is not likely to go through his entire life without a day's illness. But if we are careful and really study him, it is reasonable to hope that he will escape any severe malady, and certainly avoid any illness which could be due to our own personal ignorance or carelessness. The poodle is a very healthy, robust type of dog with no characteristics which point to any weakness such as, for instance, a very short nose which may cause a certain amount of respiratory or chest trouble, or a very long back which could mean spinal or disc trouble, or a very heavy body which could mean heart trouble in later life. On the contrary, he is an elegant, well made dog with plenty of energy who, with normal care, should avoid most canine troubles. But in spite of all that, there is bound to come the time when he will have some sort of malady which will shock you, as the owner, and cause you great anxiety, and this is the moment which may possibly call for much skill in nursing, and no one can help the poodle at such a time more than his owner, the person he knows, relies upon, and who will give him great confidence and the will to get better.

There are four points which must be observed when nursing the sick dog and it is almost impossible to say which of the four is the most important, therefore they are listed alphabetically. They are *1. cleanliness, 2. loving care, 3. peace,* and *4. warmth.*

Cleanliness means particularly the cleanliness of the nurse, that is the washing of hands before and after each treatment, the wearing of a clean protective apron. It also means the cleanliness of all feeding and drinking vessels, dosing spoons, and also hygienic beds and bedding. The removal immediately of all soiled bedding, soiled newspaper (for your dog may be too ill to go outside to relieve himself and then newspaper must be used). It also means the cleansing of sore or discharging eyes with diluted witch hazel or Murine, or diluted boracic, the sponging of genitals with mildly disinfected warm water.

Loving Care means the gentle stroking when you approach his bed, the soft and encouraging voice which comforts him and makes him feel it is worth while to get better, the anticipation of his every want as far as it is humanly possible, and when he is well on the way to recovery, loving care will mean producing especially tempting meals which he will enjoy and which will quickly build him up.

Peace is very important, and means protecting him from other people who may fuss him; from other dogs, either from the sound of them or the sight of them, for these may easily excite him to think of past enmities or past jealousies, or may retard his progress by sudden desires to be out and about with other dogs when he is not yet strong enough. Sleep is the very best healer, and if he is given peace and quiet to drift into sleep until he is recovered, he will get well that much quicker.

Warmth, or an even temperature is important for if a dog is very ill he has very little reserves of strength, and he must not have to use up these reserves in trying to keep warm. So give this a great deal of thought, and ensure that he is neither too warm nor cold. Warmth with plenty of fresh air is the best atmosphere providing there is no draught.

Nursing Aids

It is possible that a few aids to efficient nursing may come in useful when dealing with a sick poodle. If the poodle is suffering from a body wound which he will continually lick or some slight skin trouble when you do not wish him to be continually biting himself, then a linen or cotton 'hospital jacket' can be made very easily. This is also useful if you wish to keep a bandage or dressing on the tummy, as the jacket does up with tapes along the top of the back.

Another useful gadget is a very stiff cardboard collar which fastens with lacing. This is particularly useful in severe ear trouble, or eye damage, when it is essential to keep the poodle from scratching in the region of his face. It is *very* uncomfortable for the poodle to wear and is only advised when there is no other way of keeping him from scratching at the wound. Another excellent aid, which would probably be far more comfortable than the collar, is a surgical bag made from some strong material which has a draw string of tape to fasten it round the neck. It will certainly help to prevent him from nibbling or scratching at some sore or wound, and he quite quickly gets used to wearing this, particularly at night when one probably cannot watch him all the time.

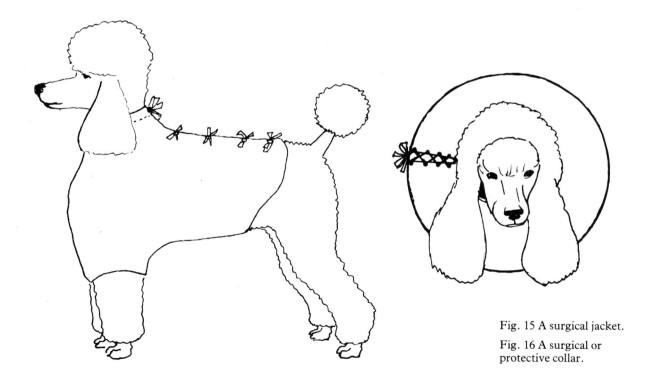

Fig. 15 A surgical jacket.

Fig. 16 A surgical or protective collar.

Equally a bag such as this made of thick towelling serves as an excellent 'Drying Bag'. If, having bathed your poodle, you are not absolutely ready to dry him or are called away for some reason, it is very useful to pop him in such a bag when he will begin to dry, and more important will not get cold and shivery.

Lastly, don't forget that your own hands are important to you, both when nursing or generally caring for dogs, so don't risk getting bitten. Dogs when in pain or when frightened may often turn round on the person who is tending them or nearest to them. It does not mean that they are vicious but it happens instinctively and then you have a nasty bite. Quite often to obviate such a bite it is prudent to 'tape' the patient. Just place a piece of 2½cm (1″) or 5cm (2″) cotton bandage round the muzzle, twist it under the chin and tie behind the ears. It will at any rate give you time to get your hands out of the way, and the soft bandage does not hurt the poodle. This kind of 'taping' is sometimes useful also when mating a bitch. If she is bad tempered, or else very nervous, one can save one's stud dog from being bitten by slipping a tape on the bitch. If a stud dog is ever badly bitten, it may put him off stud work for a very long time.

Fig. 17 A surgical or drying bag.

Fig. 18 Protective taping of muzzle.

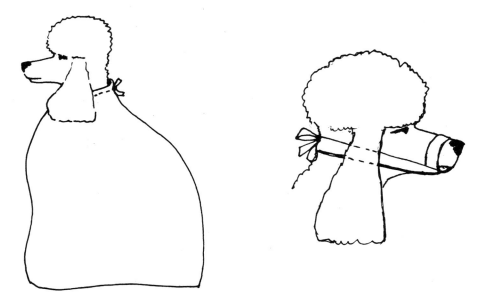

If all these points are well considered, you at any rate, will be doing everything that is possible to accelerate your poodle's return to health.

It may happen that your poodle must have an operation at some time which will involve the administration of an anaesthetic. It may only mean the extraction of some teeth or it may be for something much more serious but whatever it is there are two things you must do before he goes to the veterinary surgeon for the anaesthetic. Firstly, he must *have nothing at all* to eat and drink for *twelve hours* before he goes to the vet. This is absolutely essential for if an anaesthetic is given after recent food, he is likely to be very sick and ill. Secondly, he must empty his bowels and his bladder before starting off for the vet. Therefore leave plenty of time as this may be quite a long business if you have to walk him about for some time. If he shows no signs at all of wishing to defecate, then it will help gently to push the thermometer case, having greased it with vaseline first, up the back passage, wiggling it about a little as you do this. This usually works well, but if not then a glycerine suppository must be inserted. The size for a miniature is that suitable for a child, infant's size for toy poodles and either adult or child's size for the standard poodle.

Post-operative care also needs thought for when you go to the vet to collect your poodle after his operation he may not be quite 'round' from the anaesthetic. Have his bed ready for him at home, and leave a hot water bottle in it so that his bed is warm and cosy for him. Take a coat or a blanket with you, for he will still be more or less in a state of shock and must be kept warm. Have him near you where you can keep a constant eye on him and can reassure him whenever he wakes up and doesn't quite know where he is. A dog who is coming round after an anaesthetic reacts quite oddly at times, and may suddenly jump up from his bed to find his owner, and then may injure himself by falling flat from giddiness. So be near to him to help him if he needs it. It sometimes takes as long as twenty-four hours before he is completely round again, so he may be very 'staggery' for several hours. It is unlikely he will pass a stool for the first twenty-four hours, but he may need to be supported while he spends his pennies until he has regained control of his legs. His diet should be light and completely digestible – scrambled eggs, a milky pudding, or Complan – and then raw minced beef when he fancies it. If he has had a lot of teeth extracted, food must be soft and sloppy for a couple of days, but as dogs always swallow their food more or less whole and have a different mechanism to enable them to digest their food without initial mastication, it is surprising how quickly they will be back on 'hard tack', possibly well within a week.

Don't forget that when your poodle is well he is very self-sufficient and can deal with all comers. But when he is ill, his defences are down and he must rely entirely on you. So anticipate his wants and let him know for certain that you are there at hand whenever he needs you. Remember, the healthy poodle is the clean, well fed, well housed, and completely happy poodle.

10 First Aid

VETERINARY surgeons are very busy people and because of this they do not like being called out needlessly or for frivolous reasons. Especially they dislike unnecessary night calls, for they need a good night's sleep as much as anybody. Equally, any veterinary surgeon who really has the well being of animals at heart would never refuse to come out to a seriously ill dog. If he did refuse, then it would be unwise for the dog owner to remain on that particular vet's list.

Therefore, it is essential if the dog is to receive quick and efficient help in emergency, that the owner should not have indulged in crying 'wolf' and summoning him for a totally unnecessary reason. If a good relationship is to be built up between the poodle owner and the veterinary surgeon, the latter must be sure that something really *is* serious or he would not have been summoned. There is no doubt that as an owner, one is inclined to panic quite unnecessarily when one's dog appears ill, and forget that a dog goes up and down within a very short time. However, every veterinary surgeon will appreciate knowing as much as possible about the condition of the ailing poodle when he is first summoned.

Again the authors have turned to Mrs Ellis and her sister Miss 'Mouse' Sherry, to assist them in the following notes on first aid. These two poodle breeders have, for a number of years, assisted a London veterinary surgeon by taking over the nursing and post operational care of seriously ill dogs. They take the dogs into their own country kennels and have been responsible for saving a great number of sick dogs – and indeed, not only dogs but other animals of all kinds. Therefore, the authors felt they could not do better than draw on their specialised knowledge and experience for the following notes on recognition of symptoms and first aid treatment, and when it is necessary to call the veterinary surgeon and when it is essential that he comes at once.

But before we pass on to actual first aid, it would be as well to consider the matter of a first aid box or cabinet. This must be intelligently stocked and ready for use at a moment's notice. It rather depends on the owner and his own particular ideas as to what will be needed, but the following can certainly serve as a working basis:

The First Aid Cupboard

Smelling salts (for collapse)
Bicarbonate of soda (for wasp stings)
Vinegar (for poisons)
Brandy
Glucose
Honey
Collo-Cal-D (for whelping emergency) or Canovel calcium tablets
Disprin tablets
Salt (for cleansing)
Soda (small pieces for emetics)
Piece of string for ligature or tourniquet
Permanganate of potash crystals (for disinfectant)
Milk of magnesia (for indigestion)
Aperient such as syrup of figs or liquid paraffin
Golden Eye ointment or Brolene
In addition, several rolls of bandage
One 3cm (2½″) or 7½cm (3″) Crepe bandage
Cotton wool
Bottle of Dettol and T.C.P.
Lint
Pair of curved surgical scissors
Pair of nail clippers
Small pair of tweezers
Box of Band Aid and sticking plaster
Peroxide (for swabbing or syringing wounds and abcesses)
Boracic, for eyes
Sterzac powder or sulphonamide wound dressing
Baby kaolin mixture
Savlon antiseptic cream
Brands' chicken or beef essence (In fridge)
Bicarbonate of soda (solution for immersing in or bandaging on burns)
Elastoplast (2½cm (1″) roll)
Nuvar Top (for spraying fleas away)
Small hypodermic syringe (very useful for giving liquid doses – without using needle)
Clincal blunt-ended thermometer

In addition it would be as well to keep the following drugs and medicines handy for emergency. Some of them are on prescription and your veterinary surgeon would probably help over this, others are available at a good chemist or else to order.

Phisohex (disinfectant)
Sterzac powder (antibiotic powder)
Dapsetyn (ointment for wounds, eyes etc.)
Intermammary penicillin (ointment)
Otodex (for ears)

One point is really important. The name, address and telephone number of the veterinary surgeon must be clearly written out and put up in a prominent position. If possible, a second vet should be mentioned in case the regular vet cannot be contacted. In a sudden crisis, there is no time to have to hunt for these details.

First Aid

ABSCESS

An abscess is a pocket of pus under the skin. It is indicated by swelling, heat and pain, sometimes fever. If there is a rise in temperature over 38.8°C (102°F) consult your veterinary surgeon in the morning, otherwise deal with it under general first aid rules outlined below.

An abscess usually comes to a head rapidly, and bursts. Unless too painful, this can be speeded by hot fomentations. Once burst, there is a discharge of bloody matter and immediate relief is felt. The resulting cavity should be syringed out with warm water containing several drops of Phisohex – a hypodermic syringe, without the needle does the job very adequately – insert the nozzle well into the hole and gently press plunger. Repeat several times. Dab dry and dust area with Sterzac powder. Now squeeze into the cavity, again placing nozzle well in, either some Dapsetyn or intermammary penicillin. Repeat this treatment once or twice daily, healing will be rapid. Do not allow a scab to form, healing must come from inside.

An abscess under the tail just by the rectum is called an anal abscess and should be treated in the manner previously described. Some poodles are particularly prone to this most painful ailment, and it causes considerable distress both physical and mental. An anal abscess can be obviated by regular emptying of the gland for the animals that are prone to this trouble, and the method of emptying is this: Hold the tail erect in one hand, and with the other hand place a couple of tissues over the anus, then with the thumb one side and the forefinger the other side of the anus press the two firmly and quickly together. The anal fluid is most evil smelling, and it can be rather hard and cheesey in character or rather like pus. Once the gland is emptied, immediate relief is felt. A dust with Sterzac after a quick swab down with warm water and a drop of Dettol and any lingering smell is soon gone.

Should an abscess not burst once it has 'come to a head', then your veterinary surgeon's help must be sought without delay for unless the abscess is lanced and the poison drained, general septicaemia may set in with possible fatal results.

ARTIFICAL RESPIRATION

This is required immediately a patient ceases to breathe on his own accord. The method should be to place the dog on its right side with head extended and tongue pulled forward. Place your hand on the rib cage behind the shoulder blade and press downwards with a short sharp action. As soon as your hand is removed the chest will expand and refill with air. The pressure should be repeated at five second intervals until natural breathing is resumed, or your vet takes over.

BITES AND WOUNDS

For the treatment of bites and wounds it depends on the extent of the damage done and the degree of shock sustained whether this requires professional skill regardless of the hour or whether the matter can wait until morning. If you have any doubt of your ability to cope, S.O.S. your vet, he will not mind. If on the other hand it is something that common sense first aid can deal with until morning, remember your vet may have been up all last night with a sick animal and he is only human.

Wash any bites or wounds with warm water and a few squirts of Phisohex or peroxide or any other suitable disinfectant. If any clots have formed leave well alone, for if removed haemorrhage may occur. Cover wound with tulle gauze and bandage. For any severe bleeding see under paragraph for haemorrhage. Any bites and wounds from wire or glass large enough to gape at all, will require stitching to facilitate healing and minimise scarring.

No matter how trivial, always treat for shock, and as the poodle will probably be in pain or upset, tape his mouth so that he cannot bite *you*. You are useless if *you* have to have treatment!

DIABETES

Symptoms: Starts with excessive drinking and rapid loss of weight. Collect a urine sample and your vet will advise you. Provided you have the courage and love your pet enough to do it, there is no reason why, with the help of daily injections of insulin, the dog cannot again live a normal life as thousands of diabetic people do. Diabetes tablets don't work.

DIARRHOEA

Diarrhoea has many causes. The first worry is that in uninoculated poodles it can be a symptom of a virus infection such as distemper etc. If there is a rise in temperature above 38.8°C (102°F) S.O.S. your vet. Diarrhoea caused by tainted food will usually clear up very quickly with two or three doses of baby kaolin and one day of semi-starvation. Next day a little rice, fish, chicken, or scrambled egg.

Change of home, routine and diet will sometimes cause diarrhoea and loss of appetite.

In many animals, particularly the sensitive adult, plain nerves brought on by a worrying situation, will cause a motion so loose that it is watery and evacuated with great force. Medical term for this type of eliminating is projectile, be it for vomit or passing that type of stool and correct use of that word can help your vet in his diagnosis. This type of diarrhoea clears up with the passing of the situation that caused it.

EAR TROUBLES

Ear troubles cover a vast field usually loosely and erroneously called canker.

Symptoms: At the first sign of any head shaking or ear scratching, the ears should be examined. If there is any hair in them, gently but firmly pull out a few hairs at a time, keeping inside the ear and the fingers dusted with Sterzac (an antibiotic powder). This facilitates the grasping of the hairs and also some powder will get on to the skin and soothe the inflammation caused by plucking the hair out. The ear can then be properly examined and if there is any brown matter in it, or any squelching when the base of the ear is massaged or any odour, then the ear should be syringed out before starting further treatment. Using a hypodermic syringe *without* the needle, and a small bowl of tepid water, into which you have dissolved a few squirts of Savlon gently syringe the ear, massage the base of it to loosen any dirt, and then wipe out with a cotton wool swab or Baby Buds as it comes to the top. Repeat this until there is no more sign of anything to come up, and swab dry with cotton wool. Pour a few drops of Otodex into the ear. Do this daily for a week, and if there has not been a marked improvement consult your veterinary surgeon. Bad ears should never be neglected, they cause mental as well as physical distress. The ear drum can even be perforated causing permanent damage, such as head always on one side and lack of co-ordination in walking.

ECLAMPSIA

Eclampsia is a lack of calcium in the blood stream found in some bitches when nursing a litter. Usually occurs when the puppies are around three weeks old. Unless the bitch is given an injection of calcium within a few hours of the start of an attack of eclampsia she will pass into a coma and die.

Symptoms: Vary with every bitch, the most common symptoms however are extreme restlessness, panting and becoming very distressed, general twitching and jerking. This usually continues into convulsive movements of the legs with the bitch lying on her side unable to stand, the predominant factor being the terribly distressed breathing.

If you have a bitch showing any or all of these symptoms, nursing puppies around three weeks old (it has been known for eclampsia to occur just prior to whelping but the most common time is when the puppies are taking most out of the bitch, just prior to starting to wean at about three weeks old) – do not hesitate day or night to S.O.S. your vet, telling him the symptoms. Unless she is given an *injection* of calcium, in bad cases straight into the vein, she will be dead in a few hours.

The cause of this ailment is believed to be the inefficient functioning of a gland that controls the absorption of vitamin D, without which calcium is not absorbed into the blood stream.

If your bitch has a previous history of eclampsia she should be given Collo-Cal-D, 2ml (⅓teaspoon), three times daily by mouth. Use a syringe with *no* needle. If tablets are preferred, then Canovel Calcium is another excellent safeguard. These tablets are produced by Beechams and do the same job as Collo-Cal-D. Bitches can often be tempted to eat them like sweets. To be on the safe side Canovel may be given two weeks after mating until the puppies have been weaned.

ENTERITIS

This can occur at any age. It can be caused by a virus infection, but usually from a bacterial source such as tainted food.

Symptoms: Violent diarrhoea, sometimes tinged with blood, frequently accompanied by sickness. Usually responds rapidly to treatment with Guanamycin, a day of liquid diet only, water and glucose, followed by light diet for a couple of days. If however there is any blood in the excreta, call your vet at once.

EXCESSIVE DRINKING

Excessive drinking, although it may sound trivial, is one of the first symptoms of three serious diseases. Pyometra, diabetes and kidney diseases are the three most serious ailments of which excessive drinking is a first symptom – see under these headings. If any animal continues to drink more than usual (taking into account hot weather), over a twenty-four hour period, your veterinary surgeon should be consulted in the morning. Your forethought will be praised and appreciated if you go armed with a bottle containing a sample of urine. This is quite simply obtained by taking a small clean frying pan on the first walk of the day, and when your patient squats or lifts a leg, pop it under! If no frying pan is available any flattish dish will do, but the handle does make it easier. Bitches, in particular, are sometimes embarrassed!

EYES

Eyes are too precious to neglect. At any known injury, such as a cat scratch or a thorn, consult your vet, be it day or night.

If an eye starts to look weepy or has a discharge, or looks blue, bathe with boracic (one teaspoon to one pint of boiled water kept in the fridge). Then insert Brolene or Golden Eye ointment.

FITS

Symptoms: Fits have numerous causes. The patient will suddenly start frothing at the mouth and champing its jaws, twitching and jerking and if not restrained may gallop off, only to fall as the fit progresses. Unconsciousness may follow and the breathing may stop. Should the dog cease breathing, artificial respiration must be started at once. If there is a delay in starting artificial respiration of more than three minutes irreparable brain damage will be done. See the paragraph on artificial respiration.

The patient must be prevented from damaging himself. If he is small enough, wrap him in a blanket and hold him until the violence passes, or, if he is too big keep him in a room where there is as little chance of his crashing into furniture as possible. Keep a watch that you do not get accidently bitten, the dog in a fit does not know what he is doing any more than an epileptic person does.

Fits are a genuine reason for a day or night emergency call for your vet. He will be able to prescribe sedatives that you can give to lessen the likelihood of fits recurring and also he will investigate the probable cause – virus infection, wrong feeding, fear, worms, teething, epilepsy, etc.

HAEMORRHAGE

Haemorrhage must always be regarded as serious. A sudden and severe loss of blood apart from the obvious risk carries also the very real dangers of death from shock and also frequently from pneumonia. S.O.S. your vet, meanwhile set about your first aid.

Methods to arrest bleeding are:

1. By applying a pad, and bandaging in position – clean hanky, nylon stocking if nothing else!
2. If blood continues to seep through, apply direct pressure for a few minutes and another bandage *tied on top*.
3. The tourniquet is the last resort and obviously can only be applied to a leg. Severe bleeding from a leg usually means a vein or artery is cut and speed is essential. To apply a tourniquet make a loop, using that nylon stocking again, round the leg *above* the site of the bleeding. Insert a pencil or stick in the loop and twist until it becomes tight enough to cause the flow of blood to cease. Hold it in your hand. The reason for this caution is that if the tourniquet remains on for more than ten minutes without it being slackened,

irreparable damage will be done to blood vessels and gangrene will set in. Note the time the tourniquet is applied and loosen every ten minutes until you get to your vet.

KIDNEY INFECTIONS

These are various. **Symptoms**: In general the first symptom is thirst, sometimes trying to pass water frequently but cannot do so, or passing water with some drops of blood in it. It is essential to collect a urine sample in a *scrupulously* clean utensil and keep in a fridge until you take it to the vet. Keep on a white meat diet and give barley water to drink.

POISONS

Cases of poisoning, although not common occurrences among dogs and even more uncommon among cats, require such speed and efficiency in dealing with them if your patient is to survive, that a general outline in first aid must be read, absorbed and remembered.

The first step to be taken when suspecting that an animal has had access to or been given poison is to S.O.S. your vet, stating, if known, the type of poison, i.e. rat poison, sleeping pills etc. He will tell you what specific treatment he wants carried out until he arrives or until you can get to him. It cannot be stressed too greatly the speed with which professional help is required if the animal is to be saved.

If you are 'in the wilds' send for help and in the meantime carry out the advice outlined below.

Poisons come under four headings: *1. narcotics, 2. corrosives, 3. irritants* and *4. convulsants*. You have to decide from your knowledge, i.e. missing sleeping tablets, puppy drinking disinfectant, puppy eating rat poison. Or you may find a country dog in convulsions near mole hills – and you assume strychnine as this is used for the destruction of moles. One of the commonest accidents is the puppy getting at sleeping tablets.

1. Narcotics

Symptoms: The narcotic poison works on the nervous system producing sleep, and this must be averted at all costs. As most accidents of this type will happen in the home, remedies should be at hand. First an emetic. Give a piece of washing soda the size of a large pea or a strong solution of salt water, but never force liquids down an already unconscious animal's throat. A tablespoon of salt to a pint of water. If mixed in a tonic water bottle, the neck of the bottle can be inserted in the pouch of the dog's lips and the emetic poured *slowly* in. Care must be taken not to pour too fast or some may go down the windpipe and you may kill the poodle by trying to save its life! Owing to the sedating action of this type of drug it is sometimes impossible to make the patient sick but if the emetic works, repeat once or twice more before moving on to the next step, which is an aperient. The quickest to hand, found in most households is Milk of Magnesia tablets, six or more according to size, or any other aperient will do. Next, black coffee, with plenty of glucose or sugar, again poured down slowly. Now keep your patient awake and moving, remember if he sleeps he dies! It may sound brutal, it is brutal, but, in between copious draughts of black coffee, slap his face, push, prod, pull, *keep* him on his feet until help comes and he should live to lick your face again!

2. *Corrosives*

These are either acid or alkali. The important thing to remember is, when this type of poison is suspected, by reasons of smell, i.e. Jeyes fluid etc. on the breath of a puppy, or by signs of brown burn marks on lips or tongue, the only first aid treatment that can be given is to dilute the poison taken, *never* give an emetic. If the poodle will drink give as much as possible of any soothing fluid, milk, gruel, olive oil, which will help soothe areas burned by the poison. If you have to force the fluid down mix milk with only a little oil, as oil is inclined to make an animal choke.

3. *Irritants*

Those that irritate and inflame tissue with which they come in contact are divided into two main groups: 1. caused by decaying food; 2. chemical irritants such as arsenic found in weed killers, lead found in some paint, and phosphorous found in some rat poisons.

For treatment of group 1. see under heading: Enteritis. Group 2. arsenic, lead and phosphorous. **Symptoms**: severe and prolonged vomiting, sometimes with blood in it. These are deadly unless you can get quick help. The best you can do is to dilute with quantities of milk and treat for severe shock.

Very rarely some plants may be poisonous to dogs, for instance laburnum seeds and holly berries but it is unlikely that dogs would eat such things. More likely, the danger would occur from any substance *on* the plants such as weed-killer or slug repellant. If anything like this is suspected, the poodle must be rushed to the vet *at once*. Such preparations usually state the poison contained in the preparation and the vet will know the correct specific to use.

4. *The convulsant poisons*

These are strychnine and prussic acid and unfortunately there is nothing anyone can do. The patient is usually a country dog who has possibly eaten chicken carcasses baited for foxes and unless he can be got to a vet within minutes of eating the poison and before convulsions start there is no hope.

PYOMETRA

This is an infection of the uterus, which if neglected is a killer. It usually occurs in middle aged or elderly bitches not long after they have been on heat, and more frequently in bitches that have never had a litter.

Symptoms: Excessive drinking, swollen tummy, sometimes tender and hard, generally poorly, off food, rise in temperature. Purulent discharge, and sometimes vomiting, usually occurs within about two weeks of a prolonged oestrus. Test after two to three weeks for safety. Any bitch showing the above symptoms must have veterinary treatment at once. Your surgeon may try antibiotics at first, but if there is no improvement then the poodle will have to be operated on at once.

If you own a treasured old lady your vet can find out by taking a blood sample from her vein about six weeks after her season if she is threatening pyometra.

If the result is positive an operation before the infection flares up is very much safer, and to be recommended.

ROAD ACCIDENTS

The first thing to do on arriving at the scene of a road accident involving an animal is to organise one or two of the gaping spectators to help you.

1. Send one to telephone the nearest veterinary surgeon. Tell him you are bringing in an accident case and ask him the quickest route, getting precise directions and address.
2. Get one to arrange a car if you haven't one, shooting brake if possible.
3. Another to get something suitable to act as a stretcher – household tray, board, gate. If nothing can be found, keep the animal as flat as possible when moving.

Those three things take seconds only to detail to someone else to do. Now assess your case. If there is bleeding it must be stopped, by one or all of the methods used under the heading haemorrhage. Loss of blood is one of the causes of shock, and shock alone can prove fatal to an animal. Next, are there any obvious fractures, legs lying at impossible angles, or bone actually protruding through the skin? If so, using whatever you can obtain, providing it is reasonably clean, immobilise the limb by splinting. If a broken leg is not splinted before moving, greater pain is caused. Pain gives shock and also there is danger of the damage becoming more severe by movement. To splint a broken limb obtain a stick the same length as the leg and cover it with any sort of material handy to make it softer. Place against the leg and tie it to it starting at the top. Grasp the paw and give a firm but steady pull. Get someone else to tie just above the paw. If it is a large leg (standard poodle etc.) the splint should be tied in one or two more places taking care not to tie over the wound. If the site of the break is obvious, tie above and below it. Nylon stockings, handkerchiefs, ties, all make very handy emergency first aid items! The author once splinted a compound fracture of the left front leg of a springer spaniel with the aid of a stick from the hedge and a petticoat torn in strips by a willing donor. The spaniel was so greatly in shock it never moved.

Immediately any bleeding has been arrested and fracture splinted, slide your patient on to the stretcher if you have been able to get one, if not, try and keep him as flat as possible, place in the car, cover with coats or blankets and *get to your vet.*

If your patient is in too much pain and will not permit you to handle him without risk of being bitten, and unless you have someone you can trust who will grasp him firmly by the back of the neck and restrain him while you are carrying out your first aid, it would be safer from your point of view if a muzzle was quickly slipped over his mouth. This can be improvised by tying a knot in a nylon stocking and the loop thus formed can then be slipped over the mouth, the knot under the jaw, pulled tight and the ends then tied behind the head.

SHOCK

Shock, whether it is as a sequence to a fight, accident or sickness, requires very similar treatment to that given to human patients 'in shock' – that great British hot sweet tea, warmth and rest.

Provided you know for sure the animal will not be requiring a general anaesthetic within the next twelve hours, warm milk, sweetened preferably with glucose which is more quickly absorbed into the blood stream than sugar, or tea, if the patient prefers it, is excellent.

Cover lightly with blankets and make sure, if hot water bottles are given, that these have very adequate covers, and the most important of all just sit and be quiet with your patient. Try to create an atmosphere of comfort, for this can be very healing.

TONSILITIS

Tonsilitis, frequently called 'poodle throat' by veterinary surgeons as so many of the breed seem to get it at some time in their lives.

Symptoms: Glands in the neck just under the jaw bone become enlarged – obvious difficulty in swallowing, therefore the poodle is off his food. Sometimes a rise in temperature. If the mouth is opened and the tongue depressed, the tonsils can be seen to be red and enlarged.

A mild attack can be treated by keeping the poodle in an equable temperature, only allowing him out for a quickie to relieve himself and then only with a coat on. If they can be persuaded to take it, a light nourishing diet of rabbit, milk and honey. Complan is advisable. The attack usually passes in a few days. A few drops of T.C.P. in the drinking water is a help. If, however there is a rise in temperature above

38.8°C (102.5°F) then contact your veterinary surgeon, preferably before 10 a.m., as unless the infection is brought under control with antibiotics, the patient is laid open to secondary infections.

Provided a well stocked first aid cupboard is maintained, and you know your dog thoroughly when he is well and can therefore immediately recognise the fact when he is suddenly off colour, and provided you do your utmost to care for your poodle in the most sensible and kind manner, you should be able to help him with the least possible delay if he *should* fall ill. Speed in noting symptoms and promptitude in putting the correct first aid into operation will undoubtedly save your poodle from pain, stress and fear and may avoid many dangerous complications from ever starting.

11 Grooming, Shampooing and Drying

THE grooming, shampooing and clipping of poodles is, undoubtedly, a major undertaking. Grooming must be regular and it must be thorough. A well cared for poodle is a thing of great elegance and beauty, but a neglected poodle, dirty, matted and unclipped, is a very ugly sight. Before deciding that you wish to own a poodle, the matter of coat care must be sensibly considered. Have you time to keep your poodle reasonably well groomed? If you cannot actually clip and bath him yourself, can you afford to send him to a poodle beauty parlour? Such visits cost money, but if the owners and assistants in the parlour are knowledgeable, kind and artistic your poodle will come out looking wonderful. But equally you should be able to clip and bath your poodle yourself after a little experience and this would save you a lot of money.

In this chapter, the know-how of grooming, shampooing and drying will be explored, and advice on the right type of equipment which is necessary will be proffered for those who need it. Also the matter of the right types of shampoos and coat conditioners will be discussed in detail.

Grooming

Obviously there are a number of firms who produce excellent grooming and clipping requisites and it pays to 'shop around' at shows such as Crufts, or the breed club shows. However, we have found that Messrs. Allbrooks Ltd of Witton House, Lower Road, Chorleywood, Herts do give a most comprehensive service and their products appear to be of excellent quality. Therefore, most of the equipment mentioned as follows has been supplied by this firm. Usually, they have a stand at most of the large shows. The prices we give are a rough guide and inflation must be taken into consideration as the years go by. In any case, it would probably be a great advantage to send for a catalogue if you are starting up either as a poodle owner, breeder, or else contemplating your own beauty parlour.

Special care must be taken with some poodle coats at certain times of the year. The coat may suddenly 'teazle' almost overnight in the early spring. A poodle normally does not shed its coat as in most other breeds,

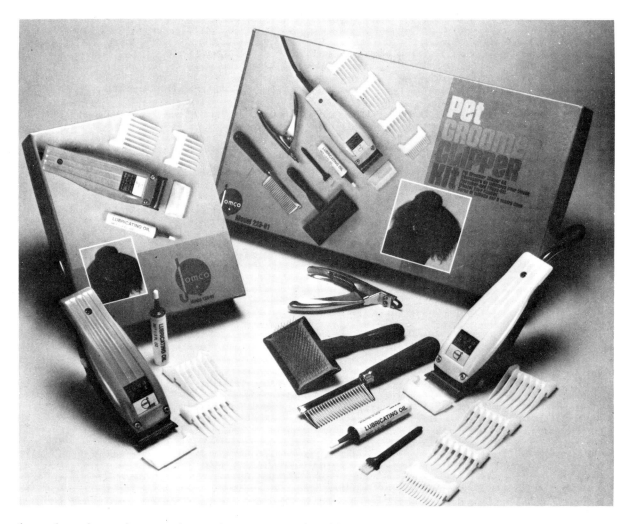

but when the spring coat is starting to grow, the old coat comes out in a multitude of little tags which are not actually shed but remain embedded in the thick coat. Daily and even twice daily brushing and combing must be carried out, to free the coat of these wretched tags. If not noticed, it is then that the coat will become unbearably matted in a matter of days. This condition does not last long – probably a week or ten days.

It pays to buy a really good, suitable brush to begin with, possibly one of pure bristle set in a pneumatic rubber base. This would cost from around £2.50 to £4, but if you want to be really extravagant there is the Kent Brush at about £10. Possibly a softer brush would be needed initially for the puppy.

Two Grooming Kits produced by Messrs. Allbrooks Ltd of Chorleywood, providing every piece of equipment needed by the beginner.

If the poodle's coat has become badly matted (a condition which should never occur with the conscientious owner!) then a wire brush might be necessary. These are fairly inexpensive. But the greatest care must be taken as the action is harsh – indeed it must be to deal with the teazles in the coat – so beware, as the last thing that you will wish to do is to put your poodle 'off' grooming for life. Certainly do not economise over brushes as some of the cheaper, obscure makes undoubtedly pull out the coat and split the ends of the hair. As a result the poodle never looks well groomed, but appears rather fluffy and untidy, and certainly will never grow a good coat.

The next consideration is a good comb. One with a handle is useful, but the teeth should not be too fine. Equally, a comb which has moderately close teeth one end and wide teeth the other is to be recommended. Prices range from £2 to £3.

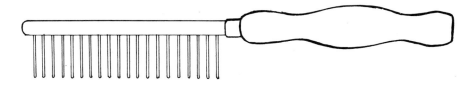

Fig. 19 Types of comb suitable for a poodle.

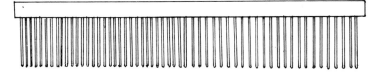

Rule number one is this: start grooming your puppy almost before he can walk. Therein lies the secret of peaceful grooming sessions throughout his entire life. A dog is a creature of routine – and none more so than the poodle – and if grooming is a natural daily happening, and has been so ever since his weaning, then he will accept it cheerfully, he may even enjoy it, and it will not occur to him to make a fuss. Firstly, a soft brushing daily and remember always to brush his coat upwards in a different direction to that in which it normally grows. From the tail to the top of the head, up the chest, up the legs from wrist to shoulder, and ankle to haunches.

As soon as the puppy is old enough and as the coat grows longer, accustom him to lying on a table on a foam or rubber mat, or if he is a tiny toy you may find it easier to make him lie on your lap. But however it is, accustom him to lie first on one side and then on the other while you give the hair a vigorous brushing and then a light combing. Raise each leg in turn by holding the toes and again brush and comb upwards, then brush the hair on the brisket and belly. Next, invite him to stand while you brush and comb his back. Finally, tell him to sit facing you and with the finer toothed comb, attend to his ears, which should be combed downwards, and his top knot which should be combed upwards and back. At last comb out the pom on the tail and the grooming procedure is accomplished.

In all, this should take at the most five to seven minutes. Not a very arduous task and yet so many poodles are never groomed from one week's end to the next, and so when they become too shoddy for words, a long and painful session is necessary. It is real pain to the poor poodle and so he objects and loses his temper, becoming really rather difficult to handle. His owner also becomes somewhat short-tempered and says 'Why on earth did I have a dog whose coat mats like this?' And yet only five minutes a day and everyone would have been happy and the result would have been a smart, elegant, nice-tempered poodle whom everyone admires with an owner basking in reflected glory and feeling really rather smug!

So remember – daily grooming is a must, the best equipment is essential, and training the poodle to lie down quietly from an early age is the keynote to a peaceful session.

Shampooing

If poodles are to be kept sweet smelling and clean they must be bathed from time to time. There is no doubt that frequent bathing *in the right shampoo* will improve the coat. Many of the most luxuriously coated show dogs are shampooed weekly. However this, of course, is not essential, and provided regular grooming takes place, a poodle will remain clean skinned for many weeks in normal circumstances.

There is no doubt that the choice of shampoo is of paramount importance if the poodle's coat is to be kept in healthy condition and always looking its best. Just any old shampoo *won't do*! It must be a shampoo which has been prepared entirely for the good of this particular coat. Some owners think that the most expensive type of shampoo prepared specifically for human hair must be all right for poodles. This is not so. Admittedly such shampoos will make the hair glossy, and also soft and luxurious, but the last thing the poodle's coat should be is soft. The correct coat should be of good, hard texture. It should be bushy and resilient so that when the hair is patted it resists the touch and springs back into position, and for it to be soft and clinging is thus incorrect. Also in some shampoos there is a great deal of detergent which tends to make the hair ends brittle and prone to splitting. Again a bad thing.

Often if the dregs of a diluted shampoo are left overnight, it will be found in the morning that any surplus water has evaporated and all that is left are sharp crystals of soda. One has only to know what soda will do to one's hands to realise what such a shampoo would do to the poodle's skin. From all this it will be realised that only the right shampoo should be used.

There are many shampoos and conditioners on the market, and those offered by Allbrooks Ltd have been well tested and found to produce good results. The Oster Protein shampoo gives a specially fine sheen to somewhat dull coats, while the Oster White Coat shampoo for all white poodles is to be recommended. It is always an advantage to use a coat conditioner as it certainly adds lustre and life to the coat. Oster also produce a shampoo for the removal of pests such as fleas, ticks and lice though hopefully the well cared for poodle should not be troubled in this way. There is one drawback here that after shampooing against pests, the poodle may lick his coat and sometimes this causes a mild tummy upset. After all, if the preparation is to kill fleas etc. it equally could have a milder action on the digestion of the poodle, so whichever is the lesser evil must be chosen. Shampoos sometimes produce sore eyes, and to obviate this a very light smear of Vaseline across the eyelids is useful, or else the use of Oster Easy-on-Eyes shampoo which is a mild wash for sensitive skins.

Clean towels are the first consideration, and these should be well laundered or washed in disinfectant from time to time. It is not enough to hang them up to dry after each shampoo. A rubber spray is another essential and these can be purchased from Boots or Woolworths and are not expensive.

Certain preparations must be made before bathing. Two towels must be ready, the sprayer fixed on the tap, a plentiful supply of hot water available, two small pieces of cotton wool laid ready for plugging the ears, and the correct amount of a suitable shampoo ready in the plastic bottle. A rubber apron for yourself is a wise precaution if your poodle is one which is likely to throw his legs around your neck when being bathed. Regarding the dog himself, it is not advisable to bath him within at least two hours of a heavy meal, and he should always be given the opportunity to relieve himself just before his bath. A thorough grooming is absolutely essential, and this must be a combing right down to the skin. The slightest mat or teazling will turn into 'felting' on the application of the shampoo and such 'felting' is difficult to remove after bathing. A small piece of cotton wool should be very gently pushed into each ear hole to keep out any water which could set up canker or an irritation – but don't forget to take out the plugs after the bath or else you will wonder why your dog appears to have become rather hard of hearing! If the poodle is to be bathed in a somewhat slippery sink or bath, then a rubber mat should be placed in the bottom. This will add to his comfort, for a slippery surface will frighten him. Take a look around before commencing the bath, to see that nothing is hanging above the sink or bath which might fall on him and scare him, such as measures, utensils etc.

He is now ready for the actual bathing. Wet his coat thoroughly starting from the tail and hindquarters and going up to the top of the neck but excluding the actual head. Poodles' coats are extremely waterproof and you may have to squeeze the hair several times to get it completely waterlogged. Now dribble a little ready mixed shampoo along the back, down the front and back legs and on the chest, and then vigorously massage his coat until a really fine lather has been produced. If he is very dirty he may need now to be rinsed and a second application of shampoo given. In any case, round the elbows, round the buttocks and between the toes will need extra massaging. Next the head should be wetted with warm water, and then well rubbed with shampoo, especially round the edges of the ear leathers. Be careful of the eyes and mouth because shampoo stings the eyes and also tastes very unpleasant and it is not really necessary to apply it in those places. Next spray the poodle very thoroughly with clean, warm water until all trace of shampoo has been removed. Turn off the water, and squeeze out the long hair to remove as much moisture as possible. It is as well to keep a restraining hand on him now for he is very likely to choose this moment to give a hearty shake, almost soaking you to the skin. Continuous commands of 'No' will usually obviate this. But he is likely to escape and have a lovely shake on your best bedspread unless carefully watched! Take him out of the bath and stand him on the table, at the same time holding a towel round him rather like a tent while you tell him to 'Shake'. He will very soon learn this word and obey, and if you shake the towel as you say this it will help him to get the message. He should now be squeezed, patted and rubbed with the towel and then wrapped up fairly tightly in a clean dry towel, with only his head and neck appearing out of the top. As he has learned to 'lie' for grooming, he will be quite happy to do this while being dried.

Drying and Dryers

Dry his head and ears thoroughly with the dryer while he is still wrapped in the towel, using either a clean brush or a comb to separate the hair as you dry. Then unwrap his back legs and dry those, finally taking the towel off the rest of his body to dry that. It will really make all the difference to his smartness and the finish of his coat if you comb the hair upwards all the time the flow of warm air is drying him. Of course, both the shampooing and the drying technique described applies more especially to miniature and toy poodles, and it is obviously more difficult to operate in this manner with a standard poodle. Here is would be more convenient to use the human bath for shampooing, and to dry on a lower bench than a table. Another method of drying is to place the dog under an infra red ray lamp until he is half dry, and then finish with a table or hand dryer, combing out the hair at the same time. But whatever method is used it is better to cope with drying the head and ears before turning to the rest of the body.

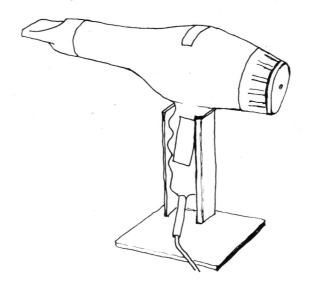

Fig. 20 A good type of hand dryer and stand.

Hand dryers are not cheap. The Braun 1000, which is more powerful than an ordinary hair dryer, and is used by many professional hairdressers, is a very good choice but it will cost around £20. It has an output of 1,000 watts and is comfortable to hold. It has two heat settings. Alternatively, the hand dryer and stand supplied by Allbrooks is excellent value at £25 as this has two heat settings and a cold blow, combined with two air speeds. The stand allows both hands to be free for combing out. If, of course, you have oodles of cash, you can pay upwards of £150 for a dryer which stands on the floor and has easy glide castors!

Quite useful in the busy beauty parlour is a drying box which has a hot air blow coming through the top and vents which can be opened or closed. Certainly this could be an advantage when there are dogs queuing up to be dried, and perhaps shivering with a wet coat until their turn comes for the hot blow. While the authors do not condemn this method of drying, providing it is constantly and efficiently supervised, they do consider that some poodles might be frightened by this method, simply because they cannot escape from it, nor do they have the reassurance

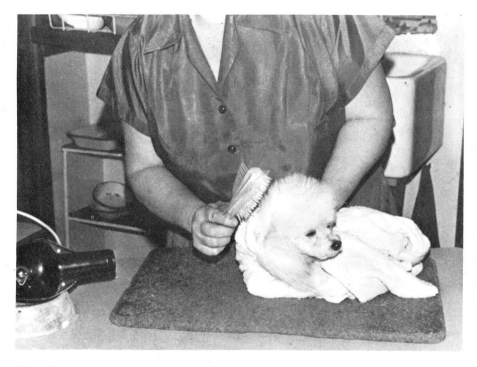

Drying the heads and ears first, while the rest of the puppy is wrapped in a warm towel.

from human hands throughout the procedure. Possibly a kinder (and indeed cheaper!) method would be to pop the poodle under an infra red ray lamp for a while or until you are ready for him; or put him in a towelling bag (see Fig. 17)

Remember, the poodle's coat is a thing of beauty, and therefore it is worth looking after. Use good quality shampoos, reliable equipment and above all groom regularly without fail. If all this sounds too much like hard work, then perhaps a short coated dog should be your choice. But there is tremendous satisfaction when taking a sparklingly clean, beautifully groomed, magnificently clipped poodle for a walk, and everyone turns round and says 'Look at that gorgeous poodle.' The poodle undoubtedly feels one hundred per cent as well!

12 Basic Clipping and Equipment

BEFORE we can begin actual clipping, it is necessary to collect a comfortable and efficient set of equipment. Unnecessary expense can be saved by giving this matter a lot of thought. For instance, is the equipment needed for just one poodle every eight weeks or so, or do you contemplate owning several poodles, or finally do you plan to set up in business and clip other people's dogs? If the first then a light pair of clippers and one or at most two pairs of scissors would serve the case, but in the last two cases heavy duty clippers will be necessary and several pairs of scissors of various types, together with such items as tooth scalers, nail clippers, grooming control stands etc. But it is pointless to spend a deal of money on equipment you may hardly use.

Clippers

An excellent new edition to the Oster range of equipment available from Allbrooks is a comprehensive clipper kit, which contains a pair of fixed-head vibratory clippers with two comb attachments for varying the length of the cut. There is also a larger kit which has an adjustable blade clipper with four comb attachments, together with a pair of guillotine nail clippers, a comb and a de-matting brush. Both of these kits are suitable for the beginner to start on, but not really for the experienced clipper or the beauty parlour. They are priced at around £18 and £29 respectively. (See photograph on p. 119.)

If you can afford electric clippers you will never regret investing in these. They make the job fast and reasonably easy, and poodles prefer this method once they get used to it. However, if it *must* be hand clippers, Allbrooks stock a medium size model at about £6.50, and also the A.1 model for which different sized blades can be obtained.

But if circumstances will allow, there is no comparison between electric and hand clippers, and once you have used the former you won't want to return to the latter. From past experience, the authors have found the Oster small animal clipper A.2 model extremely satisfactory. They have used this clipper for many years and with reasonable servicing and blade renewal have never had any trouble whatsoever. They are American manufactured and need a small transformer supplied with the

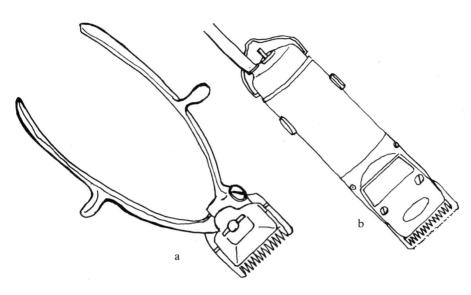

Fig. 21 Clippers
(a) Hand clippers.
(b) Oster electric
clippers.

a

b

clipper to convert the 115 A.C./D.C. voltage to the normal United Kingdom voltage. The clipper weighs only 450g (20oz) has very little vibration and is shock-proofed, and there is automatic tension and a guide plate which eliminates swivelling and skin-nipping. There is a detachable head so that instant change of blade can be carried out by a twist of the wrist. It *is* an expensive clipper and in Britain costs around £70 plus the transformer. Really the Oster A.5 is a better buy as it costs the same price but you do not need a transformer as the voltage is 220/250. Sets of blades can be purchased and for poodles it is recommended that a No. 5 is used for long hair, that is for maintaining the curly or lamb clip, No. 10 or 15 for face, feet and tails. A No. 30 blade is often used to obtain a very close clip on show dogs, but experience is necessary to avoid scraping the skin and setting up a clipper rash. There is also a very handy blade, either 16mm (⅝″) or 22mm (⅞″) which is excellent for toe work. The price of the blades is between £10 and £13.

Don't forget the higher priced clippers have *electric motors* while the cheaper models have only *vibrators*. All clippers must be carefully looked after, and blades should always be brushed over with an oily brush and wrapped in oily paper when not in use. Quite a lot of moisture emanates from the poodle's coat and if the clippers are left with hair sticking to the blades after a clipping session they are very likely to go rusty over night, and thus be quite useless – so watch for this. Clipper oil can be obtained in tubes or Three-in-One is equally suitable. Send your clippers to your supplier once a year for servicing – this is a must. Allbrooks have a very good service department which undertakes all clipper repairs as well as blade and scissor sharpening. They have Oster lapping wheels and testing equipment so you will know your equipment will be restored to maximum efficiency.

Scissors

Scissors are the next pieces of equipment to consider. Do use sharp, properly set scissors. A blunt pair will really hurt your poodle, and will make him jumpy and set up a tension whenever a clipping session is obviously in store for him. Three countries are well known for good scissors – Britain, France and Germany. Our choice is for British scissors as they are so very well balanced, light and well tempered. The 18cm (7″) size is suitable for poodles, and one of medium weight. The German made scissor is rather heavier and the balance is not so precise, but the forging is excellent. There is little difference in price. The British scissor made from Sheffield steel is excellent, though again heavier, but quite often considerably cheaper. Those with a finger rest are particularly comfortable to use.

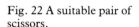
Fig. 22 A suitable pair of scissors.

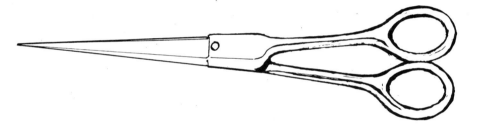

Allbrooks have a good range of scissors and the authors would recommend for poodle clipping the No. 111 light weight nickel plated pair of 16½cm (6½″) or the No. T.9 which is 18cm (7″) long. If you like a finger rest the No. 59 oxydised scissor is very good, and certainly the hook steadies one's hand and helps to a more professional finish. All these are priced around £5 to £6. Any scissors over 19cm (7½″) long, or those with wide blades are not very suitable for poodles. A pair of surgical scissors is rather essential for toework and a 13cm (5″) either curved or straight model with blunt-ended blades is good. Again scissors should always be kept oiled and wrapped in oiled paper when not in use.

Various Equipment

There are one or two other items which are needed for the poodle's toilet. Tooth scalers are often required. Tweezers are useful for specific

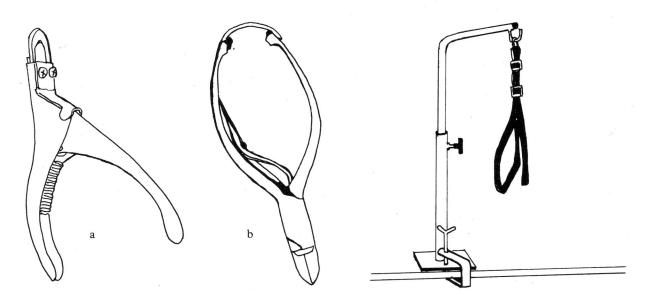

purposes, although quite frankly eyebrow tweezers intended for human use are just as good and cost one third the price. Nail clippers are an essential, and the guillotine types are the only ones which do not upset the dog and therefore are highly recommended. They are not cheap, costing about £3. Two additional pieces of equipment which are not essential but are extremely useful to have are *1. a poodle measure*. These can be either the sliding rule type, or the hoop type and produced in three sizes to measure 25½cm (10″), 28cm (11″) and 38cm (15″) and are reasonably priced. *2. A grooming stand*. A great boon to those who undertake a fair amount of clipping. They are fully adjustable and help very considerably to reassure the nervous or awkward dog. However, such grooming stands are really very expensive, and possibly an equally handy form of control such as a wooden frame clamped to the grooming table to which you can attach the dog's lead or sling would be suitable. A sling made from denim or some fairly strong material is a very good aid. This encircles the poodle between front and back legs, and the ends of the sling fix on to the wooden or metal frame. This will keep the poodle steady – generally support him, and yet will be comfortable for him and assist him to stand still for quite a time.

Be sure you get the initial equipment which will suit your special circumstances, and take expert advice from your supplier or others on this if necessary. When you have your equipment, take care of it, keep it well serviced and it will have a long and efficient life.

Now we must consider how we should use this equipment. There are such a variety of styles into which the poodle can be clipped, and in no

Fig. 23 Nail clippers
(a) Guillotine type.
(b) Open blade type.

Fig. 24 Grooming and clipping control stand.

other breed is there such a difference between the show style and the style usually adopted for the companion or pet poodle. The traditional lion cut is practically essential when showing an adult poodle. Just occasionally a poodle appears in the ring in some other clip but he will not get very far for the simple reason that he immediately loses a great number of points on lack of length of coat. The clip should make no difference to the assessing of the structural points by the judge. However, it is recognised as more or less essential for a show poodle to appear in the ring in traditional lion cut after he is one year old, and in first or second puppy clip from six months to a year.

Basic Clipping

Whichever clip one favours – lion clip, dutch clip, lamb trim, continental clip or puppy clip, the basic clipping of face, feet and tail is common to all these styles.

There is a certain knack in using a pair of clippers, whether they be electric or hand operated. It is necessary to use the clippers *against* the direction that the hair normally grows. To begin, lay the clipper head on the surface of the short hair, and then tilt the machine slightly towards the blade part so that the clippers will pick up the hair in the clipping process. It is essential to bear firmly, but one must avoid digging into the flesh for fear of grazing the skin. Equally it is no use being too light in touch or in any way skimming over the surface. The happy medium must be achieved and this is where the knack comes in. If you are able to procure some sort of an old rug or piece of sheep skin, this is invaluable in trying out the method to be used, and it is strongly recommended.

Sit the poodle on the grooming table, and with your fingers feel the dog's facial structure and with the aid of Fig. 25 make certain exactly where you wish to cut and the lines to follow, before actually working on the poodle's head.

It should be noted that the following instructions apply to right-handed people, and therefore should be reversed for those who are left-handed. It is a great advantage to be ambidextrous.

A firm hold should be taken of the poodle's head with the left hand, with the dog sitting or standing with his right side towards you. Your thumb should lie against the dog's right cheek, while your fingers clasp around the back of his head and on to his left cheek. A straight line should be cut horizontally from the orifice of the right ear (Point A) to the outside corner of the right eye (Point B). If the ear is highly set, then Point A should be slightly lower than the ear orifice.

Next ease the dog's head in an upward direction to tauten the skin at the front of the neck and then clip from Point C, up the chin, and then over the cheek to the inner corner of the eye, taking care to clip carefully

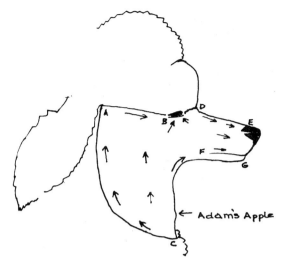

Fig. 25 Basic clipping of face.

over the adam's apple at the throat. The clipping at Point C should commence 5cm (2″) to 7½cm (3″) below the adam's apple. Next clip from Point C in a curved line as shown to Point A, clipping off any hair still remaining on the right side of the face.

The muzzle must now be clipped starting from Point F to the end of the nose at Point G. Pull the skin taut from nose towards ear with your thumb, and take great care at the corner of the lips (Point F) for here it is very easy to jag the skin. Turn the poodle round, with left side facing you, and then clip this side to match up with the right-hand side. There now only remains the top of the muzzle from Point D to Point E to be clipped, the ∧ between the eyes, and this latter is the most difficult of all. When starting one is inclined to make the ∧ much too wide. It should be narrow going from the inside corner of each eye up to an angle about 2½cm (1″) up, and the object of this is to give the impression of narrowing the head, and also to provide elegance for if the hair is left straight across from eye corner to eye corner a somewhat cloddy, glowering expression is given to the poodle. In the case of a poodle in other clips than lion cut, where the hair is rounded off rather short, the ∧ also serves the purpose of keeping the hair from dropping across the eyes. The modern trend in show poodles is to dispense with the ∧ between the eyes, taking the topknot straight back from the eyes, but in clipping styles for most companion poodles the ∧ is still the thing.

The clipping novice may find it difficult to clip the hair short immediately below the bottom eyelid. Proficiency in this comes in time, but if it cannot be achieved with the clippers, a pair of round-tipped scissors may be used, though it must be pointed out that there is less likelihood of cutting the skin with clippers than with scissors.

The late Les Watson clipping the underparts of a poodle in Dutch clip.

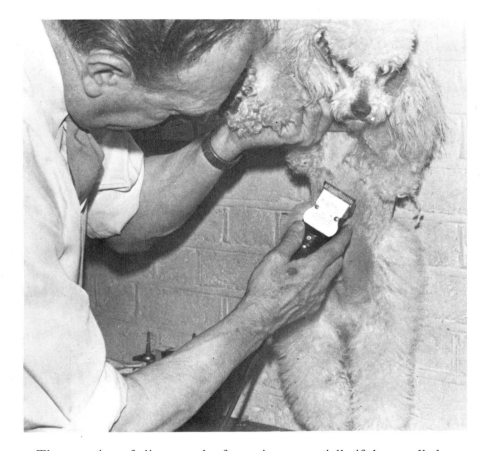

The question of clipper rash often arises, especially if the poodle has a sensitive skin. This can usually be avoided if the poodle is bathed before clipping for this obviates any infection from dirty hair. Also it pays to use Johnson's Baby Lotion, or similar preparation, on a pad of cotton wool after clipping, or else a dusting of Johnson's Baby Powder will help enormously to avoid trouble. Once a clipper rash has started it is difficult to heal but application of witch hazel or a camomile lotion will help deal with such skin irritations and troubles which unfortunately are usually due to the clumsy use of clippers and scissors. If a really unpleasant cut or graze has been made, which will develop into a serious and painful sore once the poodle starts to scratch with a dirty paw, a preparation called Betnovate is extremely useful. It is prepared by Glaxo and is in the form of a cream or an ointment, but it is only obtainable on prescription. But obviously prevention of clipper rash is so much better than cure.

Next the feet must be clipped, and here you should look at Fig. 26. Most poodles are very sensitive, or shall we say ticklish, about the toes

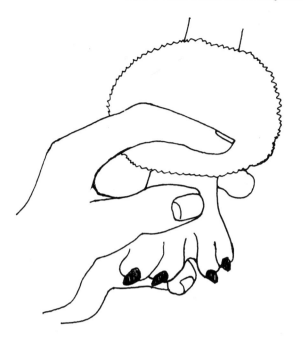

Fig. 26 Foot and toe clipping.

and therefore it is a difficult part of the body to clip. Grasp the ankle or wrist, and first clip from the toes to 2½cm (1″) or 4cm (1½″) up the leg from the ground as the poodle stands – front, sides, and back. Be careful on the front feet of the lump on the inside where the dew claw has been removed. Often a small lump is still there, and the clippers can catch it. If the dew claws, by any chance, have not been removed then extreme care is necessary, and this point should always be checked before starting the feet. The tricky part now comes for the hair must be removed from between the toes.

The toes should be separated by holding the foot as in Fig. 26 and pushing the webbed part forward from the underneath of the pad with the third finger. Then the clippers may be used on either side of each toe to remove all the hair. If it is found that the poodle objects too strongly, round tipped scissors must be used. It is also necessary to remove all the hair from the pads underneath the foot, and here a pair of scissors is the best implement. If the poodle will lie down for this part it makes it much easier, or if he is a small poodle it may simplify matters if he lies on your knee. Again all clipped areas of the feet and toes should be swabbed with baby lotion or dusted with baby powder.

The final stage in basic clipping is the tail, and the underneath of this part is by far the most sensitive on the poodle. The slightest graze, or even worse one tiny hair working up into the rectum can drive a poodle nearly mad with irritation and will really upset him for days on end. The

A poodle wearing a stocking cap to protect the ear fringes when clipping the feet.

authors always clip the hair from the tail *the same way as it grows* which invariably prevents irritation. Also the first quarter of an inch of the rectal orifice is lubricated with vaseline applied with the little finger. However, many clipping experts *do* clip tails against the normal growth but it does court trouble. Fig. 27 should be studied and it will be seen that sketch c) is the normal length of tail, while sketch a) shows the too-short docked tail and sketch b the too-long tail. In both the normal tail and the long tail, the clipped area from A to B should be approximately 4cm (1½″) for a miniature, rather less for a toy and more for a standard, but if the tail has been originally docked much too short then only about 2½cm (1″) or even less can be clipped from A to B. Obviously the normal tail is going to have the best pompom, but it is

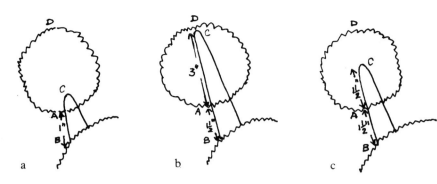

Fig. 27 Tail clipping and shaping
(a) Too short.
(b) Too long.
(c) Correct.

possible with judicious trimming to help the pom on both the too-long or too-short tail. For the too-short tail the long hair of the pom must be encouraged to grow as thick as possible, and grow a good 7½cm (3″) from A, i.e. an inch below the tail clip to end of pom at D. But even so, the short-tail pom will never be very striking and this does take away from the elegance of the poodle. A too-long tail is an easier matter, for here there is plenty of space for the long hair to grow in the 7½cm (3″) or thereabouts of the stump that is available from A to C. The normal 4cm (1½″) should be clipped from A to B, and the hair of the pom cut off immediately at the end of the stump at C. To get a well rounded effect on the pom, the ends of the tail hair should be twisted tightly and the twist cut through with scissors at the desired place, whereupon the hair when released from the twist, should fly out in a round pom.

This completes the instructions for the basic clipping which must be carried out initially in any of the many poodle styles. Novices are advised to use a coarse blade for the first two or three times for then there is little chance of cutting or marking the skin. A 10mm (3⁄8″) blade is suitable, and when a little more proficient a 15mm (5⁄8″) can be used. Anything finer than this is not used too often, unless a *very* close trim is needed for a show. Veterinary surgeons will, of course, use an extremely fine blade for shaving prior to surgery. This may be why occasionally the poodles which are clipped by the vet or by his girl assistants are almost shaved and often suffer extreme irritation as a result. It is always advisable if sending a poodle to a veterinary surgeon for clipping to ask that only moderately fine blades should be used, and not the fine surgical blades. If your poodle has ever suffered from clipper rash after clipping, you should inform whoever is undertaking the job for you, so that special precautions can be taken. It surely can be agony for the poodle for as long as a fortnight after clipping. If you are undertaking clipping personally and should nick the skin of the poodle, an immediate dab of permanganate of potash crystals will staunch the flow of blood. Ear leathers and toes can bleed very profusely and thus quick action is necessary. Unfortunately the crystals will stain a white poodle's hair a bright mauve, which will only wear off in time. On a black or other dark coloured poodle the crystals are not very noticeable.

Nail Clipping

An important part of the poodle's toilette is nail clipping. If the poodle has a lot of road walking then the hard surface will probably keep his nails short, but if exercise is mostly on grass or parkland then nails will need attention. The authors prefer the guillotine type of clipper for nails as shown in Fig. 23. These seem to cut far more neatly and it is rare indeed for a poodle to 'squeak' when these are used. The other type, called the open blade nail clipper, is rather more inclined to squash or pinch the nail before actually cutting, and poodles do seem to suffer pain from this type. Nails are not easy to trim as one cannot usually see the quick, especially in black or coloured poodles. It is certainly easier in white poodles (see Fig. 28 b). It is best to snip off a little at a time, until nearing the quick and the final end can be filed with an emery board. If the quick is nipped, dab the nail into a small tray or dish of permanganate of potash crystals, and this will stop the bleeding immediately.

Fig. 28 Nail clipping
(a) Method of handling foot and clippers.
(b) Avoiding cutting the quick.

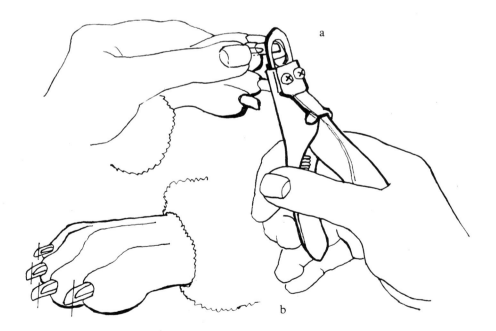

Care of the Teeth

If your poodle can chew large marrow or knuckle bones, the teeth will be preserved in clean and perfect condition and usually this will keep his breath sweet and wholesome. But not all poodles can take bones and are often troubled with upset tummies after a bone-chewing session. Thus it may be necessary to clean the teeth regularly and any good tooth powder or paste and a baby tooth brush are excellent for the job. If, however, tartar has formed on the teeth, a dental scaler must be used.

The method requires great care and gentleness. The top of the scaler should be gently pushed just under the gum, and the tartar can usually be hooked off in one piece. The secret is to attend to this when it is first noticed and before the tartar eats into the enamel and the gums start to recede.

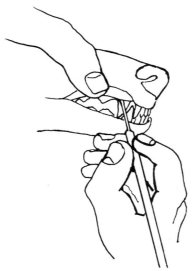

Fig. 29 Care of teeth – removing tartar with the aid of a dental scaler.

When clipping a poodle don't forget to allow him to relieve himself before you start. If he needs to go out he will be very jumpy and difficult. Also, if you are clipping other people's poodles, they will behave much better if the owner is not present. This is not a matter of trying to get rid of the owner so that cruel methods may be used. It is simply that, like children, they behave and settle down much better if 'Mum' is not there. If on the other hand you have a valid reason to suspect that your poodle has been badly treated, strung up, or doped, then do not go to that particular clipper or poodle parlour again, but find someone else whom another poodle owner thoroughly recommends. Personal recommendation counts for more than anything. On the other hand, your poodle may be extremely difficult and it may not be the fault of the clipper if he literally refuses to be clipped without some sort of control or sedative.

A final word as to the safety of your poodle. Never leave him on the table unless he is secured by a lead. A hook on the wall side with a chain short enough to prevent him from jumping is an essential. So often poodles jump down and in doing so break a leg, or put out a shoulder. So always play safe in this respect. If you are clipping other people's dogs ensure that there is a safety door in addition to the main door in the beauty parlour and that such door is locked or secured before starting work. It is so easy for a dog to take fright just as someone opens the one and only door on to the road, and the poodle disappears in a cloud of dust. It is possible, and indeed very advisable, for the professional clipper to ensure against injury to or loss of a client's dog while on the premises.

13   The Traditional Lion Clip

The Lion Clip

This is the most beautiful clip for the *sound* poodle. It gives him great dignity and tremendous elegance. The word 'sound' must, however, be strongly emphasised for it is a clip under which no faults can be hidden. Forelegs must be straight, hindlegs must be well and truly angulated, backs must be short, and in fact the poodle must have perfect balance to make the best of this clip. A long-backed-short-legged poodle will look extremely cloddy and inelegant, while bandy front legs or cow-hocked hind legs will make the poodle a laughing stock in this particular clip. The lamb clip or dutch clip can hide a lot of these faults, but it must not be deduced from this that only unsound dogs appear in clips other than the lion clip – far from it. A sound, well-made poodle will look equally magnificent in other clips, and also the shorter clips may well suit his

These two photographs illustrate the tremendous change in styling of the white miniature poodle in the 1940s and the brown toy poodle (Ch. Bartat Burnt Almond of Grayco) in the 1980s.

circumstances far better. For instance, it might be far more convenient for the country poodle to have the shorter style, and in any case not everyone likes the lion clip – many prefer the other varieties.

The lion clip is very old and has been the accepted dress for the poodle for nearly four centuries. A white poodle appears in lion clip in a German portrait as early as 1620, and another picture in the Swedish National Museum dated 1725 shows a poodle working in the reeds in this clip, and of course there are many beautiful Rockingham poodles which favour the lion clip.

Many who have not been clipping poodles for very long, fight shy of attempting the lion clip, imagining that it is too complicated for the beginner. This is not really true for if the following diagrams are carefully studied in advance, and followed throughout the clipping, it will be found that this lovely style is no more difficult to perfect than any other.

Firstly, the poodle must be very carefully groomed right down to the skin, and then shampooed in a suitable shampoo and finally well dried, being combed and brushed during the actual drying process. It is useless to try to fashion the poodle into the lion clip for the first time unless the foregoing basic work has been carried out. If he is ungroomed and somewhat grubby and sticky coated, the attempt to put him into lion clip will be disastrous – he will merely look a rag bag. It is assumed that the basic clipping of face, feet and tail has already been carried out.

Before actually beginning to cut the coat, study Fig. 30 very carefully.

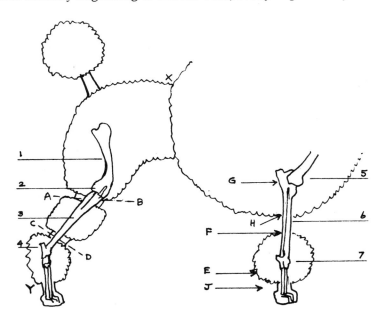

Fig. 30 Bone structure as guide to lion clip.

This shows the bone structure of the normal poodle, and it is by feeling the bones and joints that the correct places for the shaved bands, wristlets, anklets and pompoms are ascertained. From Fig. 30 it will be seen that the top clipped band A to B on the hind legs should be placed immediately below the stifle joint (2) between the tibia (1) and the femur (3) bones. The second band C to D must be shaped at an angle just above the hock (4) and the hair covers this joint. The equivalent joint on the foreleg which is the wrist joint (7) is also covered with a pom or wristlet, while the forelegs are clipped from point F (above wrist) to point G which is the elbow joint (5), with the mane falling over the clipped part down to point H. If all these points are carefully felt with the fingers on the poodle's body, they will easily be located, and this is the first step in attaining the correct result in the end.

So now, having done our homework on the poodle himself we will turn to Fig. 31 and begin the actual coat cutting. A decisive line must be worked out to ascertain where the large mane is to end, and the short part begin. On a miniature poodle this should be about 12½cm (5") from the root of the tail, and a good guide is to feel the last rib bone and regard this as the marker. However, as a start it is far better to *over estimate* the length of the mane because when carrying out the final trimming one is inclined to clip the mane back a little more and then a little more still, and end up with a mane covering only half the back instead of two-thirds.

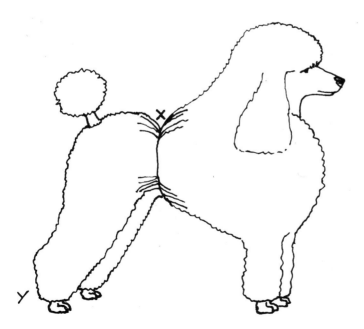

Fig. 31 First step in lion clip style.

Make an even parting with the comb round the poodle's body at point X, that is roughly at a line taken from where the hindquarters meet the hindlegs, over the back bone to the same point on the other side. Smooth the hair of the mane towards the head and then tie a piece of cloth over the mane towards the shoulders from the parting. This will ensure that the long hair of the mane does not become inadvertently clipped. This now leaves the long hair from point X to Y at the ankles, and this should be roughed off as evenly as possible to not less than 2½cm (1″) in length. Your poodle should now resemble that in Fig. 32.

Fig. 32 Second step in lion clip style.

The next stage is perhaps the most difficult of the whole undertaking, but providing you constantly check on bones and bone structure and follow Figs. 30, 31 and 32 the desired effect should be attained.

Referring to Fig. 30, gauge with your left hand a line from the root of the tail, slightly diagonally to the stifle joint and with the scissors cut a narrow line of hair about 13mm (½″) wide from points A to B. Feeling again with your hand, locate the hock joint, and cut another narrow line from points C to D, leaving the top ruffle about 7½cm (3″) wide. The line C should run downwards at a slight angle to D to accentuate the hind angulation with hocks well let down behind. The bottom anklet should measure approximately 5cm (2″) wide. Nowadays when preparing for show, the anklets and wristlets are wider, almost covering the foot. Although precise measurments are given on the diagrams, it must be stressed that these must not be taken *too* literally, and a 13mm (½″) here or there won't matter, providing both sides of the poodle tally! They apply to the miniature, and naturally will vary considerably for the standard poodle or the toy poodle, and even in various miniatures. Therefore it is better to get into the habit of working anatomically.

This has all been relatively simple so far but now the other hind leg must match, and this is why only a very narrow 13mm (½″) scissor line is advised. Eventually the band will probably be at least 2½cm (1″) wide, but the initial narrow strip will allow one to raise or lower each band if they do not match exactly. So now carry out the same procedure on the other hind leg. When you have done that, turn the poodle with his hind quarters towards you and if you have faithfully worked from the bone structure both sides should be even, but if there is a small discrepancy you can adjust until you are absolutely satisfied.

Now, still referring to Fig. 30, turn to the forelegs, and with scissors rough off the hair from the top of the wristlet at point F to the elbow joint at G. Great care must be taken here to ensure that enough hair is left on the wrist, and also that the mane is left to drop over the leg between point G and H. Grasp the poodle round the wrist bone and with your comb make a parting round the leg about 2½cm (1″) above the actual wrist joint at point F. Then with the scissors rough off the hair from F to G., still grasping the wrist so that none of the pom hair escapes. Repeat this procedure on the other leg. You have now completed the basic fashioning and both you and your poodle will need a rest and some refreshment. Your poodle will feel rather odd and off balance and will probably spend some time shaking his front legs in dismay, giving you baleful looks, but he should resemble Fig. 33.

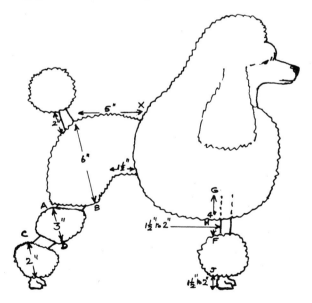

Fig. 33 Plan for lion clip.

Having satisfied yourself that both sides of your poodle are the same and that he is beginning to bear a slight resemblance to Fig. 33, the rear bands may now be clipped with the clippers, but again these must be *narrow* because the clippers always seem to take off more than you plan. The hair on the inside of the upper thigh band can be removed with scissors if it is difficult to clip this. The lower band is difficult to clip and a good tip is to press the first two fingers of your left hand on the *inside* of the band C to D, on the poodle's right leg, as this will give you a surface to clip against. Then press your fingers on the *outside* of the left leg lower band so that you can clip the inside. Turn the poodle round to face you to clip the reverse areas in the same way.

Next, grasp the dog's front leg and with the clippers remove the hair from the top of wristlet to the elbow joint all round the leg. A guide for finding out the right depth for the wristlet, is to bend the leg at the wrist and there should be 25mm (1″) to 32mm (1¼″) below and above the wrist joint, that is 5 to 6 cm (2 to 2½″) from F to J.

The next step is to trim the longer hair on the lower back and haunches from X to the end of the band at the stifle. This hair should be evenly trimmed to a length of about 13mm (½″) to 19mm (¾″) and the best method is to comb the hair upwards, and then slightly lift the comb, and scissor off the hair which is *above* the teeth of the comb. This technique will come with practice and you will find that a really plush-like effect can be achieved. The same technique is employed for the ankle pom and then with the scissors a straight line is trimmed off from the top and bottom of band A to B, and C to D. For both the anklets and the wristlets, the hair should first be combed downwards, and the 'fringe' neatly trimmed round then the hair should be combed upwards and again the fringe tipped off, then any untidy hair round the middle of the ruffle should be tidied off. This should give perfectly round lower ruffles above the feet about 38mm (1½″) from the floor.

The next part to tackle is the actual mane which is probably appearing a little untidy and uneven. The outline you wish to achieve is a round one, therefore the hair must be combed *upwards* in a line from the elbows to the end of mane at last rib, and then layers of hair must be combed down starting at point X and the untidy ends of each layer trimmed off until all the long hair right from the top of the back on each side has been so treated. The same procedure is carried out on the front of the chest. This is known as 'Tipping'. The end result should be a springy, bushy, mane of hair equally covering two-thirds of the body, the neck, shoulders and chest. This final finishing only comes with practice and experience, and while the diagrams and descriptions will assist considerably, it would help even more to go to a show and look at the prepared poodle in the flesh.

There only remains now the fashioning of the top knot and the

a

b

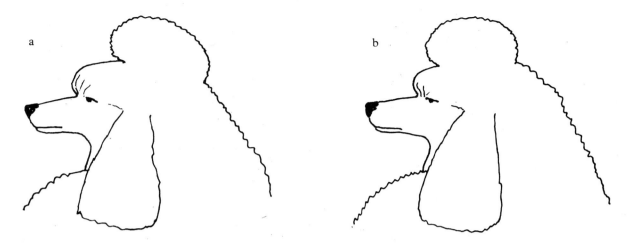

shaping of the tail pom. In the lion clip we would ask you to turn to Fig. 34 a) and b) and here you see that (a) and (b) apply to the lion clip. In a) is shown what is known as the backward look, and this aims at giving a younger and sweeter expression. It is often used to give a slightly sweeter look in bitches as opposed to males, and can also be used when there is a profuse top knot of some 10cm (4″) or 12½cm (5″) of hair. The hair is gathered up in the left hand and brushed or combed straight back, and then a *very* narrow rubber band is slipped over the hair keeping it close to the back of the head. The ends above the rubber band are then collected up in the fist and cut straight across, allowing the top knot to fan out above the band. In the forward look, often used for older dogs or perhaps for stud dogs for it gives a slightly aggressive and arrogant air, the hair all round the head is gathered up in the same manner but is drawn more forward as will be seen in the illustration b), put in a band and trimmed off. Bows made of ribbon or velvet or else candlewick yarn used to be the fashion in the show ring but are seldom seen these days. This is a pity, for the bow on the top knot has been the prerogative of the poodle for centuries, and indeed it is believed to be correct to say that poodles and Yorkshire terriers are the only two breeds who have permission from the Kennel Club to use this adornment in the show ring. Although not seen often in the ring these days, there is no reason at all why the 'with it' non-showing poodle in lion clip should not wear a ribbon.

Finally, tails. Here, we would refer you to Fig. 27 Chapter 12 which refers to the actual length of tail and not specifically to the lion clip. In any case, there should be a profuse and rounded pompom for that style and to get the right shape the tail stump itself should be approximately 7½cm (3″) from root to tip. A longer or shorter tail, which of course was

Fig. 34a Hair style for lion clip – the backward style.

Fig. 34b Hair style for lion clip – the forward look.

determined at the time of docking during the first week of the poodle's life, will present difficulties in fashioning a correct pom, but various methods can be adopted to help this state of affairs. In the normal length of tail, the clipped part from A to B should measure 4cm (1½"), while the pom itself from A to D should be approximately 7½cm (3"), so that is 11½cm (4½") from B to D overall (Fig. 27 c). To get a round effect, the hair of the pom should be twisted between the fingers, and the desired amount of hair at the end cut off straight with scissors. When released the hair will spring back as desired to form a pom. However, if the tail stump has been docked too short as in Fig. 27 (a) it is difficult to achieve a reasonably profuse pompom. Certainly 2½cm (1") must be clipped from A to B, otherwise the poodle will lose all elegance and balance in his rear end! And it can only be hoped that as much hair as possible will grow on the small amount of stump left for this purpose. The too-long tail as in Fig. 27 b) is not so bad, for here the pompom is trimmed short up against the end of the stump and will not be too noticeable, providing of course that this too-long tail does not become 'gay' or tend to curl over the back. But as far as trimming is concerned, the diagram should be carefully studied and shaping carried out as necessary.

Your poodle should now be in a presentable lion clip and each time you clip and trim him you will improve in technique. There are one or two points for the beginner to note carefully. Ear fringes should be allowed to grow as long as possible. If the ends become wispy and untidy, these ends may be trimmed off very sparingly. Moustaches are *not* worn with the lion clip. Hair must never be cut short above the eyes, except for an inverted 'V' between the eyes, but in clipping for show this inverted 'V' is seldom seen.

It is interesting to note how very much the style of the traditional lion clip has altered with the years. In the 1920–40 period the ruffles on the ankles and wrists were very sparse and short. In the 1940–70 period much more attention was paid to profusion of coat, and the ruffles were longer and fuller. Also the head styling was different as there was an accentuated 'V' between the eyes and the hair was pulled back rather flat to the head and then gathered into the band of the top knot. Now the ruffles are enormous, as is the tail pom, and the mane resembles one large round ball and almost meets the ruffles at the wrist. The neck is closely clipped far lower down the neck. There is no inverted 'V' between the eyes and the hair of the topknot is rather pulled forward before being secured in the band. The authors would refer readers to the photograph of one of the Rothara poodles as he was prepared for show about 1956, and then look at the photograph of Ch. Burnt Almond of Grayco, and the difference in style is patently obvious. Certainly the emphasis is now on an immense coat. (See page 139.)

There are two variations of the lion clip – the continental clip and the

English saddle clip. As its name implies, the continental clip is used almost exclusively in foreign show rings, particularly in Germany and France, but more and more the standard poodle is appearing in this clip in the English show rings. The English saddle clip, oddly enough, is mostly used in the United States of America and in Canada.

The Continental Clip

The forward half of the body, that is the mane, front legs, head and ears are clipped identically with the traditional lion clip. The hindquarters, however, are closely clipped from above the ankle ruffles on the hind legs, up the thighs and over the loins and lower back to the point where the mane commences. Quite often two rosettes or circles of hair are left on the lower back, usually just covering the haunch bones. These must be exactly the same size, and quite a good tip is to place an upturned wine glass or tumbler on the exact spot and then either mark round with chalk or else snip round with the scissors. The rosette should be moderate in length of hair, about 13mm (½″) to 19mm (¾″) and should measure about 6½cm (2½″) in diameter on a miniature, and proportionately more or less on a standard or a toy poodle. Sometimes other designs are fashioned such as a pair of hearts or diamonds. A very small, chic French moustache on the upper lip is quite often worn, though it is more usual for the muzzle to be clean shaven. The mane is tipped slightly shorter in length and the topknot is styled so that the hair is a little shorter and is swept up and back, and often no band or tie is used. Needless to say, this is a clip that may only be worn with success by the completely sound poodle, since any defects or oddities in the hind quarters are shown up at once. It is a very elegant clip for the poodle with long legs, well covered (but not fat) body and a racy, springy gait. The rather stout, short-legged poodle is by no means enhanced by this clip. (See photograph on p. 207.)

The English Saddle Clip

This resembles the traditional lion clip far more than the continental clip, the only difference being that a crescent shaped patch is shaved between the haunches and the mane on either side of the body. The ruffles on legs, the mane, and the head style are all identical with the lion clip.

Don't despair if your efforts are not one hundred per cent for the first time. Poodle clipping needs practice, but many beginners achieve championship show finish in a surprisingly short time. Persevere, and work on bone structure. Don't panic if you go wrong – poodle hair grows very quickly.

14 Royal Dutch Clip and Lamb Clip

Royal Dutch Clip

The reason for the word 'Royal' is somewhat obscure, but the 'Dutch' is supposed to refer to the baggy trousers traditionally connected with Dutch national dress. If it is well done, and provided the poodle has a profuse and springy coat then this clip can look most attractive. But if the hair is rather thin and wispy, and the poodle is structurally not well built, this clip would not show the poodle to the best advantage. It is no easier, nor more difficult, to fashion than the lion clip, but as will be seen from the diagram it is really as different as chalk from cheese. It is a clip which could be employed to hide certain leg faults such as bandy legs, cow-hocked rear quarters as can readily be appreciated whereas no 'faking' is possible in the lion clip. However, the sounder the dog, the better he will look in either clip, and any type of poodle-faking is to be deplored.

'Sindy Lou Sunshine', owned by Miss Drake. A lovely black miniature youngster expertly styled in Dutch clip by the owner.

METHOD OF CLIPPING

In the Dutch clip it is essential to work to measurement rather than by bone structure. We will assume that the basic clipping of face, feet and tail has been carried out. The next step is to cut with scissors a straight line from the root of the tail, up the backbone to the nape of the neck. Look at Fig. 35 and you will see this strip marked with a dotted line from A to B. Next clip a similar line right round the body of the poodle C to D. These strips can be initially about 2½cm (1″) wide. With the scissors now round off the shoulder pads E to F on both sides and the hip pads S to T on both sides. The distance between shoulder pads at point W should remain narrow, also the piece immediately above the tail at point A. Scissor off the hair to form a round at the nape of the neck just above point B, and continue round the neck and across the throat to where the basic face clipping has been done. Now stand your poodle up on his hind legs with his back towards you and check that the parts you have clipped with scissors are symmetrical and resemble Fig. 35. When you are quite happy with the design, you can clip these parts with the clippers.

Now you will need to fashion the long trousers of both front and hind legs and for this you should turn to Fig. 36. The measurements given refer to a normal miniature poodle, and therefore must be adjusted accordingly for a standard poodle and a toy poodle. The Dutch clip requires that the hair on the top part of both shoulder and hip pads shall be moderately long, about 4cm (1½″) in length, and that this should taper down to wrist and ankle joints. Therefore the hair should be left at its longest between L and K which should measure approximately 15cm

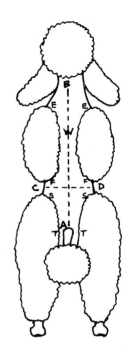

Fig. 35 Dutch clip. Basic lines for clipping.

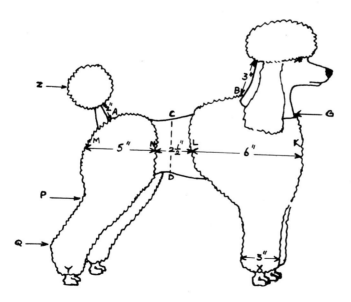

Fig. 36 Dutch clip. Completed styling with measurements.

(6″) across, and from M to N which should be about 12½cm (5″) across, down to point Y and X which should be approximately 7½cm (3″) across and with hair 13mm (½″) to 19mm (¾″) long. The angulation of the hind leg should be followed, thus a slight cutting in should be made at P, with hair left longer at point Q and slanting downwards to the ankle at Y. The front legs should be straight and parallel with hair about 13mm (½″) to 19mm (¾″) long at the wrist. This tapering is difficult, and the best method is to pick up the hair in layers with the comb in the left hand, and then snip evenly with scissors in the right hand, removing the hair *above* the teeth of the comb so that the desired length of hair is left. It is better to start at the ankle or wrist and work upwards towards the back progressively, leaving the hair a little longer until you have a profuse, full pad at both shoulder and haunch.

Having completed the tapering, you will now need to cope with the 'finish' of the body. You may need to make the clipped band (C to D) round the body, a little wider, say up to 6½cm (2½″), and also the band from A to B may need widening. This depends entirely on how your poodle looks, and this is where your own individual artistry comes in for no hard and fast rules can be laid down. Round off the hair evenly wherever the longer coat meets the clipped part. A good guide for ascertaining the neck line B to G is to hang a collar loosely round the poodle's neck and take this as the border line between long and short hair. The hair on the front of the chest should be trimmed to a length of about 19mm (¾″). Don't worry too much if you do not get the measurements quite even the first time – this will come with practice and the hair soon grows to hide your mistakes!

TOP KNOTS

The top knot resembles as much as anything a round cap and should be as profuse as possible. The hair should be about 6½cm (2½″) long, tapering at the temples and down the back of the neck. The hair can either be tapered into a 'V' at the back of the head or rounded at the base. An inverted 'V' between the eyes helps to keep the hair out of the eyes but *never* must the hair be clipped from the head *above* the eyes. A good way to achieve a smart top knot (and it is always difficult to get it right) is to comb the hair outwards from the crown of the head (i.e. from the very centre of the top of the head) then trim with the scissors about 13mm (½″), or whatever is necessary, off the ends. Then comb the hair upwards and you should have a reasonably good top knot. All that is necessary now is to trim slightly with the poodle facing you, and then trim the back and sides with him seated with his back towards you.

TAIL POMS

A slightly different method is employed when shaping the tail pom and

Fig. 37 Dutch clip. The rounded topknot.

as this is the same as in the lion clip, it is suggested you turn back to Fig. 27 Chapter 12 for advice about this particular point.

The Lamb Clip

There are various names for this clip such as the lamb clip or the astrakhan clip. It is a moderately easy clip to fashion and a very workmanlike one. It is generally used in kennels for brood bitches or for those poodles which are not actually being shown. The normal basic clipping of face, feet and tail is carried out. The rest of the hair all over the poodle is either cut with scissors or else clipped with a coarse clipper blade to a length of approximately 7mm (¼″) to 15mm (½″) long. If scissors are employed, then the comb method should be used, that is picking up layers of hair with the comb, raising the comb just slightly to give the length of hair required, and then cutting off the unwanted ends of hair which appear *above* the teeth of the comb. With this method the hair by the shoulders at point A and over the hips at point B can be left a little longer. If clippers are employed, a 5mm (⅜″) blade is correct and the hair cut in the direction in which it grows – i.e. from neck to tail. If a shorter clip is required, then the hair can be cut in the reverse direction from tail to neck. It is not usual in this clip to use clippers on the front legs, and the hair should be cut with scissors, leaving the hair approximately 19mm (¾″) long. The top knot can be a little shorter than in the Dutch clip and tapers into the short hair at the back of the neck, point C. Ears should be left naturally with good fringes. However the extreme ends of the fringes may be tidied if they are wispy or uneven. To do this twist the ends of the fringes between finger and thumb, and then cut off the end of the twist. This is undoubtedly a very serviceable style, simple to do, cool in summer, and very easy to keep groomed, and most poodles

Rothara the White Bouquet demonstrating the curly clip. Basic clipping for face, feet and tail, while the hair on the body is scissored to about 7mm (¼in.) or 15mm (½in.), or maybe a little longer.

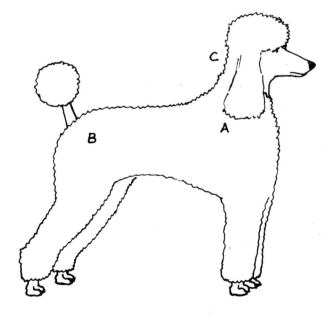

Fig. 38 The lamb or curly clip.

look very attractive in it. The coat of any poodle if it is thin or soft or generally poor will be very much improved with short clipping. To improve the condition of the coat, the Oster coat conditioner may be used when shampooing, or else the Oster Aerosol conditioner, both obtainable from Allbrooks.

Clown Clip

This is a slight misnomer, and the authors much prefer to call it 'Summer Clip'. It is most attractive and provided the structure of the poodle is correct and he does not have very short legs, then it is very elegant. The entire body is clipped short with the 5mm (⅜″) blade or even the 10mm (¾″), but fairly profuse ruffles are left on wrists at the front and ankles at the back, together with a large pom on the tail and as profuse a top knot as possible. This is an excellent clip for poodles in hot countries, or in a really hot English summer, but the coat needs to be left longer if it gets somewhat chilly in the autumn. It is not very suitable for winter weather as the longer ruffles pick up wet mud, and also ball up if there is snow.

It must be stressed that all the foregoing styles are used for companion poodles, and are not suitable for the show ring.

Penpens Firefly of Dorlin wearing the summer clip when retired from the show ring. The body is clipped right down with a 5mm (⅜″) blade for coolness, with fairly large ruffles left on ankles, wrists and tail. Ears full and long, and head neatly shaped.

15   Other Styles of Clipping

THERE are so many styles of clipping for the poodle. No other breed is such a child of fashion which is obviously why there are so many poodle beauty parlours, and also why the poodle's coiffure can be such a costly business. Before purchasing a poodle it is a point which needs thinking about – can you afford frequent visits to the poodle parlour which cost anything from £3 to £5 a visit? If not, then you will have to apply yourself to learning the art of clipping. The most popular styles have already been described in detail, but there are many more. Some are useful and completely down to earth such as the country clip, some which apply to various ages such as the puppy clip and the second puppy clip, while others are bizarre, grotesque and odd, to say the least of it. These include the monkey clip, the cowboy clip, the sailor boy clip, the hillbilly clip, and the baby doll clip. None of this last group can really be recommended and surely only serve to make the poodle a laughing stock. However, they are seen occasionally and poodle owners may wish to know what they are like.

The Country Clip

This is a very simple clip, serviceable and clean but does rather tend to destroy the poodle 'image'. It could equally be used for almost any long haired breed of dog. The method is simply this: the hair is clipped short with 5mm (⅜″), blade *all over*, that means legs as well as body. The face, feet and tail are not basically clipped short as in other styles, but clipped to the same length as the body. The tail has no pom but is clipped short all over the tail stump. There is no top knot, and the hair is scissored fairly short. The ears are clipped or scissored close to the ear leather, and no fringes are left. It is a useful clip for any poodle who is used for the gun, since there is very little hair which can become matted or torn.

Puppy Clip

This is normally used for the puppy between six and twelve months of age which is exhibited in the show ring. In this clip (see Fig. 39) after the basic clipping of face, feet and tail has been done, the long hair is

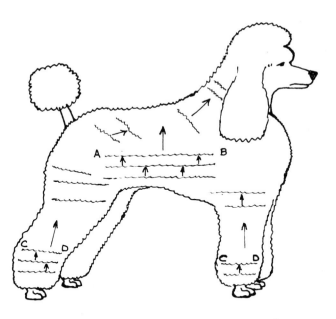

Fig. 39 Puppy clip, showing direction of combing to achieve layering with scissors.

combed out sideways in layers starting at the bottom of the ribs each side of the body and also from ankle and wrist upwards (see A to B, and C to D) and working in layers up to the top of the back. When each layer is combed out sideways, about 13mm (½″) of the thinning ends of the hair are 'tipped' in a straight line horizontally, and then the layer combed downwards to join the rest of the coat, and the next layer higher up treated in the same way. This should give a very neat, bushy appearance. The chest is treated in layers in the same way. A normal pom on the tail is grown, and the fringes on the ear leathers left as long as possible. The top knot is also grown as long as it will, and secured back with a slide to keep the hair from falling forwards. A typical puppy hair-do is illustrated here:

Fig. 40 Puppy clip – head and topknot styling.

The Second Puppy Clip

This is really a transitional clip, bridging the gap between puppy clip and lion clip, and is sometimes used for puppies in the show ring between nine and twelve months of age. In this clip, we would refer you to the Fig. 32 in Chapter 13 relating to the first stages of the lion clip to make the points clear. The coat from point X over the body, shoulders and chest is treated as for the puppy clip described above. But from point X over the hips, down the hind legs to the ankle, the hair is scissored evenly to about 2½cm (1") in length. The hair then settles down normally for the next few weeks until the puppy reaches the age of twelve months or perhaps younger when it is necessary for him to be put into an adult clip, for instance the lion or continental clip if he is to be shown. The lower half of his body then has hair of approximately 2½cm (1") which is ready for the fashioning of rings and ruffles of the traditional clip. It must be repeated that the hair on the front legs is left long and is *not* clipped. It should be explained here that the ages referred to for various clips are not obligatory insofar that many youngsters are shown in the adult lion clip as early as six months which is the time they may enter the show ring, but no show dog *over* twelve months should appear in any form of puppy clip.

Other Styles of Clipping

The Monkey Clip has most of his body clipped short, but has a semi-mane of hair round the shoulders, ruffles on wrists, and a three-quarter length of long hair left on hind quarters from haunch to ankle with a clipped rump and a pom on the tail. A small round cap of hair on top of the head, with a band clipped above the eyes, leathers clipped closed with a small tassel on the bottom of each leather.

The Cowboy Clip resembles the Dutch clip in body with profuse 'Cowboy Trousers'. However the face is covered with long hair in the form of mutton chop whiskers with just the eyes clipped round, and the ear leathers clipped close.

The Baby Doll. A very feminine clip and must be worn only by bitches, surely? It is really a mixture of the continental clip and the Dutch clip but the mane is worn rather nonchalantly resembling a mink wrap, with the neck clipped closely giving a somewhat off the shoulder effect. Usually a gold or diamond collar is worn, and this style is not very often seen other than in Central Park, New York!

And so, you see, there is tremendous scope if you have a flair for hairdressing, but don't forget the poodle is an elegant animal, and he is also sensitive. He hates to be laughed *at* although he adores to laugh with you. Don't make him a laughing stock by snipping him into any grotesque shape. Remember he is really a gun dog, and he must not be made to blush when rubbing shoulders with the spaniel or the retriever!

Clipping Puppies For Sale

One final word about clipping. It will very much enhance the value of poodle puppies which are offered for sale if the basic clipping style is adopted. A small puppy looks so smart and delightful when his little face is clipped, and also his tiny feet and tail. It immediately turns the puppy into a poodle, whereas the unclipped puppy could be *any* breed. It is advisable to leave the muzzle unclipped and with a neat moustache, for many intending purchasers so often don't like a shaven face in the baby, and once you have taken off the whiskers you can't put them back and this could lose you a good sale. It is very easy to clip off whiskers and moustache in a second if the buyer does not like them. It also pays good dividends to bath a puppy before offering for sale. They look so very sweet and cuddly when newly shampooed, and in any case puppies should not go to their new homes unless spotlessly clean and clipped for the first time.

16 Planning a Litter and Mating

IF you own a bitch, or perhaps a small kennel of poodles, the time may come when you feel you would like to breed a litter or two. This should not be entered into casually for there are a great many points to consider so that your bitch or bitches will produce the very best type of puppies – in fact the careful and ambitious breeder will always aim at producing puppies which are better in quality than the sire or dam, though of course in practice this may not always come about!

Early Planning

Certainly 'family planning' must be considered, and here hereditary factors as against environmental characteristics must be taken into account. To this end it is essential to have a good working knowledge of both the sire's and the dam's forebears. It is not enough to look at a potential sire and say: 'Ah, yes – he'll do nicely for my bitch. He has a long head and she fails in head; his coat is nothing to look at but her coat is so dense that she will make up for that.' Those are only the very superficial thoughts one must have when planning a litter. One must delve back as far as possible to the grandsires and grandams to see if the good points are really characteristic of the chosen stud dog's line and not just flukes in that particular generation. If the past generations, say of the stud dog, do not quite fulfil your aims then you must be sure that your bitch's forebears are strong in these particular points, otherwise you will be doubling up on the undesirable characteristics. Roughly speaking a puppy inherits 50 per cent of characteristics, both good and bad, from both sire and dam – 25 per cent from the four grandparents – 12 per cent from the eight great-grandparents and so on. But it is always important to know which are inherited attributes and faults, and which are due entirely to environment. For instance, a dog may have been reared in a loving and secure home and never known fear or anxiety, and thus have a placid, sweet nature. But he may have been sired by a dog who is anything but pleasant natured, and who stems from a line of ill-natured dogs, and this may well skip a generation and crop up in the grandchildren. Equally, the brother of the placid dog may have been 'knocked about', may have been kennelled away from people all his life, and have developed a nervous, unreliable temper simply because his environment has made him look out for himself and has stifled his natural good nature. One's instinct would be to say 'I don't want to use *that* dog on my sweet bitch,' and yet he may produce lovely puppies if they are given the chance of a secure and happy upbringing. It is all very difficult and if one is to be really serious it needs a lot of research. It is essential to delve into the past histories of both sire and dam and not take either dogs at their face value.

Another point when choosing a suitable mate for the bitch is to try to see some of the progeny he has already sired, for many mediocre dogs can sire outstanding puppies, and conversely the fabulous, top winning dog may have just nothing to pass on.

All this research takes time and it is not too early to start when your bitch puppy is perhaps only eight weeks old, and you have another sixteen or eighteen months ahead of you before the actual mating.

Line Breeding

There are three possible principles when planning a litter. One can follow either the principle of line-breeding, in-breeding or out-crossing. In line-breeding, dogs of a similar line or family are bred together so that it is likely that *both* sides will carry the genes for various good points which it is hoped to incorporate in the ensuing puppies. If carried out with care and great selection it can be a most successful method, but *only animals who have few faults should be mated together* for while the good points will be doubled, equally so will the faults. The selection should be carried out by mating dogs who have certain outstandingly good and desirable attributes which have been handed down through several generations, to bitches who are related but not too closely and who have equally good points in moderation. The mating of grandson to grand-mother, grandfather to granddaughter, nephews to aunts, nieces to uncles, and also half-brothers and sisters – that is dogs and bitches with the same sire and different dams and vice versa – are all suitable. To use line-breeding as a method you must know your line extremely well and you *must* only choose dogs and bitches with the least number of common faults and the greatest number of shared attributes.

In-breeding

In-breeding, on the other hand is when two very closely related dogs are bred together such as mother and son, father and daughter, brother and sister. In such case, the sire and dam contribute 50 per cent each of all good points and, of course, the same proportion of all undesirable points. It is not to be recommended in the normal way, for it is very easy to fix firmly an almost ineradicable fault into a strain by these means. It is done by knowledgeable breeders from time to time and admittedly has produced champions where it was needed to establish some outstanding good point, but close breeding such as this runs the risk of producing weak fertility or even sterility, and may be the harbinger of monorchidism or cryptorchidism. Certainly it is strongly advised that the novice does not dabble in in-breeding.

Out-crossing

Out-crossing is just the reverse for it is mating together dogs and bitches of entirely different lines or strains. This can be used to bring in some good point in which either the dog or bitch is weak, or it may happen in a somewhat haphazard mating when the chosen dog is selected because he happens to be available or perhaps lives next door. Again, unknown bad points may be brought in and will be difficult to eradicate. These have a habit of cropping up throughout the generations. Also when considering the breeding of toy poodles, use of an out-cross is inclined to produce larger puppies which develop into larger-than-desired toys. In line-breeding, like breeds to like, and size is thus likely to remain the same. By the same token, in-breeding can produce very tiny specimens if the parents stem from stock which has been reducing in size over the generations – but at a cost!

Special Breeding Formula

The authors worked to a special breeding formula many times with their miniature poodles, and this certainly produced a great many outstanding winners. It was a modified form of line-breeding and was built up thus: an outstandingly good dog was selected, and when he had produced a very good bitch puppy, this puppy was in time mated to a *son* of a daughter of the same outstanding dog. This formula produced the authors' lovely bitch Rothara The Gamine who became an English champion with four challenge certificates before going to the United States where she became a triple international champion. Many outstanding winning Rothara dogs were bred on these lines. The pedigree of Gamine is given here and to simplify the formula the key sire is marked as 'A' with his daughter as 'D', the son as 'C' and the other daughter of the key dog as 'B'. In this case, the key dog was Ch. Blakeen Oscar of the Waldorf, originally owned by Mrs Sherman Hoyt in the States, and imported into England by Mrs Hall of the Wychwood Kennels.

It will be noticed that this is also an example of line-breeding for Gamine was the result of a mating where her sire was a *grandson* of Blakeen Oscar, and her dam was a *daughter* of the same dog, Oscar.

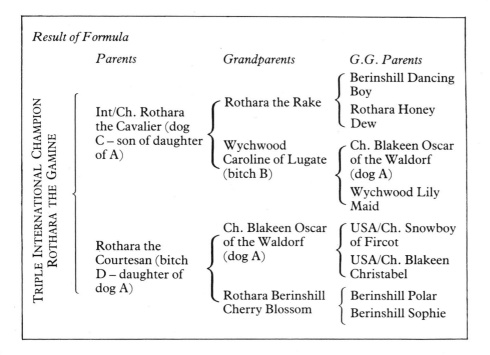

Result of Formula

	Parents	Grandparents	G.G. Parents
TRIPLE INTERNATIONAL CHAMPION ROTHARA THE GAMINE	Int/Ch. Rothara the Cavalier (dog C – son of daughter of A)	Rothara the Rake	Berinshill Dancing Boy
			Rothara Honey Dew
		Wychwood Caroline of Lugate (bitch B)	Ch. Blakeen Oscar of the Waldorf (dog A)
			Wychwood Lily Maid
	Rothara the Courtesan (bitch D – daughter of dog A)	Ch. Blakeen Oscar of the Waldorf (dog A)	USA/Ch. Snowboy of Fircot
			USA/Ch. Blakeen Christabel
		Rothara Berinshill Cherry Blossom	Berinshill Polar
			Berinshill Sophie

The Stud Dog

But now to turn to the stud dog which after all these considerations, has been selected as being the most suitable in every way. It is essential that the potential stud dog should be carefully reared from puppyhood and the keynote of such rearing should be *confidence*. He should never be scolded for his natural curiosity in bitches even at an early age. If he is eventually to be used at stud, he must always regard this act as natural and right, for it is very easy to instil into a poodle a guilt complex which will prevent him, when the time comes, from being a quick and efficient force. So never scold him for being amorous, rather take the bitch away for the time being. A poodle dog should be started on his stud life fairly early, possibly mating his first bitch at about ten months of age. If possible, provide him with a bitch who is docile and one who has been mated before. It is essential that there is no risk of him being attacked or snarled at. It is advisable for the dog to serve the bitch twice on consecutive days for he may not be fertile at the first time. After this initial mating he should be rested for two months, and then if possible he should be used again, then another month's rest and after that he can be used at normal intervals.

A popular poodle stud dog is usually much in demand, but a service on an average once a week is not too exhausting, providing – and this is really important – that he receives a high protein diet of good red meat, eggs, cheese and milk with a certain amount of fat included in the form of butter or oil. As a conditioner, he should have a high dosage of vitamin E possibly in the form of wheat germ oil, and also Bemax daily.

The poodle, if at public stud, must be kept in a constant state of cleanliness and smartness, ready for inspection at any moment. Owners of bitches have a habit of dropping in to look at stud dogs without appointment and therefore one must be ready at all times. Prior to serving a bitch, a stud dog should have at least two hours rest in his kennel after a light meal. He should always be given the opportunity to relieve himself both immediately before and after a service. He should not be fed for two hours afterwards. The best time of day for a mating is the morning or early afternoon. It is not advisable to use a stud dog within two hours of his normal dinner time for if he is really fond of his food his thoughts may be more on that than on his lady love! Equally the evening is not ideal, for a dog is a creature of routine, and as most stud dogs are often kennel dogs, they go to bed fairly early and thus the evening is not their most active time.

To launch a dog on his stud career he must first be proved – that is, it must have been proved that he is fertile and thus can sire a litter of puppies. Quite often to 'prove' a dog, a free service is offered, but in this case the chosen bitch must herself have had a litter. When a reasonably good litter results, the owner of the bitch may decide to be generous and give the stud dog owner one of the puppies or else a moderate fee, but this is not obligatory. Once the stud dog is proved, an advertisement can be inserted either in one of the canine journals or else in the local paper, and he is open to accept 'dates' at an agreed fee. Here we should say that a well-bred, healthy dog is worth a reasonable fee. It is difficult to lay down any scale, but a fee from £25 to £35 is usual, while for a champion or particularly popular sire the fee could be upwards of £60. It is not fair on other breeders to drop the fee, and it certainly would not pay if the stud dog is to be fed, reared and housed as he should be. A stud dog can continue stud work until eight or nine years of age – indeed, poodles much older than that have sired satisfactory litters, but after the age of about eight years the progeny may tend to become a little weedy. When the dog has proved himself, stud cards should be prepared, and these usually take the form of printed cards, perhaps with a photograph of the dog, bearing the details of the first three generations of his pedigree, his date of birth, his Kennel Club registration or stud book number, and the stud fee. He must, of course, have been registered at the Kennel Club on the Active Register before being put at stud, so that any puppies he may sire can be officially registered when the litter is born. A receipt is given with information as to when the bitch is due to whelp, which is sixty-two days after mating. It is usual for the stud dog owner to agree that should the bitch not conceive a litter, a free service will be given at the following heat providing the stud dog is still in the same ownership. That is *not* obligatory, but is a nicety which is practically universal.

Occasionally the owner of the stud dog may agree to accept the pick from the ensuing litter in lieu of the payment of a stud fee. In this case the bitch must be of good quality, and a stipulation is usually laid down that she is herself a proved breeder. Sometimes a small fee is charged for the actual service in the above case, and such fee is refunded when the pick of the litter is handed over. This means that if there is no litter, then the owner of the stud dog will not have had his dog used for absolutely nothing. If a dog is proved and placed at public stud it is assumed that he is completely reliable and that any failure in conception would be the fault of the bitch.

The Brood Bitch

Now to consider the brood bitch. The menstrual cycle comes round once every six months, the first season or 'heat' being when the bitch is approximately eight to ten-months-old. Standard poodles quite often commence their first heat as early as six months, while tiny toy poodles may not start until twelve-months-old or even later. The oestrum period lasts for approximately twenty-one days. Warning that the season is about to begin is shown by a swelling of the vulva, and sometimes a slight clear, colourless discharge. Also the bitch may act rather strangely for a day or so beforehand by becoming unusually restless and 'het up'. The first day of the heat should be counted from the first show of actual colour, which will then be bright red and profuse for about nine or ten days. After that the vulva becomes larger and softer, and the discharge changes to a pinkish shade and this is the normal sign that the bitch is ready to be served, and usually she will remain in this state for at least six days. Another guide to ascertain her readiness to mate is to touch her tail at the root, when she will turn or wave the tail from side to side at the same time arching her back. This is called 'tailing' and is an almost infallible sign that she is ready to accept the dog. The season will normally die down between the eighteenth and twenty-first day, but this must not be entirely relied upon, for often a bitch has been known to accept a dog – indeed search for a dog – as long as twenty-four to twenty-seven days after commencement of the heat. So if you don't want her to mate – lock her up securely. It can happen in a flash, and with co-operation from the bitch, a keen dog almost seems to get through a keyhole!

The pre-mating of the bitch is important. She should be in tip-top physical condition, not too fat and yet nicely covered, with a healthy loose skin. Raw meat, if she will take it, if not grilled or baked meat which retains the goodness, should be regularly fed for several weeks before the heat is due with a goodly proportion of eggs, cheese and milk included in the diet. Enough good quality biscuit to provide roughage without putting on weight, and vitamin E, either in tablet form, or as wheat germ oil will help a normal conception.

It is not usually advantageous to mate at the first season. For one thing the bitch is not sufficiently mature to take on the strain of pregnancy and motherhood and therefore it is inconsiderate. Equally it is likely that only one puppy may be conceived, and consequently this may be a large one. It certainly seems to pay to wait until the second season when the normal bitch should be just right for reproducing herself. The only time this might not apply could be if the bitch did not come into season for the first time until well after a year. It must be remembered that the grossly overweight bitch runs a strong risk of non-conception, as equally does the too-thin, weedy, somewhat nervy type of bitch. The ideal type of poodle for breeding is one in first class physical and mental condition – one who has a bright springy coat, moderately hard muscle, sparkling eye and a hearty appetite, and one who is placid, intelligent and affectionate.

The bitch can usually be mated between the tenth and fourteenth day of her season, and ideally between the eleventh and thirteenth day. It does happen, however, in some rare cases that a bitch is only in the right state to conceive during a period of twenty-four hours during her season. In this case, it might be well-nigh impossible to catch just the right moment, and she may be labelled after several attempts as barren. A remedy is sometimes to let her run with the dog almost consistently from the tenth day until mating occurs. Certainly heavy daily administration of vitamin E will help if given several weeks before the season is expected. Although it is the bitch who governs the number of puppies she will conceive, since the dog injects several million sperm at a service, it sometimes happens that a certain dog and a certain bitch simply do not suit each other and never will conceive a litter. In that case it is always advisable to try another stud dog for that particular bitch, although the dog himself may have sired puppies to other bitches, and therefore be quite reliable. It is just a matter of incompatibility.

The bitch should receive the same treatment as the dog prior to mating. She should rest before and after mating, and she should have the opportunity to relieve herself before introduction to the dog, but definitely should be prevented from urinating for at least half an hour *after* mating, otherwise the sperm may be washed away before it has the chance of fertilising the eggs. If she has come on a journey by car, plane or train, she needs time to settle herself before the mating.

A maiden bitch is sometimes difficult to mate, and needs particularly gentle handling. She is likely to be scared of the somewhat boisterous advances of the stud dog. It always helps the maiden bitch if her owner is able to hold her head while the service is in progress as she may be fussed by the handling of a stranger coupled with the fear of a strange dog. If possible, the bitch should be allowed time to get to know the stud dog. It is likely, however ready she is, that she may snap or growl at him to begin with. The normal keen stud dog does not mind this a bit, in fact it spurs him on, and after a short period of playing 'hard to get' the bitch will also become skittish and amorous and then all is set fair for a successful mating. But if the bitch is really bad tempered, and non-co-operative then the stud dog owner cannot afford to risk injury to his dog, and in this case the bitch may need to have a tape secured around her muzzle and her collar tightly held to obviate any turning-round on the dog. In the case of a pathetically nervous, shy bitch, the owner can do so much by a gentle voice and reassurance. Secure firm holding of the bitch will help to reassure her during the actual mating, and even though there may be absolutely no co-operation or reaction from the bitch, the result can be completely satisfactory.

Mating

The actual mating may take anything from two minutes to an hour. After the preliminary advances, the dog will mount the bitch and after one or two attempts will enter her. Whereupon in most cases the dog 'ties' with the bitch, and they will remain securely together until the genital organs of both deflate and this allows the dog to withdraw. After the dog has entered the bitch, she may suddenly react by whimpering and crying, and try to throw herself from side to side, in a state of excitement and perhaps in an effort to free herself. Whoever is holding the bitch must be prepared for this and hold on to her very tightly, otherwise she may injure the dog by twisting him. After this, the couple usually become fairly lethargic and it is now a matter of waiting for the dog to withdraw, but meanwhile both dog and bitch must be held. As the 'tie' may well be a long one, some breeders assist the dog to turn. This means steadying him while he removes his front legs to one side of the bitch, and then assisting him very gently to turn round so that dog and bitch now stand stern-to-stern until the dog finally withdraws himself. When the bitch is free, she should be held upside down in her owner's arms, or if too large for this, she should be held on her forelegs with her stern pointing upwards in order that the sperm can move in the right direction. The bitch should be held in this position for at least ten minutes. It is advisable not to wash the bitch before mating, for this will remove the scent to a certain extent which causes the dog to be not so keen as he might be. And, of course, no deodorant or anti-mating lotion or tablets must be given to the bitch for at least forty-eight hours before the mating.

Misalliance

Some owners fondly believe that once mated, the bitch will have no further desire for a dog and vice versa. This is certainly a fallacy, and a bitch will be even more keen to find a mate for several more days. In the event of a misalliance, conception can be nullified by an injection given by the vet within forty-eight hours of the mating. This will immediately kill the sperm, but equally it will cause the bitch to come into season again for a further three weeks, and she will again become attractive to the males between the ninth and fifteenth days after the injection. At this time, she could be in a condition for another mating but it is fairly unlikely that she will conceive again. However, she might do so and the possibility must not be ruled out. Some owners hold the opinion that if a bitch has once been mis-mated and has borne puppies to a mongrel dog or a dog of another breed, that she will be valueless as a pure-bred bitch thereafter. This is a complete fallacy and it would have no bearing whatsoever on future litters. This theory is called telegony.

Dual Conception

Dual conception is a point upon which authorities are inclined to differ. Some breeders feel sure that if a bitch is mated by two or more dogs during her heat, that she will conceive puppies some of which will be sired by one dog and some by another, and thus dual and even multiple conception can take place. Equally, others hold the belief that once the ova have been fertilised by the sperm from the first dog, the channel is automatically closed and sperm from another dog cannot enter in to fertilise other eggs.

At the time of the service both the dog and the bitch should be treated with the utmost gentleness. Some breeders become a little callous when supervising a number of stud engagements. It should be remembered that for the bitch in particular it is a strange and in some cases very frightening experience, therefore extreme gentleness and reassurance should be given. She must have time to settle down and get to know both her surroundings and the dog himself. All too often the dog is brought in, the bitch is held, and they are expected to get on the job straight away. While this probably suits the male, it can be very frightening indeed for the bitch.

Consideration and gentleness are essential, and also much reassurance if the bitch appears to be apprehensive. Fear and tension can prevent conception, and if both these states are present during a service it is strongly recommended that where possible a second mating should be carried out within the next forty-eight hours, when the bitch will feel far less strange and fearful. Of course, some bitches approach the matter with avidity and show no signs of fear and apprehension, and in these cases the foregoing remarks would not apply. After the service, both dog and bitch should be made much of and encouraged to realise that you are pleased with them.

Also owners of busy stud dogs are inclined to forget that it is a big day for the *owner* of a single bitch, and he or she may well be very apprehensive and upset as she may feel the bitch is being hurt or treated callously. So kindness and consideration all round is most essential.

17 Pregnancy and Preparations

THE bitch carries her litter for sixty-two days, but poodles are rather inclined not to run their full time of nine weeks and may produce their puppies anything up to a week earlier with no ill effects whatever. If they are early, the puppies will be slightly smaller and not quite so fully developed, and rather more care must be taken during the first few days. It is unusual for poodles to go much after their time, but it does sometimes happen. The puppies then are much more advanced, and of course unfortunately that much bigger for the bitch to produce.

For the first month after mating little change is necessary in the bitch's normal way of life. Her usual diet can be followed, and she may be exercised in the same way. It is unlikely that the breeder will be able to be sure the bitch is carrying puppies until four weeks have elapsed, although if the litter is going to be large a 'bulge' may be felt earlier. The veterinary surgeon is usually able to make sure on the twenty-eighth day after mating. Examination by X-ray was often employed but most vets have dropped this procedure as it was considered that it might be detrimental to both bitch and puppies.

Around the third week of pregnancy the bitch may seem a little off colour insofar as she may be very lethargic and 'tucked-up'. She will probably go off her food for some days. Although this will worry the owner considerably, he or she must remember that this is the time when the puppies are quickening, and it is therefore a fairly reliable sign that puppies are really on the way. The bitch may also suffer from 'morning sickness', again another good sign. Her usual food should be put down for her, but if she does not want this then do not force her, and try not to worry yourself. She knows how she feels, and as soon as the quickening process is over she will come back on her food naturally, and for the second half of her pregnancy it may be quite difficult to keep pace with her insatiable demands for food.

Feeding

At this time, care must be taken over her diet to ensure that she does not put on a lot of extra weight, especially if she is normally a well-covered good 'doer'. For the last two weeks of her pregnancy, divide her meat meal into two meals, giving her one at midday and one at evening time. Give her plenty of milk to drink. Many poodles, however, do not seem to like milk or milky drinks, but as soon as the babies actually arrive they forget this little phobia and usually drink as much as they are given. A scrambled egg with a little brown bread for breakfast is very nourishing and a few small knobs of cheese at bedtime will obviate any feeling of night starvation. But don't forget that good quality lean raw meat to eat, and fresh cold water to drink are the best possible milk-producers.

Exercise

Exercise for the last four weeks should be modified, but she must not become lazy. She will whelp far more easily if she keeps moving up to the very last minute, so ensure that she has at least two walks each day but as the time goes on let *her* set the pace. Don't allow her to race madly after other dogs, nor after a ball, nor up and down steep inclines. As her time approaches, her exercise will probably have slowed down to little more than a slow toddle and this is as it should be. If she is a tiny poodle and is carrying quite a large litter she may need help in getting up and down steps or stairs. Her bed or basket should be quite low on the ground so that she does not have to jump in and out.

There is also the psychological aspect, and possibly not enough attention is paid to this side of the bitch's pregnancy in some cases. The keynote of this trying time for her must be safety, security and serenity. Some bitches when in whelp suffer much irritation, and sometimes even fear, at the attention of other dogs. Dogs know she is not quite 'right' and may mistake her condition as that of being in season. They will continually sniff at her, which she resents, and may also try to ride her. One cannot really blame the dog, but the bitch must be protected from such annoyances. If she is a kennel dog it is wise at this time to let her choose her own companions. Quite often a bitch will turn against a dog or bitch which has been her constant companion before this, and take up with another poodle, often another bitch in whelp. Whether or not they get together dreamily to discuss the knitting of baby woollies one doesn't know! But certainly it will help their serenity to choose their own friend or friends. With the only house pet, the bitch will become increasingly possessive and affectionate, and she will certainly need much love and affection from her owner. This reliance on human affection lasts until the moment the puppies are born, when usually to the dismay and chagrin the owner finds that the bitch completely changes, even growling if her precious babies are touched or approached. This is quite hurtful to many owners when they have spent nine weeks doing everything possible for the bitch and basking in her love and reliance! However, once the puppies are five or six-weeks-old she is likely to grow heartily sick of them, and will return whole heartedly to her owner.

At this time she is also particularly vulnerable to attack from other dogs. She is slower and a little clumsy and she just cannot cope with attack in any form. It is advisable for the last two or three weeks to take her for walks on a lead so that any attempt at a fight is prevented before it starts. If she is set on she can easily abort her puppies at this time.

Punctual Meals

Feeding time is also important for, from mid-way through pregnancy she has probably a voracious appetite and thinks a lot about the next meal. Therefore this meal must be there on time, for dogs certainly know to a split second when it should arrive. A bitch in whelp must not be allowed to fuss and get in a state through the unpunctual appearance of her dinner. Also feeding conditions must be studied, for above all she must have her meal in peace and quiet and alone. She must not fear that another dog is able to steal her food. Such conditions (which apply to feeding of all dogs) must be faithfully studied such as not feeding in a cold draught, or scorching sun, or in the rain. Above all make her comfortable and secure.

Grooming

Grooming is another burden to the in-whelp bitch and because she possibly does not like being groomed at this time, the easy course is taken and she is left until a few days before the expected birth. It is much kinder in the long run to cut her coat down moderately short so that it is easier to brush and comb, and then be sure to groom her daily. This should only take a minute or two as against a three or four hour session if she has been neglected and become full of tags and knots, and as it will be a daily routine job she will be used to it and take it fairly philosophically.

Cleanliness

One final point which makes pregnancy easier for the bitch is to help her over cleanliness. She may not be able to get through the night without passing water, and therefore if there is an accident above all she must not be scolded. She simply cannot help it especially if she is carrying a large litter and is near her time. So put down thick layers of paper near her bed or box – she will know what they are for and no great harm will be done anyway. If she tries to hold herself through fear of the consequences she will become extremely jumpy and this could well upset her nerves for the imminent whelping. So tell her she has been a good girl.

Whelping Bedding

The provision of the right type of bed is another matter for thought. She needs a larger-than-usual bed where she can stretch out and is in no way cramped. Also she needs soft bedding. The bitch who lives in the house will appreciate a thick latex foam cushion or pad which will ensure that she has quiet and restful nights obviating the tossing and turning occasioned by hard boards and old cardigans for bedding. The foam mattresses can be covered with a cotton slip and changed as necessary. For the kennel dog possibly a deep bed of wood wool is the most satisfactory. Straw can be used but is hard and spikey, while hay is definitely inadvisable as it will generate far too much heat.

Obviously, if all possible steps are taken to reassure the bitch, protect her, make her comfortable, and generally cosset her during this period, she is going to be mentally and physically in excellent health for producing and rearing a litter of puppies one can reasonably hope will be strong in both nerves and bodies, and free from temperamental inhibitions.

Poodles are usually very easy whelpers, for the puppies have slim heads with fine bones, and thus there is not so much danger that the bitch will have difficulty in expelling each puppy as there might be in the case of perhaps a pekinese or a bulldog. Complications do occur from time to time such as a difficult breech birth, or the puppy which is completely wrongly presented and becomes lodged broadside on, occasioning a caesarean section. But usually everything is plain sailing.

The actual whelping place should be decided two weeks at least before the due date. If possible a small kennel is probably ideal which has a door at the front, and a top opening lid. This ensures that the bitch will have her puppies in one place, and will not, if she is slightly agitated, tend to have them in different places.

The top hinged opening will allow examination of her and the litter at frequent intervals and yet will keep her comfortably in her place. She should be encouraged to sleep in her whelping quarters well in advance and should be accustomed to having her meals in the new place. By this means she will get used to it and we hope regard it as her own 'den'. However, this does not mean to say that, being a poodle, she may not have her own very definite ideas on where she would *like* to produce her litter. The most popular place is your own bed for the eiderdown or duvet make a very cosy nest, or else the best chair in the sitting-room!

Warmth

Poodle puppies at the time of birth need a lot of warmth, and more puppies die from cold than almost anything else. The use of an infra-red ray lamp is probably the best way of supplying an even, regular heat.

There are many types on the market which can be obtained at either ironmongers, pet stores or through chemists. It is advisable to obtain one of approximately 250 watts, and also one with a dull emitter rather than the bright red bulb, for the latter is not good for the puppies' eyes. A certain amount of testing should be carried out in advance to ensure that the lamp is fixed at the correct height above the whelping box to ensure that the puppies are kept at the right temperature. Fix the lamp above the whelping box so that the rays fall on to the area on which the puppies will lie. Suspend the lamp from either a beam, or the ceiling or an angled bracket, *and hang with a chain*. It is not safe to use cord or a flex for if this is overheated and burned through the lamp could fall on the puppies. Place a thermometer in the whelping box directly under the lamp, and thus test the temperature, raising or lowering the lamp until correct. But the thermometer should be used at approximately the height of the bitch's back when she would be lying with the pups. If the thermometer is placed on the floor, this might mean that although right for the pups it would be too hot for the bitch and make her uncomfortable. For the first three or four days the temperature should be approximately 24°C (75°F), and then as the pups progress the temperature can be lowered by *raising* the lamp every few days until around the 15°C (60°F) mark. After the puppies are a few-weeks-old the lamp can be turned off in the day, and only used at night, and at six weeks they will not need more than the usual room temperature either by day or night.

Coat Preparation

Some breeders advocate shampooing the bitch immediately before labour actually commences. Certainly this relaxes the bitch, and ensures that she starts off as clean as possible. However it is sometimes difficult to know exactly when the bitch *is* only a few hours off labour, and certainly she must not be washed once labour has started. Possibly in the majority of cases, shampooing a week before the expected date of birth would be better, especially if the bitch does not like being bathed very much. A quick bath is necessary in not too hot water. No disinfectant should be used and a mild bland shampoo should be chosen.

The bitch should only be in the bath for a matter of two or three minutes, and then gently dried with a hair dryer and warm towels. Nails should be cut as short as possible, for if she is the type of bitch who scratches about in her bedding just before whelping, long nails can do quite a lot of damage. The hair on her belly, and particularly around each teat, should be clipped or scissor trimmed quite closely; also the hair around the vulva and anus should be scissored moderately short. This will all assist the bitch to keep herself clean throughout the whelping process. Immediately before labour commences, it will help to rub a little olive oil on each teat as this will soften them and make it easier for the puppies to suckle.

Last Minute Preparations

Certain other pre-whelping preparations should be made. First, the veterinary surgeon should be informed of the due date and it is wiser to tell him if you think the bitch, from various signs, looks like whelping early. The vet will then probably be able to tell you where he is likely to be so that you can get hold of him without delay in an emergency. For the actual whelping it is advisable to have prepared a clinical thermometer, a pair of sharp scissors which have been sterilised (boil for at least five minutes in a saucepan of water), cotton wool, a tube of vaseline, a bottle of T.C.P. or similar mild antiseptic preparation, some pieces of clean towelling, a tin of Sherley's Lactol, an eye dropper in case the babies have to be hand-fed for any reason, and a reel of white cotton. It is a good idea to have prepared a small box possibly about 30cm (12") square, lined with cotton wool in which to pop the puppies while the bitch attends to the birth of further puppies. Also quite a stack of newspaper which will be required both as bedding for the bitch during the birth, and also to wrap up garbage and rubbish such as soiled dressings, after-births and such like. A flask of coffee and some biscuits for yourself in case labour is very protracted and you do not wish to leave the bitch. Also some prepared Lactol to which has been added some glucose in case the bitch needs some sustenance during her ordeal. Have her lead and collar ready to hand in case she needs to go out during the whelping – she must be kept under control at this time in case she rushes into inaccessible bushes to produce another puppy.

Nothing else remains now but to keep a watchful eye on her and be ready for the very first signs of the impending arrival. Get some sleep yourself for you will probably be almost as exhausted as she is when matters have been brought to a successful conclusion!

False Pregnancy

Perhaps before concluding this chapter a word should be said about false pregnancy – a distressing event for the bitch and a disappointing one for the breeder. This may happen with nervous rather highly strung bitches. The bitch appears in every way to be pregnant, growing larger as the weeks go on, until at the end of the gestation period there may appear a slight discharge, and the bitch gradually returns to her normal size without producing any pups. She may produce quite a lot of milk. Some breeders hold the theory that the puppies were indeed there and have been absorbed, while others contend that the whole affair was imagination. But bitches are inclined to repeat these false pregnancies, and the veterinary surgeon should be consulted for often the administration of special hormones will prevent a re-occurrence. This type of false pregnancy only happens when the bitch has in fact been mated, but many bitches go through all the symptoms of producing puppies when they have not been covered by a dog. This is called a phantom birth, and happens about the ninth week after her season. She is excitable, endeavours to make a bed, and will purloin any toy or object which she then cuddles and tries to nurse. She is very distrait and odd at this time, eating practically nothing, and lying for hours in a would-be nest cuddling perhaps a slipper, or a scrubbing brush, or anything like that which she obviously imagines is her puppy. This can go on for a week or two, and once a bitch has this phobia it may happen after every heat. If she is a kennel dog and other puppies need a foster-mother she will certainly help out and can even produce milk to assist with the feeding.

False Heat

False heat is another disturbing oddity in the breeding cycle for this is very difficult to recognise since the bitch will produce a coloured discharge, will stand for service to a dog, but will not conceive puppies but comes into a genuine season some weeks later, when if mated she will conceive normally. There is also the abnormality of too frequent seasons when the bitch comes into season every three or four months instead of every six months. Usually this calls for hormones to regularise the matter. These are all irregularities in the breeding cycle which are irritating to the breeder but can generally be cleared up or obviated on the advice of the clever vet.

18 Whelping a Litter

EVERYTHING is ready and it is very difficult to curb one's impatience. One longs for the bitch to start her labour and yet one dreads it! Have we thought of everything? Will something go wrong? Why did we mate her anyway? Anticipation and dread go hand in hand, at least for the first two or three litters, and even when one is an 'old hand' there always seems to be trepidation and anxiety.

Imminent Labour

A sure guide to the imminence of the commencement of labour is a sudden drop in her temperature. If this drops by about 2° from her normal 38.4°C (101.2°F), then it is fairly certain she will whelp within twenty-four hours. Equally, if there is a sudden rise in her normal temperature and she seems off her food and generally uncomfortable, then the vet should be alerted right away as this may mean that some complication has arisen. As a precaution, check her temperature daily during the last week of pregnancy.

Other indications that she is very near her time, are that she may refuse all food and drink, turning her face away or pushing the dish away. Or she may appear pre-occupied and very busy in her mind and oblivious to you, her owner. She will wander about, poking about in corners, lying down and sleeping quite heavily for half-an-hour and then prowling restlessly again. She may need to relieve herself frequently. She may give a scratch or two to the carpet or a cushion. This is the moment to put her firmly in her whelping box or pen with quite a number of sheets of newspaper. She may whimper and whine, tearing the paper to shreds, and panting at intervals. All this is quite normal and the more she moves about in her efforts to tear the paper, the better for her. It keeps her busy and provides the necessary stimulation. She may like to be alone, but the majority of poodles prefer to have their owners about with them at this time. If you are with her, you will probably notice that she becomes quite still for a moment or so, and during this brief lull possibly a ripple will pass down her back from neck to tail, and she may give a slight grunt, immediately afterwards returning to the business of paper tearing. This is her very first strain and you will know she has really started her labour in earnest.

Normal Birth

Providing a normal whelping takes place the contractions should become stronger and more pronounced at intervals of approximately ten minutes. However, these contractions will become more frequent until the water bag appears at the vulva or entrance to the vagina. The water bag resembles a rather reddish, muddy coloured balloon about the size of a small egg, and in due course this will burst during a contraction, letting loose a flood of water tinged with blood. Once the water has broken the first puppy should not be long in arriving. In fact, one would hope the puppy would present itself well within half-an-hour because once the bag has burst the puppy is no longer cushioned, and subsequent straining, if this continues for too long, is likely to bruise the puppy considerably. Although the contractions are not quite so strong immediately after the bag has burst because the pressure is somewhat relieved, the straining will soon build up again until finally the bitch appears to be almost turning herself inside out. If the puppy is normally presented the head will pop out first, and as the body and legs are smaller, the entire puppy should need very little more to arrive completely. The entire foetus is wrapped in a strong sac, looking as much as anything like a polythene bag. The bitch will usually turn quickly and by licking and nibbling, free the squirming puppy, but if this is her first litter she may not know what to do, or may be completely exhausted. It is of the utmost importance to free the puppy's head as quickly as possible. It is probably not necessary to remind breeders that hands should be spotlessly clean with nails well scrubbed before whelping a bitch. The sac must now be ripped open without delay and the puppy's face and mouth wiped over with a clean piece of towel. If the pup is strong and lively he will cry and struggle, and as soon as any mucous has been removed from his nose and mouth, he must be given back to his dam. He will, of course, still be attached by the umbilical cord to the placenta or after birth. This placenta may, ideally have been passed by the bitch, but equally it may still be lodged in the vagina. If it has been passed out, the bitch may be biting and pulling at the communicating cord as her instinct tells her. She needs watching at this point as she could nibble too close to the puppy's navel and must be restrained from doing this. If the placenta has not yet been passed from the bitch, this could be very gently pulled in a downward direction and will usually slip out. Great care must be taken to ensure that the cord is not pulled *away* from the puppy as this could easily cause a hernia. When both puppy and placenta are lying side by side, and if the bitch is obviously going to do nothing about separating them, then a piece of cotton should be tied tightly round the cord about two inches from the puppy's navel, and the cord neatly snipped with scissors on the far side of the cotton, that is furthest away from the pup's abdomen or else neatly severed with one's fingers (see Fig. 41.). The after-birth

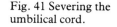

Fig. 41 Severing the umbilical cord.

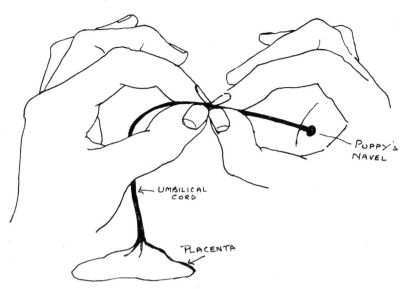

should be wrapped in paper and thrown away. Some bitches are very quick to get hold of the after-birth and eat it. It is not really a good idea as she may very likely vomit afterwards which exhausts her, although some breeders feel that the consumption of the placenta gives a bitch the necessary strength and nourishment to produce the next puppy. It is a matter of opinion but most definitely every possible effort should be made to ensure that the placenta does not slip away back into the vagina, for this could produce a bad infection. Count the after-births as they are brought out, one to every puppy, and if any have slipped back inform the vet of this when the entire whelping is completed.

After the birth of the first puppy there is often quite a long interval of half-an-hour or even an hour, during which the bitch may probably sleep in quite an exhausted manner with the puppy already nuzzling her and becoming glued to a teat. After this interval of rest, she will start her labour pains and contractions again and so it goes on.

Some Complications

This, of course, is the trouble-free whelping and things do not always go so happily. Complications of one kind and another occur. Sometimes the interval between the bursting of the water bag and appearance of the puppy is too long and then the vet must be summoned. A stimulant will be given to hurry things up. Equally a bitch may start her labour and will be straining well, but nothing seems to be on its way. After perhaps an hour or even more, the contractions will become less frequent and weaker. This usually means that the bitch is suffering from uterine inertia, and this again calls for veterinary advice for possibly a caesarian operation may be indicated, and in a case like this no time at all should be lost. Another complication may occur when a puppy is breech presented and hind legs and body have appeared from the vulva but the head of the puppy is stuck, and no amount of straining from the bitch seems to shift it. Usually the breeder can help by grasping the hind legs and body of the puppy firmly in a piece of dry towelling, and with the bitch standing the puppy can be pulled *very gently downwards*, each slight pull being carried out at the same time that the bitch strains. However the vet should have been called immediately the legs of the puppy are seen, and the above measures should only be carried out pending his arrival. Unless the puppy can be removed within quite a short while there is little hope of it still being alive or capable of resuscitation.

Another complication may be that a puppy is born apparently lifeless, but the brave and competent breeder can do a great deal to bring the puppy to life. Possibly the 'kiss of life' is the best method. First the puppy should be *really roughly* rubbed with a towel right under the infra-red lamp, and at the same time he should be vigorously shaken head downwards in an endeavour to get rid of fluid which may be in the lungs. Then the breeder should take the puppy between both hands, taking the whole of the puppy's mouth and nose into the human mouth, a human breath is breathed into and expelled out of the puppy's lungs at a rate of approximately sixteen times a minute. This can be continued for as long as ten minutes and still be successful. At intervals the little chest can be gently massaged with the first two fingers. The excitement of a successful result is wonderful, and the authors have had this experience several times. First a little toe twitches, or perhaps an ear. One can hardly believe it – then there is a definite kick from one back leg. This is the moment to carry on at all costs, for suddenly there will be a gasp and then a little cry and your efforts are crowned with success. But the massage and rubbing must be continued for some time until the little puppy is obviously breathing deeply and evenly. The puppy which is born bluish in colour has the best chance even though he may be quite limp and apparently lifeless. The puppy who seems completely flat and flaccid with white gums, toes and abdomen has less chance. But it is always so very worth while to try – and to keep on trying for a long time. It is a lovely sight to see the nose, ears, gums, pads and abdomen flesh of an apparently lifeless puppy turning from a sickly greenish-white to a bright rose pink and know that by your own efforts you have brought him to life.

The reader is referred to the photographs of the various stages of whelping. These photographs were, of course, taken during an actual whelping and were possible due to the bitch's very placid and easy temperament, and also because she appreciated the fact that we, as her owners, wanted to give her all the help and reassurance we could. With this particular whelping there were no complications, except that the last puppy needed to be given the 'kiss of life' and came to life within about five minutes.

1. The night before the birth of the puppies.

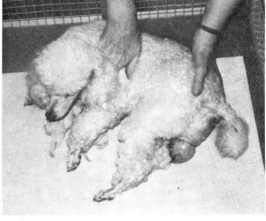

2. The puppy is about to be born.

3. The puppy is born, though still in the membrane sac and attached by the umbilical cord.

4. It is sometimes necessary to rub the puppy with a piece of towelling to get it going.

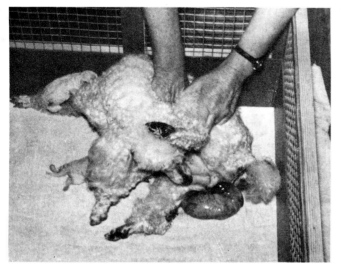

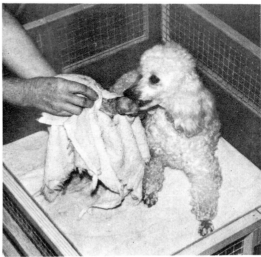

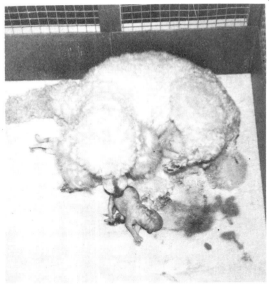

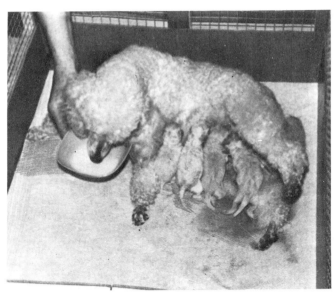

5. The bitch now cleans up the puppy, and with her tongue stimulates life.

6. The puppies are now comfortably feeding and the bitch needs a milky drink.

7. 'The Kiss of Life'.
Sometimes necessary if the puppy appears lifeless.

8. Heart Massage. Gentle massaging of the heart area, often helps a puppy who is having trouble with breathing.

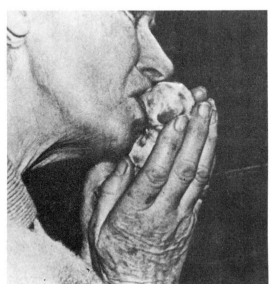

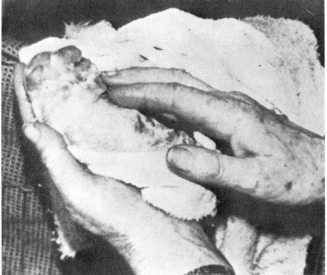

A problem often occurs after whelping in that the bitch may develop a state of excitability twenty-four to forty-eight hours after the birth of the puppy. The milk usually comes through in full force within twelve hours of the birth and often the puppies do not take a great deal until at least two-days-old. Therefore the milk builds up and the breasts become swollen and painful, and the bitch suffers both physical pain and mental 'fuss', with an accompanying rise in temperature. Usually the condition subsides after a couple of days when the puppies are suckling better and clearing the 'milk bar' satisfactorily. But it is a very anxious time, for in severe cases the bitch will carry her puppies about in her mouth whining piteously and she will have bouts of excessive excitability when she scratches madly in the corners of her box, sending the little things in the nest flying in all directions. All this is very bad for the pups and sets them back. In some cases it weakens them so much that they give up the unequal struggle. A darkened room, a very light diet, and as much quietude as possible are essentials at this time, and *definitely no visitors* either in the form of children or other animals. Crookes Laboratories manufacture an excellent preparation called Collo-Cal-D and correct doses of this three times a day will do a great deal to ease the situation. It is certainly a preparation which should be obtained in advance of a whelping, kept handy and administered at the least sign of over-excitability. It depends on the severity of the state as to whether the veterinary surgeon should be called, but if anything approaching eclampsia (milk fever) is suspected, professional help and advice must be obtained immediately. If, however, the condition appears moderately mild then it may upset the bitch less if the vet is not called. It rather depends on the vet and the bitch's relationship with him. Some dogs love the vet while others shiver and shake at his approach.

Milk Complications

When there is excessive lactation, the milk glands often become hard, lumpy and very fiery, with the bottom and two top teats being only partially effective. It may be necessary to draw off a little milk from these teats night and morning to relieve the pressure. If the teats and the area around them are gently massaged with warm salad oil, this will greatly help with the 'milking' process.

Converseley, there may be a very small supply of milk or even no supply at all. In the first case the puppies must have supplementary feeding during the day at any rate, and in the second case complete hand rearing must be employed – an onerous task indeed! But in these days the veterinary surgeon can inject to bring in a better supply of milk.

If, by any awful chance, the puppies should die at birth or soon after, the breeder may be faced with the problem of a heavy milk supply which will give the bitch a lot of pain, in addition to her agony at losing her babies. Mastitis can easily develop unless great care is taken, and here the milk becomes lumpy, dry and cheesy. An abscess may occur. It is certainly a case where the vet must be called, and to ease the condition fluids must be restricted. This is difficult as the bitch will be feverish and therefore very thirsty. But these are all complications which do not normally occur, and therefore need not bother the breeder too much. But it is as well to know about them so that initial symptoms may be recognised and help obtained.

Supplementary Feeding

Supplementary feeding of poodle puppies, particularly of the toys, is sometimes essential for the first forty-eight hours. So often a lovely strong litter is born and then within six hours they are fretful and grizzly, and within twelve to eighteen hours they are obviously doing badly. The coats become stary, little ribs begin to show, and they are lethargic with continual thin, whining crying. And yet they are continually hanging on to a teat, until they become too weak to take a grip. The inexperienced breeder may not realise, that although the puppies *look* as if they are suckling there is, in fact, no milk in the teats. Little bellies should be watched carefully, and if these are not round, soft and obviously full, then supplementary feeding must be started. Sherley's Lactol must therefore be ready. Prepare exactly as prescribed on the tin for the age and size of breed and DO NOT OVERFEED. If half a teaspoonful of the prepared milk is advised, then give just that at the correct intervals. A blunt-ended eye or medicine dropper is the best thing for this kind of feeding. Advice from the veterinary surgeon should also be sought for he will be able to give the bitch the correct treatment to stimulate the flow of milk. This type of supplementary feeding is not really very onerous for usually the bitch will be able to cope on a reduced scale through the night and will also clean the puppies and keep them cuddled up and warm.

Disposal of Puppies

She still has to face the unhappiness of her puppies leaving home. It can be such an agonising time for her especially if all the puppies go on the same day. For the sake of her peace of mind the puppies should be taken away one by one. It is such a pathetic sight to see a bitch searching everywhere for her puppies which have been sold *en bloc* to a pet shop or dealer. She has tended them with such a willing heart, and the least we can do is to make the parting as easy as possible.

Breeding puppies is the greatest fun, in spite of the anxiety and the hard work. Such pride can be taken in a contented happy bitch serenely nursing a strong, healthy litter. If the bitch is a house pet, and the only one, it is extremely satisfactory to be able to keep one of her daughters as her companion and as a follow-on for when she grows old and has to go. Mother and daughter usually grow up to be great friends and there is seldom any friction in this relationship.

One final word regarding the after care of the bitch who has produced a litter. While she was pregnant she was fed on the best nourishing food, and she was protected from all stress and strain. While she was suckling her litter perhaps even more care was taken over her diet and she was certainly given all comfort and facilities for bringing up a litter. But the business of bringing up a litter will have been a strain even though she may look in excellent health and condition. She will need just that little extra for the next few weeks, and a course of vitamins will do her a power of good. Possibly a daily dose of Abidec, a vitamin tonic and also a course of Vetzyme tablets, will build her up mentally and physically. So often bitches are reduced abruptly to one meal a day as soon as the puppies are weaned and gone. Admittedly she will need less fluids at this time and possibly less bulk, but she must have tempting and particularly nourishing meals, with the odd tit-bit of something she especially likes. After all, she has worked very hard for fifteen or sixteen weeks – she is due for a lot of careful consideration. A very good diet for the bitch for a few weeks after weaning would be:

Breakfast: Scrambled egg with a little brown bread.
Lunch: A drink of Casilan mixture.
Supper: A good helping of raw or cooked meat varied with liver, heart, or fish with brown bread or rusk added.
Bedtime: A knob of cheese is quite often relished.

More about weaning the puppies and caring for them during their helpless time, and also consideration of methods of hand-rearing from birth will be dealt with in the following chapter. The distressing state of eclampsia is dealt with in Chapter 10 and the notes on symptoms and first aid should be studied well in case of a sudden emergency.

19 Hand-rearing and Weaning

COMPLETE hand-rearing from birth is indeed hard work, and often accompanied by disappointment for the puppies may fade away after a couple of weeks in spite of all one's care. One or two golden rules should be observed for they will do much to ensure the rearing of a really healthy litter. These rules may be listed thus: 1. regularity of feeding, 2. strict compliance with preparations and feeding instructions of the product which is used, 3. absolute cleanliness of all feeding vessels, 4. correct temperature of food, 5. even, steady warmth of puppies.

Regular Feeds

Regarding the time of feeding, to begin with tiny amounts of Lactol should be given two-hourly, day and night – and there comes the rub! It is no use thinking half-an-hour either way won't matter, because it will. The tiny digestions won't wait longer than the correct interval, nor will they take another meal until the first is properly digested. An alarm clock must be employed at night, and after forty-eight hours, usually three-hourly feeds throughout the night are perfectly all right. It is absolutely essential that the correct amount of milk food is given. It is a temptation to give another sip or two when a puppy is taking it well and seems really hungry. But it won't pay because the puppy will become bloated and his digestion will become upset and then weakening diarrhoea occurs and the puppy so quickly gives up.

Hygiene

All preparation spoons, droppers, etc., must be sterilised after each meal and all bowls, cups, dishes, etc., washed in boiling water. If a baby's bottle is used this must be sterilised every time it is used, and all teats or droppers kept in a dish of cold, boiled water until needed again. Needless to say, hands, blankets, towels, etc., must be very clean at all times. Another vital point is the temperature of all fluids – these must be neither too hot nor too cold – either is extremely risky with a new-born puppy. A good guide is to feed the milky liquid at around 38°C (100°F). If there is a sizeable litter to feed, stand the bottle or cup of fluid in a

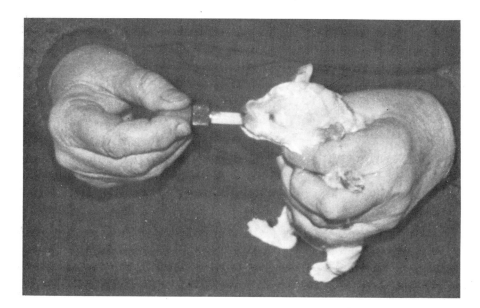

Hand rearing or supplementary feeding with the aid of a medicine dropper.

Teaching the very young puppy to lap.

bowl of hot water so that the temperature remains correct, and check this before feeding each puppy. For night feeding, two thermos flasks can be used, one for the milk at right heat, and one for hot water in which to stand the food bowl.

Weighing soon after birth, and thereafter every other day, will keep a check on the puppy's progress.

Warmth

The puppies must be kept warm, and at an even temperature. Certainly an infra-red ray lamp is of the greatest value, and if one is going to embark on the hand-rearing of a motherless litter it is worth the extra expense. Finally, the matter of the puppies' toilets, for in the normal way the mother licks the babies every so often and always after they have been suckling, and the warmth and dampness of her tongue encourages the puppy to urinate and pass motions. So the breeder must stimulate this procedure and to do this the penis or vulva, and also the anus, of each puppy must be stroked with a piece of cotton wool which has been moistened with warm water. This seldom fails to bring about the desired result, and is essential after every meal. To do this the puppy should be placed on his back in the palm of the hand with hind legs slightly lower than the head. If any pink soreness occurs, a little vaseline rubbed on will soon cure this. Mouths and noses must also be swabbed with damp cotton wool after each meal. A clean towel secured at the four corners of a box is usually the best type of bed, and the towel must be changed daily as necessary.

First Solids

Hand reared puppies can go on to solids at an earlier date than normal bitch-fed puppies, and indeed they will take to solid food much more readily. Usually at about three-weeks-old, the puppies can start on scraped raw meat, but the quantity must be really small. A small ball the size of a marble for miniatures, and even less for toys, and this should be given once a day to start. Make the puppy fight for the food by holding the ball of meat in the closed palm of the hand so that the puppy can push and nuzzle to get at the meat in between thumb and first finger. He will soon get the message and will push strongly. A little later he can be introduced to his meat in a *very* shallow dish and if a little warm water is added he can pick up the meat more easily. He will also by then be lapping his milk from a dish. It will help the puppies considerably if a stand 2½cm (1″) to 5cm (2″) high is made in which to place the dish. The puppy can soon be taught to stand squarely at the table and this avoids the contretemps of his sprawling in the drink or else waddling clumsily into it and spilling it. Meat can be given twice a day with milky feeds in between and by the time the pups are five-weeks-old they can have graduated to a little crumbled brown bread or a Farley's rusk, and other food such as boiled fish or scrambled egg. By the time they are eight-weeks-old they should be ready to go out into the world, quite self-sufficient, and the breeder can give a big sigh of relief and take a holiday on the proceeds!

Tail Docking

Tail docking and removal of dew claws is a necessary evil with poodle puppies, and should be carried out between fourth and tenth days of their lives, and most breeders will attend to it themselves. There are two methods of tail docking, either by amputation or by the rubber band system. After years of experience, the authors have no doubt that the latter is the kindest and most trouble free method. In the case of a miniature poodle it is necessary to remove the tail about 2½cm (1″) from the root (or the width of a 5p piece) and for a toy poodle about 13mm (½″) to 19mm (¾″) (or the width of a 1p piece). When the correct place has been marked, a narrow ring of hair should be snipped off round the tail with a pair of scissors. Then a small rubber band, about 13mm (½″) in diameter should be twisted on to the tail, at the mark as tightly as possible with several turns, thus stopping the circulation of blood to the unwanted end piece of tail. The puppy will give a little squeak as the tail is pinched. After twenty-four hours the end piece will be limp and at right angles to the main tail stump, and within ten days will have withered and will drop off, leaving a clean, healed stump end to the tail.

If it is preferred to amputate, then a tight ligature (such as a piece of narrow bandage knotted tightly) must be fixed at the desired mark, and the tail then snipped off below the ligature (i.e. furthest from root of tail) with a very sharp pair of scissors. The stump-end is then dipped into permanganate of potash crystals. The puppy will cry a lot, and will obviously be in pain for several hours after the operation, and this is why the rubber band method is usually preferred. But it is, of course, a matter of opinion.

Removal of Dew Claws

Poodle puppies usually have dew claws on the forefeet, and quite often on the hind feet as well. These are really extra fifth toes or thumbs. For the removal of these, the puppy should be held in the palm of the hand on his back. To remove the claw, a pair of rounded surgical scissors should be used. It is essential for an assistant to hold the puppy, for the puppy's foot must be held with the left hand and squeezed between finger and thumb to stop the flow of blood, and then the end of the scissors dug in fairly deeply to cut out the actual claw. If the incision is not deep enough the claw will grow again in time. Before allowing the circulation to return, press a pinch of finely powdered permanganate of potash crystals into the wound and this will cauterise the place and obviate any bleeding. The puppy will cry for a moment or so, but will quickly forget its troubles when returned to its mother. It is essential that the bitch be taken out of earshot while these operations are taking place, otherwise it will upset her greatly and she will suffer much anxiety. Better still, take each puppy into another room and then return him to her when it is over, and take away the next one. It is most important that the dew claws and the tails (if amputated) should be examined every hour for a little while to ensure that there is no question of bleeding. In the case of amputation and the use of a ligature, such ligature must be snipped off after ten to twelve hours. If the novice breeder is appalled at the thought of docking tails and removing dew claws, the help or advice of an experienced poodle breeder should be sought. Most experienced breeders know exactly what to do and how to do it, and are generally willing to help.

During the lactation period it is most essential that from birth onwards the puppies' nails should be snipped short. Novice breeders may often wonder why the bitch, after a while, is restless when the puppies are feeding and even turns on them with a fierce growl. They are inclined to think the bitch is a bad mother. The real truth is that each puppy is kneading the bitch's breasts with eight needle-like nails, pricking her and making her really sore. Is it any wonder she turns round on them from sheer pain? So these sharp little tips to the nails must be snipped off regularly once a week. If any of the nails bleed when cut, a pinch of powdered permanganate of potash will staunch the flow at once.

Weaning

Weaning can be a difficult time, but mostly follows a trouble-free course. It really isn't much good trying to wean the puppies if the bitch still has an abundant flow of milk and can go to her puppies when she pleases. They always prefer mother's milk and so they will not look at any other food until the milk supply becomes scarce. But there is one exception and this occurs when the mother regurgitates her food for her whelps. Not all bitches do this, but most really good mothers do so, and the puppies cannot get to this pre-digested food fast enough. This then prepares them for the usual puppy meal of soaked brown bread and meat. Novice breeders may at first be sure that the bitch is being sick and are horrified when the puppies rush to eat what has been produced. The breeder quickly shovels up the 'excreta' to the disappointment of the puppies. The puppies really should be allowed this first food and the breeder should consider himself or herself lucky to have such a good mother in the bitch. It usually happens when the puppies are around five to six weeks, in fact when they should be weaning. If it happens, don't forget that the bitch has received no nourishment herself from the meal, and she should therefore be given a second similar meal for her own benefit, and then kept away from the babies for an hour or so. Most puppies love raw meat, and this should be given to them finely scraped in the form of a ball in the closed fist, as mentioned earlier, so that they have to fight to get the meat. After a few days, minced meat may take the place of scraped, and when they have some teeth and are well on the way to feeding themselves small cut-up pieces may be given. Fluids form the other part of the weaning diet, and the authors concocted a very good weaning mixture which can be given two or three times a day and is usually most acceptable to puppies. This is called the Casilan mixture, and is a wonderful stand-by being equally good for the pregnant and nursing bitch, the convalescent poodle or the aged poodle. This is it:

1 heaped tablespoon of Farex
1 heaped dessertspoon of Casilan } all made by Glaxo
1 heaped teaspoon of Glucodin

Mix these three powders with 200ml (1/3rd pint) of hot water to the consistency of *thick* cream. Then add to this 200ml (1/3rd pint) cold milk, so that the consistency is now that of *thin* cream. The drink should then be lukewarm and just right for feeding straight away.

Another very useful weaning food is a Farley rusk either broken up as it is, or soaked in milk or gravy and given with the meat. Or else fingers of brown bread baked in the oven are usually very acceptable.

It is not cheap to feed a litter of puppies, as all breeders will know, but it is far better to feed the litter on highly nourishing food which will promote fine hard condition, shining coats, bright eyes, and regular 'tummies', and puppies reared like that should always command a good price. Obviously the puppies offered for sale at a very cheap bargain price cannot have been healthily reared (or else the breeder is a millionaire!) and though cheap at the time of buying will, as often as not, prove to be a bad buy later on when they are continually ailing and are constantly in the vet's surgery. So if you are selling, 'do' your puppies as well as you possibly can and ask a reasonable price. If you are buying, avoid the very cheap puppy for you will only buy trouble.

20 Documentation

BEFORE we can think about showing poodles, there is a matter to which we must attend first, and that is documentation. This sometimes causes panic in the heart of the would-be exhibitor for he or she may have the impression that registrations and transfers are complicated and certainly in many respects they are *not* easy to understand.

Every poodle puppy should be registered though this is not legally obligatory. However, registration means that the pedigree of the dog has been checked and verified by the Kennel Club. All shows in England, Scotland and Wales are held under Kennel Club rules and therefore it is as well to obtain a copy of such rules before entering the dog for a show. A copy is obtainable from the Kennel Club free of charge.

Registrations

A dog or puppy to be eligible for entering a show *must* be on the active register of the Kennel Club, and before this can take place several procedures must be understood and carefully carried out.

1. The breeder of the hoped-for litter must send confirmation to the Kennel Club of the mating of the bitch to a named sire, such confirmation being signed by the owner of the stud dog. The stud dog himself must already be on the active register.

2. The breeder must record the birth of the litter as soon as possible after the whelping and the fee for this is £5. At the same time, on the same form, each puppy may be registered by name for a fee of £1 each. If, however, the breeder has only recorded the litter and not registered one or more puppies, then a puppy should be registered at a later date for a fee of £5 by the new owner.

3. If the breeder has already registered your new puppy (and most reputable breeders do register their stock before selling them) then a transfer of ownership must be applied for and this is £4. The application to put the puppy in your own name must be signed by the breeder.

4. When all the above has been satisfactorily accomplished then your puppy will be placed on the active register without further charge and you are eligible to enter the poodle at a show.

Endorsements and Change of Name

However, it sometimes happens that a breeder for some reason thinks fit to place an endorsement on the puppy's documents, and he may state that the dog or puppy 1. is not eligible for entry at shows (i.e. is sold as a pet only), or that 2. any progeny is not eligible for registration, or 3. that an export pedigree may not be granted. There is no fee for the above conditions. The breeder may wish an endorsement to the effect that the new owner may not apply for change of name which means adding your own affix or kennel name. The fee for such endorsement is £2. If no such endorsement appears then you, as the new owner, may apply for change of name which means adding your own affix or kennel name and nothing else, and the fee is £5.

Registration of Affix

If you wish to register your own affix (or kennel name) which means you can use the name on all puppies you breed, or on your stud dogs and brood bitches etc. and in this case this would be your registered name and no one else could use it, then you can apply for this and the fee is £35, plus a yearly maintenance fee of £10.

While all these regulations appear very complicated, and are inclined to send breeders and exhibitors up the wall, they do serve a useful purpose. For one thing, the regulations protect the intending buyer from acquiring very inferior and unregistered stock when it is purported to be of 'show quality' and provided the buyer asks to see the registration documents of the litter or of the sire and dam and checks that these are backed by the Kennel Club, then he should know, at least, that he has a potentially well-bred dog or puppy offered to him. Also, since a stud dog must be on the active register for the puppies also to be so registered this also prevents the use of any dog from 'round the corner' whose progeny cannot be registered since he himself is not registered. And this applies equally to brood bitches. Therefore, although one may fume and grudge the time that must be spent on documentation, it would appear that it is all in the cause of breeding better poodles than has, perhaps, been achieved in the past.

The one drawback is that this somewhat complicated documentation takes a lot of time to administer at the Kennel Club and very irritatingly long delays occur as a result. However, if your registrations, changes of ownership etc. do not arrive before you have to send in the entry form for a show you may put after the name of the dog the letters 'N.A.F.' (name applied for) or 'C.A.F.' (change of name applied for) and this usually covers you.

In these days of inflation, owners and breeders who wish to take out any form of registration at the Kennel Club are strongly urged to write first asking for the current scale of fees. Fees are changed frequently and if the wrong amount is remitted this will lead to even more delay, and may mean that you cannot compete (or might be disqualified after gaining an award) at a show for which you particularly wanted to enter.

The Kennel Club publish a most excellent year book which no intending breeder or exhibitor should fail to read. This contains all the official rules and regulations in detail, including definitions of classes at every type of show, regulations pertaining to the preparation of dogs for exhibition, scale of fees charged for registration, transfers and various other services. This booklet is not expensive and can be obtained from the Kennel Club, 1 Clarges Street, London, W1. All application forms for registrations, transfers, changes of name and granting of prefixes can be obtained free of charge also on application to the Kennel Club.

21   Showing the Poodle

SO now we can turn to showing the poodle. He must, of course, be six months or older before he can be shown and it is as well to try him out at a small show to begin with, progressing to the larger shows, if he proves to have real promise. But whatever show he is to attend he must have received initial show training. It is just no good taking a wild and uncontrolled puppy into the ring, nor a very apprehensive or nervous one. Showing is a strain on any dog to begin with and he must have been well trained so that he knows what to expect and how to behave. Sometimes an exhibitor will enter the ring with a puppy which dashes backwards and forwards, never having all four feet on the ground at the same time, and who rushes up to all the other exhibits, upsetting them completely. That is not the way to enter a puppy. Equally, a puppy who might be slightly apprehensive may lose his nerve completely when faced with the ring, and will spend his time being dragged round with his tail down and his eyes nearly popping out of his head – certainly not displaying the points of the perfect poodle to their best advantage! But if both these puppies had been carefully and kindly trained for some time beforehand, they would have carried out their normal routine and also have been interested in what was going on and enjoyed the sensation of a 'day out'. It is not too early to start the puppy on his show training at six weeks of age. He should be 'stood out' on a table (if a miniature or toy, and on the floor if a standard) with his front legs straight and his hocks well out behind. His head must be held up with the right hand, and his tail held up with the left hand. At first he will struggle and wriggle, but he will quickly get the message and after the first few short lessons he will stand in this normal show position quite unaided and with his eye watching you for further instructions and a tit-bit. Next, he must learn to walk, and he must do this quietly and yet with eagerness, head and tail up. It must be imagined that the judge is watching the poodle and thus you, as handler, must walk ten to fifteen yards away in a straight line with your dog on your left side. At the top, stop and give the poodle time to turn about and then return in a straight line to the judge. The poodle should be taught to 'stand' in the correct show position in front of the judge, until instructions as to where to stand next are given. While other exhibits are being judged, the poodle can relax completely, sitting or

lying down, but at a word from you such as 'stand' or 'ready' or 'up' (or any word you have taught him) he must immediately stand in position, showing himself to his best advantage. During training it is essential that he should have met other dogs and have been handled by strangers. In order to know exactly what is required of both handler and exhibit, it is essential to attend a few shows and watch exactly what takes place so that in turn you can do the right thing yourself and also train the poodle correctly. If you can get some friends to bring their dogs, and all walk round an imaginary ring this will help enormously, finally asking your friends to 'examine' your dog – that is, feel his coat, lift up a paw and look at his feet, pull back his lips and look at his teeth, and in fact copy the actions of the judge – and train your dog passively to accept this inquisition, then you are half-way there. There is no doubt at all, that providing you have a sound, well balanced poodle to begin with you are going to have much more success (and incidentally, much more fun) if

Best in Show – a great day! Mrs L.E. Ellis with Ch. Merrymorn Golden Sorrell, the lovely little apricot toy poodle gaining the top honour. Centre is the judge, Mrs Bertha Matthews.

Mrs Margaret Worth making the most of her home-bred Miniature Poodle Ch. Piccoli Polichinelle by presenting him in an alert and correct stance for the judge to make his assessment.

you have trained both yourself and your poodle beforehand.

There are various points to be borne in mind when showing a poodle. Firstly, he must be comfortable in himself. He must have had plenty of time to relieve himself fully before entering the ring. A poodle who is occupied with thoughts about doing his business is going to be jumpy and stupid. He must have been adequately fed and watered before the show, though not given a heavy meal which will make him sleepy and slow. If he is not a good traveller, plenty of time must be allowed so that he can calm down before he actually goes into the ring. He must be comfortably settled either on his bench or on a warm rug on the floor while he awaits his class. It must be remembered that if you want him to win, then you must cosset him, you must make him happy and comfortable so that he regards show days as treats. Give him special tit-bits which he comes to associate with showing, and a country scamper on the way home. Most poodles if properly trained and kindly treated will love to show themselves off to the best advantage, and will soon learn to know when they have done something especially pleasing to their owner when a prize card is handed out. The authors were quite convinced that their white show miniatures knew the colour of a first prize card and definitely put on a gratified and somewhat smug air when they had won the hoped-for red card!

While training is of paramount importance, certainly preparation of the poodle's coat for show is equally so. The authors have asked Margaret Watson to give us the benefit of her great experience in this sphere by writing the following section on the importance of show preparation and how to achieve that band-box elegance. Margaret is a true artist for her Bidabo miniatures and Petitbrun toys have always been in the top rank of the most beautifully prepared poodles exhibited in the ring for many years. She and her late husband were a joy to watch when turning a tatty poodle into a thing of beauty and elegance. The very fact that 'Mick' Watson was invited to judge the toy poodles at Crufts in 1982 speaks for itself, and her sound judgement and unbiased selection was borne out in the fact that she chose as her best toy poodle the lovely little chocolate bitch Champion Grayco Hazelnut, owned and shown by Leslie Howard. This choice of best of breed was not only confirmed by the utility group judge, Rita Price-Jones, who gave her top place, but Hazelnut went on to be judged Supreme Best in Show all breeds in extremely fierce competition, beating the German Shepherd dog. There could be no doubt as to the worthiness of this little bitch for the highest honour of the show, since the best in show judge, Mr Reg Gadsden, drew her out from all the groups for the supreme award after several nail-biting final minutes. Therefore, all congratulations to 'Mick' for appreciating the potential of Hazelnut in the first instance, and the authors feel there is no better person to help exhibitors as follows:

THE FINAL TOUCH

Margaret Watson

Fashion decrees the changing styles in clothes and it is a mistake to suppose that it does not also play a big part in the presentation of the poodle for the show ring.

In the olden days, exhibitors presented their poodles very differently. The mane appeared to have been bathed a week or more before the show, with the consequence that the hairs would acquire a slight wave or kink. On the pack, the hair would revert to tight astrakhan curls. Length of coat was of secondary importance, density and texture being the primary consideration. Bracelets, more often than not, took on a triangular appearance and were on the small side.

Whether this mode of presentation was dictated by the fact that kennels were bigger, I do not know. Today, fewer dogs seem to be kept by a breeder, therefore each poodle can have more care lavished upon it.

Density and quality of coat today are, to a certain extent, sacrificed upon the altar of high-powered presentation. It is no longer the fashion to sally forth into a show ring with your poodle looking ready for a good run through the fields, or, to put it more clearly, as though it had never been touched with a brush or comb for the past fortnight! To do any sizeable winning, the poodle must present an all over eye-catching picture of a dog whose every hair has been coddled into a finished state of length and whose coat is in healthy, sparkling condition. Proof of this exists in the show rings today – comparatively few badly presented poodles ever reach the top and it therefore follows that even if one might deplore the exaggeration in length of coat or mourn the dearth of good, thick, crisp coats, if one wants to win, one must march with the times.

The root of all good presentation lies in the bathing. Any woman who goes to the hairdresser's salon has her hair shampooed not once, but twice. The same procedure should be applied in the case of bathing the show poodle. The first shampoo loosens the dirt, most of which is then rinsed off. The second makes sure that no dirt at all is left in the coat and the final, more painstaking rinse ensures that no soap is left and that the coat ends up in immaculately clean condition.

The type of shampoo naturally depends upon your dog's colour. For blacks and browns, any shampoo – medicated, lemon-egg or what you will – can suffice. My choice of shampoo is also dependent upon the quality of the dog's coat – is it oily, brittle, inclined to be scurfy? I select a shampoo accordingly, just as I would for my own hair.

Whites look best when bathed in one of the special blue doggy shampoos on sale for them, though on the other hand I knew an exhibitor who always bathed her whites in a famous blue washing

Twenty five years ago, at Crufts with the best miniature dog and bitch. Margaret Watson with her black miniature (left), Margaret Sheldon (judge), Barbara Lockwood (steward) and Mrs Ringrose with her white miniature (far right).

powder. Silvers too have their own especial shampoos made for them by a well known firm, and readers are referred to Chapter 11.

Once the coat has been well rinsed after the second shampoo, squeeze off excess moisture, then apply conditioning cream. But whatever you use, the secret is that the cream must be well rubbed in all over the coat with the finger-tips, bearing in mind that the massaging is doing the roots good at the same time. When this in its turn is rinsed off, add the finishing touch by putting a little vinegar or beer in the rinsing water for the browns and blacks and a spot or two of blue for the whites and silvers.

Each stage in the bathing of your dog will enhance its coat if done carefully. Bear in mind that the longer the coat, the better it will be. Therefore brush the coat constantly as you dry it so that as far as possible, it dries straight. Dry the back first, then tail pompom and bracelets, not forgetting those on the front legs as well. When fairly dry, run a small steel comb through the hairs. Now lay the poodle on its side and dry the underneath part of the mane. This is where you want the hair really long, therefore you must dry it, brushing all the time, so that it ends up completely straight.

Next comes the top knot and, just as important, the neck hair behind the top knot which helps to build it up. The remainder of the coat is then dried, after which the whole is brushed through in layers, and combed with that same small comb as you go through it. Get right to the roots everywhere, so that there is no semblance of a matt or tangle. The entire coat, provided you have done the job properly, should have a glow and each hair should give the impression of springing straightly and cleanly from the root with no suspicion of a curl at all.

The clipping having been done before the bath, you will only need your scissors. We usually shape the mane at home, finishing it off at the show, and we definitely find this is the best procedure, for a poodle looks at its best when it has just been freshly scissored.

The type of finished picture you wish to present for the judge's opinion is a matter of personal choice. Some like the mane to be free and flowing, which means that apart from the snipping of any odd hairs that stick out, you hardly use your scissors at all. Before going into the ring and when actually *in* the ring, the coat where it meets the pack is continually brushed towards the back of the head, giving the effect of layers of hair being folded on top of one another. This style certainly shows off length, but it can be most taxing to the patience of judge and exhibitor alike, at the alfresco shows, for the wind can play havoc with it.

Others prefer the more tailored look when the hair of the mane is scissored into a definite shape. All styles, however, are entirely dependent upon the shape or conformation of your dog and when you are accustomed to presenting one different dog after another, you learn that style for each individual is a matter for experiment until you find the one which suits the poodle best.

In my own case, when I have a short-backed dog, I prefer the triangular method of presenting the big coat. This consists of scissoring the mane from the pack towards the head like the long side of a triangle, starting almost at zero from the pack and building steeply up to meet the back of the top knot. This is perhaps the most spectacular cut of all, but I do warn you that your dog must be short-backed – and I do not mean short-backed by reason of having long legs! Even more essential, the dog must have a very long neck, otherwise this style, so difficult for the dog to carry off if not the right shape for it, can be a ghastly mistake.

Another style is that of the whole coat being rounded off everywhere so that the whole forms one ball as far as is possible. I once had a tiny brown toy who was as fat as butter. To my mind, she never showed up to the best advantage until we scissored her coat in this round style, when she looked absolutely delightful, completely different from all the others and therefore really caught one's eye. This style helps those poodles who are inclined to be short of neck and who are neither short nor long in back but somewhere in between. To do this cut, imagine a ball and starting from the top knot, standing your dog against the light, scissor the outline of a circle. Let the dog keep on shaking so that you can snip off any hairs that fall out of alignment.

For any cut, you must have as much length of coat as you can grow. For instance, a long-backed poodle will look even longer unless he has plenty of hair beneath his tummy. The circular or triangle styles will not suit a dog like this. For him, try scissoring the coat so that its first step rises from the pack for about 5cm (2″), then merely graduate the hair beneath the stomach – if you shape it, the dog will look longer. Just snip off any odd hair so that you do not see a ragged line under the dog.

Grooming the poodle through is your first job at the actual show. Next comes the touching up preparatory to going into the ring. Let the dog shake, then remove any hairs that have come out to destroy the outline you have chosen. Tidy up the tail pom and the bracelets. For the former, aim at a completely rounded pom, as big and thick as you can – you cannot exaggerate this too much. As to the bracelets, again they are shaped according to the conformation of your exhibit. Remember that no two poodles are the same, so it stands to reason that the presentation of one will differ from the other.

Two schools of thought exist over the final finishing off of the bracelets. The majority of people work on the assumption that if you shape a bracelet with the scissors, then the hair will remain in place because it has been cut that way. Other exhibitors favour a more modern way of coping with the bracelets. The hair is grown as long as possible and at the show, each bracelet is back-combed just as you back-comb your own hair. Then the bracelets are cut into shape and will appear far more solid and most certainly will stay rigid. If your dog's coat is inclined to be soft and floppy, this is a method of making bracelets look thick and bushy.

The pack, having been combed through, is tidied up with scissors. If your dog is too thin, build the pack out at the sides to give the illusion of plumpness. If your dog is short in neck, try leaving the hair directly above the tail slightly longer than that part of the pack which meets the mane. You will find this will help.

The last chore before you take your dog into the ring is the putting in of the top knot. Gone are the days of tying this back in a prettily coloured ribbon fashioned into a bow. Plain rubber bands are now the vogue and keeping the hair, once fastened up, smooth and flat is no longer done by using white of egg or even lacquer, but by using the sticky side of a plain luggage label. This holds the hair in position well, appears more natural than lacquer and lasts efficiently. Once the hair has been slicked back with the moistened label, take your scissors and snip off any hairs that protrude from the line where the hair of the top knot meets the cheeks.

In recent years, exhibitors have used lacquer extensively on the show poodle's coat. This was sprayed through the mane as it was groomed into its final desired position at the show bench. Nowadays, however, this is strictly forbidden by the Kennel Club, who have on odd occasions instituted a check to ensure this rule is not being infringed. Moreover, it has been known for a judge to send an exhibit from the ring, its handler being asked to remove all lacquer. I cannot think this rule is a disaster – to my mind it should not be necessary to use lacquer if you have styled the mane correctly. Where it *can* present a problem is the topknot and the hair at the back of the neck immediately behind this. The hair should ultimately appear in the shape of a huge ruff, culminating in the built up hair of the topknot thus framing the face attractively. Topknot hair can be scissored in the layer method, exactly the same as is used for your own hair if you have it trimmed in a short style. If despite any shaping, this and the neck hair is still inclined to flop, the trick is to back comb it from the shoulders to the back of the head. Then brush over the top of the back combing very gently, more or less individually placing small wodges of the hair exactly where and how you want it to present the final picture. In other words, the very same way a hairdresser would finish by back combing and styling your own set – and I have never yet found a hairdresser who was not more than willing to help by showing you the basic principle of back combing should you not be able to cope. Once you have finished exhibiting, do remember to brush out any back combing which if done carefully will not entail any loss of coat.

Finally, to impart a glossy sheen on the coat, the minute before you go into the ring, use one of the preparations you will find manufactured for the purpose, (and one of the best is that called St. Aubrey's). There are several to choose from, but as you spray the dog's coat, follow the directions carefully, otherwise you will end up with a greasy looking exhibit because you have used the spray too close to the coat.

Any job that is worth doing is worth doing well, so they say, and this is especially true of presenting a poodle. Put the maximum of time and trouble into this, and your poodle will present a really elegant and attractive picture.

Now it only remains to find a suitable show at which to exhibit the well-trained, beautifully coiffured poodle, and announcements of such shows can be found each week in the canine newspapers *Our Dogs* and *Dog World*. When the right show has been chosen, a card to the secretary will bring a copy of the schedule which will tell you exactly what classes there are, and will also give a list of the definitions of the classes which will help you to make up your mind as to which classes would be most suitable for your poodle. If he is a puppy both the puppy class and the maiden (or novice) class would be suitable. If he is older, he might do well in a rather more advanced class, but don't enter him in too many classes and don't enter him to begin with in too high a class where the competition might be beyond his capabilities. Let the more difficult

classes, such as the open class, come later when he, and you, are more expert at the job of showing.

Entries must be posted off before the closing date and the entry fees enclosed with the form. On the day of the show, make sure that you know exactly where it is to be held, and get there in really good time so that both you and your dog can be well settled in before your first class is announced. Don't forget to take with you food and water for your poodle, a rug for him to lie on, all the grooming equipment you may need, and also some food and drink for yourself in case refreshments are not available. When you arrive, buy a catalogue and check that your entries are detailed correctly. Then you have only to groom your poodle and wait for your class to be called. When you enter the ring be very careful that your poodle is not frightened in any way by other dogs or stepped on by other exhibitors. Your main duty is to get him into the ring comfortably and without fuss. The ring steward will give you your ring number which corresponds to your number in the catalogue, and this you should pin on your coat so that it can be seen easily by the judge. Have a show clip or safety pin for fixing your ring number. It will help to move your poodle up and down the ring now as this will loosen him up. The steward will then intimate that the judge is ready, and then you will be able to put your show training into actual practice.

There are various types of licensed shows held under Kennel Club rules and regulations, and these are described in ascending order for it is

Crufts 1982. Mrs Margaret Watson (centre) judging the toy poodle dogs with Ch. Suraliam Boogy Woogy from Velveteen, (C.C. winner) owned by Miss P. Morris (left), and Ch. Malibu Son of a Bear of Tuttlebees, (Res. C.C.) owned by Mr Norman Butcher (right).

better to start showing, if you are a novice, in the smaller shows and work up in due course to the highest type of show which is the championship.

Exemption Shows

Exemption show, as its title suggests, is exempt from Kennel Club rules and regulations and dogs need not even be registered to enter such a show. They are mainly organised at charity events and can be great fun. Also they are of great value for trying out your dog, assessing whether he has a show temperament, and seeing how he behaves in the company of other dogs and on being handled by a judge. There can only be four classes for pedigree dogs; but usually there are several 'fun' classes, such as dog with longest coat, dog with most soulful eyes, dog with best trick and ad infinitum.

Primary Shows

This is the first type of official show and is another good one to start your dog or puppy on his show career. Such shows are restricted to members only of the association, club or society which is promoting the show, and there must not be more than eight classes scheduled. Such shows may not start earlier than 5 p.m., except on Saturdays and Sundays when they may start at 2 p.m. Entries may be made on a special entry form issued, and such entries will be accepted on the day of the show. Special prize cards must be issued which are white and overprinted with the words 'Primary Show'.

As such a show is held under Kennel Club rules and regulations, dogs must be registered. The competition is not particularly high since no dog which has already won a first prize may enter. However, as any winning *puppies* can be entered, you may be up against extremely strong competition in this particular age bracket of between six months and twelve months.

Sanction Shows

This is the next type of show up the scale and again they are confined to members of an association, club or society and must not start earlier than 5 p.m., except on Saturdays and Sundays when the commencement may be 12.30 p.m. If the show is confined to one breed then not more than ten classes may be scheduled, but if more than one breed then not more than 25 classes. Minor limit, mid limit, limit and open classes may not be included in the schedule. All entrants must, of course, be registered at the Kennel Club.

Standard poodle puppies waiting for the judge at Crufts 1982. Mrs M.A.P. Startup's Trial Blaze from Vanitonia (*left*); Mr R. McAuley's Warwells Machoman; and Miss S. Pine's Vicmars Devil's Disciple (*right*).

Championship and Open Shows

These are the two most advanced types of show since they are open to all comers. Championship shows are those at which Kennel Club challenge certificates are offered. There is also another sub-division which is for shows limited to members of clubs or societies or to exhibitors resident within specified areas and these are called Limited shows.

In any of the above the size of the ring is laid down and this is dependent on the number of exhibits and the breeds. There are various other regulations, all noted in the relevant show schedule. Wins in variety classes do not count for entry in breed classes, but when entering for variety classes, wins in *both* breed and variety classes must be counted. In estimating the number of prizes won, all wins up to seven days *before* the closing date of entries must be counted. In breed classes at championship shows where no challenge certificates are on offer, wins are counted as at open shows.

Challenge Certificates

A judge at a championship show awards a challenge certificate to the best of each sex, and also a reserve challenge certificate for the two reserve bests of sex. And then the best of breed (i.e. of either sex) is adjudged. To become a champion a dog or bitch must have won three challenge certificates after it is a year old. If one of the challenge certificates is gained when it is still a puppy, then four challenge certificates must be clocked up.

Then finally there is the award for the best in show. At a show where dogs of only one group are scheduled, the dogs eligible to compete for best in show are those who have been judged best of breed (*provided* they have not been beaten in a variety class) and the best of the unbeaten winning dogs from the variety classes. If the show is for dogs from more than one group, then judging for best of show must be carried out on a group system, i.e. the best of breeds in each group if they have not been beaten in a variety class, and the best unbeaten winning dog from the variety classes. Then the Best in Show is chosen from the best of the groups. This all sounds very complicated to the beginner but it all follows logically and the ring stewards are there to advise you if you think you might be eligible to compete for any of these high awards.

Benching

Where it is stated in the schedule that dogs will be benched, this means that each dog will be allotted a wire pen (for small breeds) or an open fronted bench (for larger dogs), and dogs must remain on their benches for the duration of the show except for the time they are in the judging rings, or when it is necessary to give them short periods for exercising and relieving themselves. Each pen or bench is numbered and this number coincides with the number in the catalogue, and the ring number which the exhibitor or handler wears. All miniature and toy poodles must be measured by the judge before any award can be made. (See Fig. 14 a) & b) Chapter 4) Therefore it is very important that your dog is well accustomed to being both secured on a lead to some sort of bench, and is not upset when he is measured.

From all the foregoing it will be realised that dog showing can become most absorbing – in fact, it is often said that showing is a disease for which there is no cure! Perhaps that is true, but it is a benign disease providing sportsmanship remains well in evidence. It only becomes a malignant disease when the sporting spirit vanishes, and back-biting, faking and greed take over. At times the exhibitor may feel depressed and cast down, and then at the next show his luck may change and the sky becomes rosy and bright. All the strain and stress, the long hours of training and grooming, the miles of driving or travelling in trains will suddenly have become worth while for he has brought his dog to the top at last. It is exciting indeed when this happens – but does the exhibitor always remember that without the co-operation of his dog he could not have tasted this sweet success? The thoughtless exhibitor may well celebrate on the way home by treating himself to a jolly good dinner

'Can't help smiling!' Prue showing her feelings after winning her first cup. Also demonstrating a very smart continental clip.

while the poor poodle is left shut in the car in his travelling box, probably a little cold and longing for his own dinner and his own cosy bed. When you experience the thrill of a winning day, when everything goes your way and you simply cannot put a foot wrong, remember that without your dog none of this success would be yours. Give him the chance to celebrate too. He has earned V.I.P. treatment more than anyone else!

The Poodle Council

The Poodle Council represents all the combined poodle clubs in major matters, and the Council representative conveys the decisions reached by the committees of the various clubs to bodies such as the Kennel Club or the British Veterinary Association, and the Poodle Council is able to act in such cases and take decisions for the poodle clubs in general. The secretary is Mrs S.M. Coupe, 'San Juan', Doddinghurst Road, Doddinghurst, Brentwood, Essex.

Poodle Clubs

There are a number of poodle clubs to cater for the needs of poodle folk. Most of these stage one championship show during the year, and also an open show, possibly a couple of members' shows, and a number of matches, poodle parties and get-togethers. Often lectures and clipping demonstrations are arranged throughout the year, and it is certainly worth while to join one of these clubs. The two oldest and largest clubs which cater for all three sizes are The Poodle Club (secretary – Mr Norman Butcher, Tinoth Lodge, Lambourne End, Nr. Romford, Essex) and The International Poodle Club (secretary – Miss K. Rees, The Well House, Binfield Heath, Henley-on-Thames, Oxon) both of which cover the whole of the British Isles. In addition it pays to join one of the regional clubs nearest to your own particular area, or else one which is especially intended for the variety you are interested in – standard, miniature or toy. Here is a list of these clubs, and the secretaries' names and addresses, but it is as well to check on these from time to time, as of course secretaries do change quite frequently. They are usually very helpful people and will help the beginner wherever possible, but a stamped and addressed envelope should always be included with any letter, as most clubs are not endowed with much in the way of cash for postages, telephone calls and the like.

POODLE CLUBS
British Toy Poodle Club
Mrs S. Cox, White Oak, Ducks Hill Road, Northwood, Middx

Eastern Counties Poodle Club
Mrs M. Iggulden-Cobb, Highlands Cottage, Brick Spring Lane, Great Totham, Maldon, Essex

International Poodle Club
Miss K. Rees, The Well House, Binfield Heath, Henley-on-Thames, Oxon

London and Home Counties Toy Poodle Club
Mrs B. Perry, 51a Central Road, Worcester Park, Surrey

Mercia Toy Poodle Association
Mr D. Broom, 24 Alexander Road, Bentley, Walsall WS2 0HS

Midland Counties Poodle Club
Mrs M. Worth, The Orchard, 61 Glover Street, Redditch, Worcs

Miniature Poodle Club
Mrs P. Rose, 50 Circus Road, London NW8 9SE

Northern Ireland Poodle Club
Mrs J. Acheson, 67 Mountain Road, Newtownards, Co. Down, Northern Ireland

Northern Toy Poodle Club
Mrs A. Eyre, 'Bronte', 400 Queens Promenade, Norbrech, Blackpool North, Lancashire

Northumbria Poodle Club
Mr J.B. Mack, Hedgeley Hall, Powburn, Alnwick, Northumberland

North Western Poodle Club
Mr C.T. Gray, 31 Aldersgate, New Mills, Stockport, Cheshire

Poodle Club
Mr and Mrs N.E. Butcher, Tinoth Lodge, Lambourne End, near Romford, Essex

Poodle Club of Scotland
Mrs B.G. Currie, 74 Henson Avenue, South Shore, Blackpool, Lancs

Poodle Club of Wales
Mrs P.M. Cox, 87 Alexandra Road, Gorsein On, Swansea, S. Wales

South Western Poodle Club
Mrs M. Howarth, Kings Hyde Farm, Mount Pleasant, Lymington, Hants

Standard Poodle Club
Mrs A. Rawlinson, Viewswood Kennels, Buxted Park, Near Uckfield, E. Sussex

Trent to Tweed Poodle Club
Mr J. Outterside, 46 Scotchman Road, Bradford, Yorks

Obviously there is now no dearth of poodle clubs and the poodle enthusiast has plenty of choice and opportunity if he wishes to know more about the breed and also meet others with the same aim.

Groomers' Association.

An interesting non-profit making organisation has fairly recently emerged called the Groomers' Association which from time to time holds seminars, demonstrations and competitions for those interested in clipping. Admittedly, the Association covers all breeds but obviously a large percentage of activities are concerned with poodle clipping. Various regional clipping competitions are held, culminating in a national contest at the Alexandra Palace in London. All dogs which are entered must be shampooed and brushed, ears cleaned, and nails clipped prior to the contest, but all clipping, scissoring, hand stripping etc. must be done in front of the judges. All dogs must have at least six weeks' growth of hair. In the case of poodles, the judge will take into consideration the degree and difficulty of the clip and its suitability to

Competitors working
away on their models
during a Clipping
Competition at a
Groomers' Association
session.

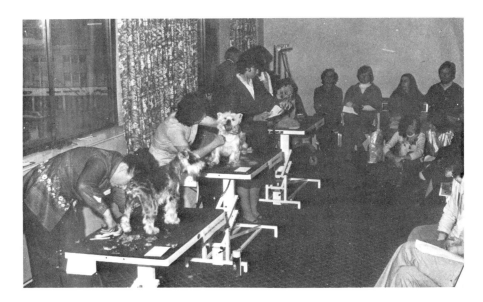

the conformation of the dog. Rough handling of any dog would be viewed very unfavourably by the judge. The competitors are allowed one hour for clipping a miniature or a toy poodle, and two hours for a standard poodle. The entry fee is £5 per competitor, and the regional winners' prizes are £50 and a trophy, while for the national winner the prize is £100 and a handsome cup. Welcome though the cash may be, it is possibly the prospect of a grooming award to show to customers which will surely be the big attraction to professional clippers and those owning beauty parlours. It would certainly be an advantage to join the Groomers' Association for a newsheet appears from time to time, and various concessions such as a 10 per cent discount for members is available on the Dog Breeders' Insurance Policy for the beauty parlour. The policy covers misfortunes to animals in the care of the policyholder for grooming purposes for which the insured is legally liable. It also covers negligence of employees and is operative on the premises and elsewhere, including collection and delivery where this is undertaken. So if you are interested in the Groomers' Association get in touch with Mr R.D. Cook, the chairman, and his address is c/o Messrs. Allbrooks Ltd., Witton House, Lower Road, Chorleywood, Herts WD3 5LZ.

To conclude this chapter on the ins and outs of showing, it really is important to join at least one club, to go to as many shows as possible and to spend time watching the way the winners are clipped and presented, how they are handled, and to gain as much knowledge as you possibly can by reading up all there is to know of this most delightful and intelligent breed.

22 Poodle Tales

WE have coped with the serious side of poodles from every angle, so perhaps now would be the moment to recount some of the comic and peculiar events connected with the authors' various poodles over the years.

Margaret Sheldon and Barbara Lockwood started their show career with their first bitch April Sun of Toy Town way back in 1946. We had decided to enter this little bitch who was only about nine-months-old and atrociously clipped, in a very small sanction show which was confined to members within a ten-mile limit, so the competition was, to say the least, not very high. Roxie, our ewe lamb was entered in every single class for which she was eligible, including open dog or bitch. She pranced into the ring each time, with her owners full of hope, but our hope gradually dwindled as she was always tossed out with the rubbish. But in the last class which was for 'dog or bitch never having been placed at any show', Roxie was placed fourth. Possibly the judge was sick of seeing this little white bitch coming into every class, so in pity or perhaps desperation he gave her a card. We returned home in great jubilation, feeling our name was made! With great pride, we telephoned a friend who was a top name in boxers to say we had won a reserve. She replied, 'The reserve challenge certificate oh well done! You'll soon make her up to champion'. But the owners had to admit very humbly that it was only a meagre reserve or fourth place. But from Roxie came all the succeeding Rotharas – Rothara the Rake, Rothara the Roysterer, Rothara the Gamine and so many others. In the heady later days challenge certificates were always appreciated but a reserve challenge certificate was considered somewhat of a disappointment!

An amusing incident happened at one show. A lovely white Rothara dog was entered, and that grand old lady of poodles, Mrs Campbell Inglis was the judge. The winners were being picked out and Mrs Inglis came over to Margaret Sheldon, patted her arm, and said 'Now, my dear, I have a nice place ready for you' and put her at the top of the line, which was where we were happily thinking we should be with six other poodles below us. Mrs Inglis then walked to the other end and started to give out the cards with ourselves thus placed sixth! Only the week before our Rothara dog had won the open dog class and been judged best in show – but that's show biz!!

When we travelled to shows in the winter we had a very small caravan. The two or three show dogs we usually had with us each had very cosy beds in the back of our estate car, and each dog wore a voluminous dressing gown made of fur fabric. On one of these outings, we came out of our caravan in the morning to find the car and caravan surrounded by at least a foot of rainwater. The show poodles with their immaculate white coats and ruffles could not possibly go out in that. But there was a tiny mound about two feet out of the ground with a small bush growing on it. We donned our gum boots, and carried each dog over to this mound where they solemnly spent their pennies, and more, and their gorgeous coiffure was unsoiled.

In the very early days of breeding poodles, we acquired a very nice, black miniature poodle bitch which we had successfully nursed through hard pad. She attended Bath championship show, where she did well, but unfortunately she also managed to pick up hard pad and brought it back to infect most of her fifteen or so kennel companions. However, all these poodles recovered with no ill effects at all, having been nursed almost twenty-four hours a day for five weeks and given nothing but frequent meals of honey and water and garlic. At the end they were very thin, but fighting fit and cheerful.

Not long after this, Jessica was successfully mated to a lovely black winning dog, and for the first four or five weeks all went well. Then, to the panic of her owners, Jessica disappeared. A tremendous search was carried out and this very self-determined bitch was located under a completely unremovable shed. She had burrowed under the shed and by the light of a torch we could see that she had made herself a neatly hollowed, cosy nest. What could we do? The shed could not possibly have been taken down. So we decided to put food out for her, and a good diet of red meat, milk and eggs were placed by her shed twice a day. She came out for this food as soon as we had retreated a little way but kept a wary eye on us and completely refused to be caught. At that stage we did not even know if she was in whelp or not, but we increased her food in case she was and in due course we could see from her teats from a distance that she had indeed produced puppies. In the end, Jessica proudly walked out one day followed by four little pups staggering after her across the grass, and as fat as butter. She returned to normal kennel life and seemed to have no further interest in the shed, and the next time she was to have a litter she decided that the comforts of indoor whelping with an infra-red lamp and all the other gadgets were probably preferable to being a 'drop out' and sleeping rough.

Incidentally, Margaret Geddes' first miniature bitch Rothara Pilgrim's Penny was a daughter of Jessica (not from the shed litter!) and the founder of her Penpens poodles. Margaret Geddes has always had tremendous rapport with her poodles, and quite literally would ask their

Three generations. Grandma Rothara Pilgrim's Penny (left), the puppies Penpens Paulina and Penpens Perdita, and on right Penpens Portia (their mother). (See the story of Grandma to the rescue).

advice on certain matters. Penny's daughter, Portia was on the brink of whelping and Margaret had everything ready in the kitchen – a low table, antiseptic, scissors, ligatures, towels, small box for the puppies. This was in the days when Margaret was living in a very small studio in London and because there was no garden the poodles were trained to the use of newspaper in the hall in case of dire necessity. Portia had started her labour, and suddenly felt something was due to happen. Thinking she must get to the newspaper, she rushed from the kitchen and promptly popped out a puppy. As she decided it was right to stand for this curious event, the puppy was swinging from side to side on the umbilical cord. In complete panic, Margaret rushed to her aid and there she was squatting on the ground holding the still-attached puppy in her hand with no means of getting to her whelping aids in the kitchen. In agony she turned to Penny, (grandmother of the bitch) who was watching the pantomine with great interest and cried 'Oh Penny, whatever shall I do?' Penny very quietly walked over to Portia and neatly nipped off the cord with her teeth. She returned to her chair rather disdainfully for all the world as if to say 'Really, what fools these young Mums are! Call me when the next one comes!'

Throughout our poodle showing life Margaret Geddes has several times helped us out of a difficulty. Once the authors wanted to go for a short holiday and Margaret said she would come and look after our

The Heavenly Twins. A photogenic pair of toy poodles, who were the constant companions of the authors, and very keen boating dogs.

poodles while we were away. This didn't start off very well because at that time we were living in a fifteenth century cottage with many old beams. We were all three having breakfast before leaving for our holiday, when a mouse lost his footing from a beam and fell into the middle of Margaret's cereal. She gulped and with a bright smile said 'It's quite all right. I'm quite used to that!' It was a terrible week for it rained and rained and the garden and kennels were flooded, and as a result the septic tank also flooded, and the loo overflowed into the kitchen and dining room! We had left our very precious first champion Rothara the Gamine (who was midway through her pregnancy) with Margaret when to her complete panic Gamine suddenly went off her food and her temperature dropped alarmingly. Margaret thought Gamine was going to whelp prematurely. The vet was also on holiday and only a very raw student was standing in as locum. Gamine's trouble proved to be a very nasty abscess on the behind, and Margaret felt the treatment prescribed was quite wrong. So she rushed up to London to her own vet, the right treatment was prescribed and Gamine was quickly herself again. Margaret had had visions of a virus disease, or perhaps a miscarriage with subsequent septicaemia. It was a week she never forgot!

Many Rothara poodles have been exported to other countries, though only to friends or friends of friends. Mostly to Canada, the States, Norway, France and Germany – never to Japan or any of the Eastern or

Triple International Champion Rothara the Gamine considers she deserves the comfort of the best chair.

very hot countries. However, the authors did have a letter from a very high-up personage in the Japanese royal household, asking for a very short coated show poodle because, as this gentleman said in his letter, 'Me lazy man'. Needless to say, no poodle was available.

However, a very lovely white miniature dog was going to a friend in Chicago, U.S.A. We took Racketeer to the airport and on arrival a newspaper photographer asked if he might take a picture. Naturally, we agreed and Margaret Sheldon combed the dog, and then combed her own hair and put on her lipstick. To her mortification, the photographer said 'I wonder if you would mind if this very pretty air hostess held the dog!' That night the photograph *did* appear splashed across *The Evening News* with the caption 'Rothara the Racketeer flies West with a price on his head'. Racketeer quite soon after that gained his championship.

Perhaps one of our most exciting escapades was when we were due the next day to start off for Crufts. As so often in February, the weather was appalling and by lunchtime it was snowing heavily. We were advised by the A.A. that if we wished to get to Crufts in time for the next day's judging we should start at once and stay in London overnight. We had entered eleven dogs, and our manageress, Miss Jackson, was coming with us, also Mrs Margaret Worth of the Piccoli poodles was coming to help with the grooming, preparation and handling of such a large string of poodles. So we loaded up the two cars and set off not knowing where we were going to sleep. We went to a hotel just off Piccadilly which was very comfortable and where we had stayed before. Of course, the verdict was 'no dogs allowed'! We were in despair and sought out the hall porter. After a great deal of chat behind our hands, the transference of quite a lot of money, he told us to book in to two bedrooms with a communicating bathroom and then come round to the back of the hotel where the fire escape stairs were situated. We surreptitiously complied with all this and the hall porter was magnificent, supplying us with mountains of newspaper for the bathroom floor and even a lidded dustbin. So four adults and eleven dogs slept in this London hotel, one couple taking it in turns to go to the dining room for dinner and breakfast, while the other couple looked after the dogs. And there was not a sound from any one of those dogs throughout our stay. They obviously took to hotel life.

The authors were once attending a championship show and an amusing incident occurred. A somewhat vain, and very inexperienced exhibitor who always thought more of her own looks than of the presentation of her poodle, was prinking round the ring more or less ogling the male judge. She thought she had her poodle on the end of her lead, though she had never looked to see. In fact the poodle had escaped and was sitting by the ringside watching her owner circling the ring dangling an empty collar and lead. Titters were heard from the spectators, growing into loud laughter, until someone was generous

The tenth anniversary party at the Rothara Kennels, showing seven generations of direct line breeding.

enough to draw the exhibitor's attention to what had happened, and was her face red! A perfect example of how *not* to show a poodle!

After ten years of poodle breeding and showing and judging, the authors felt it was time for a party. As we had seven generations of our white miniature poodles in our kennels at that time, we had a special stand built on which stood a representative from each generation. We and our kennel maids wore specially embroidered aprons, and the dogs of course had been most carefully shampooed, groomed and clipped and were really looking lovely. Unfortunately the aged founder bitch of the Kennel, Roxanne, had sadly died just a few days before the party, so a small plaque on which her name was inscribed was placed at the end of the stand. Roxie was very sadly missed. We sent out invitations to all our poodle friends and well over forty were able to come to our garden party open day including the late Mr and Mrs Mantovani (whose daughter, Paula, was undergoing a training course with us at the time), Mrs Campbell Inglis (Mannerhead), Mr and Mrs Longworth Birch (Tarry-wood), Mrs Coventon and Miss Butt (Adastra), Mrs Price-Jones (Frenches), Mrs Diana Waugh (Berinshill), Lady Stanier (Seahorses), Mrs Ellis and Miss Sherry (Merrymorn) and so many more top poodle breeders of that time. It was a glorious day, and the garden looked lovely – and the poodles had the time of their lives gobbling cocktail sausages, cheese, ham, biscuits and all the things they were not usually allowed to have.

So you see, poodle breeding and showing is not all hard work and disappointment – it has its moments of unadulterated hilarity!

'Really!' All these stories are enough to make one laugh one's head off.'

23 The Aged Friend and Conclusion

THE time comes when our beloved poodle must leave us. It is inevitable and it is heart breaking. Some owners are lucky and have their dog with them as long as seventeen or eighteen years, while others are bereft after only a few years of wonderful companionship and friendship. When this time of overwhelming sadness comes to us we are sure we can never again have a poodle and that we must own another breed which is as different as possible. And then we see a wicked little poodle pup, bursting with mischief and yet so irresistibly appealing – and that is it! We start all over again, not with a new poodle to take the old one's place, for that is an impossibility, but for the simple reason that once we have owned a poodle, no other breed is for us. Perhaps the best way is to take on a young poodle when the older one is beginning to age a little. This may make the sadness, when it comes, a little less severe. But does the ageing poodle appreciate a youngster around the place? Probably not. Does not a young poodle with his boundless energy, his teasing, his disrespect for other poodles' property such as baskets, bones and even dinners, his appropriation of the beloved owner perhaps cause the old dog or the old bitch rather a lot of irritation and exasperation, and let's face it, an awful lot of jealousy? So perhaps we should not be selfish over this matter.

Aches and Pains

But before the unhappy day arrives, we can do much to make the last years of our poodle's life a happy time. Age will bring with it aches and pains such as rheumatism, arthritis, toothache and earache. We probably cannot entirely cure such conditions but we can ensure that the first two can be lessened by the provision of warmth and freedom from draughts. A basket or bed which is tucked away out of draughts, and which has really soft bedding. Old bones notice hard floors and sharp corners, and therefore thick foam rubber in the bed helps. A knitted rug makes this bed additionally cosy and if an old mohair cardigan can be spared this will give great comfort. Unfortunately a dog cannot tell us when he is suffering pain, and unless we are extremely observant he may suffer in silence without our knowledge. Many old poodles have more than their share of toothache. Usually one can get an idea as to whether those molars are giving trouble by touching the teeth with a finger-nail. If the poodle resists and flinches and then paws his mouth one can be pretty sure he is suffering much pain. Have those teeth extracted whether it spoils his beauty or not. He will be a new dog, and if he is fed on sloppy food such as milk pudding, scrambled egg and the like for only a couple of days after the extractions, he will quickly recover his appetite, and after a week he will be relishing his meat, and to your astonishment will be attacking even a bone or a biscuit! Gone is his pain and up go his spirits. Earache is more complicated for there is so little one can do. In fact the only really useful advice is that from puppyhood one should have kept his ears clean and sweet smelling. Any suspicion of canker should be dealt with without any delay at all, and as a preventative a dusting with a good quality canker powder once a week throughout his life may save him from pain in his old age.

Loving Care

Above all, feed him sensibly. Don't let him get fat – and certainly this is difficult with an old poodle. Don't give him cake, sugar lumps or chocolate – just one chocolate drop a day for his morale! Protect him from cold winds, rain and fog. It is better for him to stay about the house when this kind of weather is forecast, but if he must go out, then let him wear a thick woollen or blanket coat. Be thoughtful over steps and stairs. The old poodle's legs are not what they were, and if he *has* put on weight then his legs are inclined to buckle when he has to climb steps. Perhaps a ramp could be erected for him, and he will soon gratefully learn to use this. Be careful not to moither him for old dogs do get a bit confused especially if they are spoken to sharply or made to hurry. So be gentle and patient with the old fellow. He may well become completely deaf and also rather blind. If so, you must be even more gentle, and when you need to communicate with him or wake him, just touch him gently and lead him wherever you want him to go. Never shout at him, this only confuses him more, and never wake him from sleep suddenly for old dogs need a little time to get back into life. This all makes for slowness, and when one is in a hurry, impatience begins to boil up. But remember him in his youth, count six, and by that time he will have caught up with you again.

Hygiene

Old dogs do occasionally become incontinent. They cannot help it and it is just that their bladders are becoming worn out. Help him as much as

'It's nice to sit in front of the fire and dream when you're getting old.'

you can over these troubles by putting thick pads of paper down at night and letting him understand that you are not cross. If he is afraid he will be scolded, he will have even less control.

Some elderly poodles' coats become a little smelly. It doesn't worry them, of course, but may be a little obnoxious in the house. The coat becomes rather thin, and the skin is a little greasy or flaky and in this case a sponge soaked in one pint of warm water to which half a teaspoonful of Dettol or Milton has been added will prove very helpful. Half squeeze the sponge out and then wipe over the poodle's back and quarters, rinsing the sponge as necessary. Finally, squeeze the sponge almost dry and again wipe the coat down again. Rinsing with clean water is unnecessary. Dry the old dog thoroughly with a hand dryer or else in front of a fire, and don't let him outdoors for several hours. This will keep him sweet smelling and sanitary.

A Peaceful End

But the day will come when we must lose him. However reluctant we are, we must not keep him if he is in real pain and ill. It is the hardest possible decision to make, but we owe it to him for he has no power to decide for himself. Whatever happens, take him to the vet yourself or if you really cannot face this then let him be taken by someone he loves and trusts. *Don't let him die with apprehension in the hands of strangers.* He won't know that the end is about to come and all that is important to him is that he is comfortable and with someone he knows well. It is an upsetting business and one never gets used to it. The authors have taken so many poodles belonging to friends to the vet, and have been able to reassure these poor old dogs in their last moments. Usually a chicken leg (a completely forbidden luxury in normal circumstances!) is produced, and the old chap just drops off to sleep chewing a succulent piece of chicken meat. There is no use in dwelling on this further – we shall be heart broken for our poodle has gone – but he will have drifted away from all pain with a friend by his side.

We have tried to take you and your poodle through all the phases of his life. We like to think we may have suggested a few things which have made life more pleasant for him and also for you, the reader. But whatever we can do for our poodle, we can never repay him for all the love, devotion and companionship that he gives us. What should we do without dogs in our lives? Life would be empty indeed.

Index